THE
TREASURE CHEST

THIS
BOOK BELONGS TO

THE TREASURE CHEST

*A Heritage Album Containing 1064 Familiar and Inspirational
Quotations, Poems, Sentiments, and Prayers
From Great Minds of 2500 Years*

Edited by

Charles L. Wallis

Photographs by Catherine Hopkins

1817

HARPER & ROW, PUBLISHERS, San Francisco
Cambridge, Hagerstown, New York, Philadelphia
London, Mexico City, São Paulo, Sydney

Acknowledgment is made to the following for permission to reprint copyrighted material:

ABINGDON PRESS for extract from *Lift Up Your Hearts* by Walter Russell Bowie, copyright © 1939, 1956 by Pierce and Washabaugh; extract from *Sermons for Special Days* by Charles M. Crowe, copyright © 1951 by Pierce and Smith; extracts from *Leaves from a Spiritual Notebook* by Thomas S. Kepler, copyright © 1960 by Abingdon Press; extract from *The Diary of Peter Parson*, copyright © 1957 by W. B. J. Martin; extract from *God's Way with Man* by Roger Hazelton; extracts by Anderson M. Baten, S. G. Fisher, Abba Hillel Silver, E. A. Stanistreet, and Charles Wagner from *A Treasury of Sermon Illustrations*, ed. by Charles L. Wallis, copyright © 1950 by Pierce and Smith; extract from Newell W. Edson from *Speakers' Illustrations for Special Days*, ed. by Charles L. Wallis, copyright © 1956 by Pierce and Washabaugh.

DODD, MEAD & COMPANY for extract from "The Wise Men" in *The Collected Poems of G. K. Chesterton*, copyright © 1932 by Dodd, Mead & Company, Inc.; "Motto for a Front Hall" from *Silver Saturday* by Nancy Byrd Turner, copyright © 1937 by Dodd, Mead & Company, Inc.

DOUBLEDAY & COMPANY, INC., for extract from *The Secret of Happiness* by Billy Graham, copyright © 1955 by Billy Graham; extract from "Love's Lantern" in *Trees and Other Poems* by Joyce Kilmer, copyright © 1914 by George H. Doran Company.

E. P. DUTTON & COMPANY, INC., for "House Blessing" and "A Poet's Proverb" from *Death and General Putnam and 101 Other Poems* by Arthur Guiterman, copyright © 1935 by E. P. Dutton & Company, Inc., 1963 by Vida Lindo Guiterman.

NORMA MILLAY ELLIS for "God's World" from *Collected Poems* by Edna St. Vincent Millay, published by Harper & Row, copyright © 1913, 1940 by Edna St. Vincent Millay.

HARCOURT, BRACE & WORLD, INC., for extract from *The Family Portrait* in *The Complete Poems and Plays* by T. S. Eliot, copyright © 1952 by Harcourt, Brace & World, Inc.; extract from *Abraham Lincoln: The Prairie Years* by Carl Sandburg, copyright © 1954 by Carl Sandburg; extract from *Remembrance Rock* by Carl Sandburg, copyright © 1948 by Carl Sandburg.

HOLT, RINEHART AND WINSTON, INC., for "Desert Places," "The Gift Outright," "Mending Wall," and "Stopping by Woods on a Snowy Evening" from *Complete Poems of Robert Frost*, copyright © 1923, 1930, 1939 by Holt, Rinehart and Winston, Inc., copyright © 1936, 1942, 1951, 1958 by Robert Frost, copyright © 1964 by Lesley Frost Ballantine; extract from "The Road Not Taken" from *Complete Poems of Robert Frost*, copyright © 1916, 1921 by Holt, Rinehart and Winston, Inc., copyright © 1944 by Robert Frost; "Heroism" from *The Selected Poems of Lizette Woodworth Reese*, copyright © 1926 by Holt, Rinehart and Winston, Inc., copyright © 1954 by C. Reese Dietrich; "Loveliest of Trees" from *A Shropshire Lad* (Authorized Edition) in *The Collected Poems of A. E. Housman*, copyright © 1940 by Holt, Rinehart and Winston, Inc.

ALFRED A. KNOPF, INC., for extracts from *The Prophet* by Kahlil Gibran, copyright © 1923 by Kahlil Gibran, 1951 by Administrators C.T.A. of Kahlil Gibran Estate and Mary G. Gibran; extract from *Pity for Women* by Henri de Montherlant, copyright © 1937 by Alfred A. Knopf, Inc.

J. B. LIPPINCOTT COMPANY for extract from *A Few Missing Buttons* by James T. Fisher and Lowell S. Hawley, copyright © 1951 by J. B. Lippincott Company.

THE MACMILLAN COMPANY for extract from *Windswept* by Mary Ellen Chase, copyright © 1941 by Mary Ellen Chase;

extract from *Mirage and Truth* by M. C. D'Arcy, copyright © 1935; extract from *Power to Become* by Lewis L. Dunnington, copyright © 1956; "Undaunted by Decembers" from *Collected Poems of John G. Neihardt*, copyright by The Macmillan Company; extract from *The Philosophy of Civilization* by Albert Schweitzer, copyright © 1949; "Prayer for Strength" from *Gitanjali* by Rabindranath Tagore; "Alchemy" and "Barter" from *The Collected Poems of Sara Teasdale*, copyright © 1937 by The Macmillan Company; extract from *No Sign Shall Be Given* by Hugh Stevenson Tigner, copyright © 1942.

WILLIAM MORROW AND COMPANY, INC., for extract from *Emotional Problems and What You Can Do About Them* by William B. Terhune, copyright © 1955.

NEW ENGLAND MUTUAL LIFE INSURANCE COMPANY for "What Is a Girl?" by Alan Beck, copyright © 1950 by New England Mutual Life Insurance Company.

W. W. NORTON & COMPANY for extract from *The Echo of Greece* by Edith Hamilton, copyright © 1957 by W. W. Norton & Company; "Stubborn Ounces" from *Hands Laid Upon the Wind* by Bonaro W. Overstreet, copyright © 1955 by W. W. Norton & Company; extract from *The Mind Goes Forth* by Harry and Bonaro Overstreet, copyright © 1956 by W. W. Norton & Company.

PANTHEON BOOKS, INC., for extract from *Doctor Zhivago* by Boris Pasternak, copyright © 1958 by Pantheon Books, Inc.

PRENTICE-HALL, INC., for extract from *Stay Alive All Your Life* by Norman Vincent Peale, copyright © 1957 by Prentice-Hall, Inc.

PUTNAM'S & COWARD-MCCANN for extract from *Alone* by Richard E. Byrd, copyright © 1938 by Richard E. Byrd.

RANDOM HOUSE, INC., for extract from *The Brothers Karamazov* by Fyodor Dostoevski, tr. by Constance Garnet, copyright ©

1943 by Random House, Inc.; extract from *The Faulkner Reader*, copyright © 1954 by William Faulkner; extract from *Where Angels Fear to Tread* by E. M. Forster, copyright © 1920 by Random House; extract from *The Great God Brown* by Eugene O'Neill, copyright © 1926 by Eugene O'Neill; extract from *Remembrance of Things Past* by Marcel Proust, copyright © 1934 by Random House.

THE REILLY & LEE COMPANY for "Courage," "My Creed," and extract from "Prayer for the Home" from *The Collected Verse of Edgar A. Guest*, copyright © 1934 by the Reilly & Lee Company.

FLEMING H. REVELL COMPANY for extract from *Healing Words* by Charles L. Allen, copyright © 1961 by Fleming H. Revell Company; extract from *Prayer Changes Things* by Charles L. Allen, copyright © 1964 by Fleming H. Revell Company.

MARIE RODELL AGENCY for extract from *Help Your Child to Wonder* by Rachel L. Carson, copyright © 1956 by Rachel L. Carson.

ROTARY INTERNATIONAL for "Ten Marks of a Good Citizen" by H. J. Taylor, copyright © 1954 by Rotary International.

SIMON AND SCHUSTER, INC., for extract from *Love or Perish* by Smiley Blanton, copyright © 1956 by Simon and Schuster, Inc.; extract from *Peace of Mind* by Joshua Loth Liebman, copyright © 1946 by Joshua Loth Liebman; extracts from *The Art of Living* by Wilferd A. Peterson, copyright © 1960, 1961 by Wilferd A. Peterson; extract from *One World* by Wendell L. Willkie, copyright © 1943 by Wendell Willkie.

THIS WEEK for "Just for Today" by Kenneth L. Holmes, copyright © 1953 by the United Newspapers Magazine Corporation.

THE VIKING PRESS for extract from *East of Eden* by John Steinbeck, copyright © 1952 by John Steinbeck.

A. WATKINS, INC., for "Atlantic Charter: 1620-1942" from *The Island* by Francis Brett Young, copyright © 1944 by Francis Brett Young.

CONTENTS

Inscribed to my father
ROBERT SCOTT WALLIS

PREFACE

"A word fitly spoken," said Solomon, "is like apples of gold in pictures of silver." Such a word is a recipe for happiness, a challenging guidepost along our journey through life, a bright star to which we may hitch our wagon, or perhaps a vine-covered arbor under which we may find peace, poise, and contentment.

The words quoted in this book reflect the experiences of our common life and by an uncommon grace of expression mirror what most of us have thought or felt or aspire to think and feel. To inspire means literally to breathe into and infuse with life. Inspiring words influence our thinking, enliven our sensitivity to life's meanings, arouse us from lethargy, and exalt us by strengthening the heart and restoring the soul. A perennially vivacious sentiment gives breadth of vision and stretches the heart's sympathies.

This abundant harvest of the wisdom of many centuries follows no predetermined editorial pattern or arbitrary method of choice. In many gardens of prose and verse I have plucked here a red rose and there a golden apple. What I have enjoyed reading I hope others will find to be equally delightful. Where I have found refreshing spring water I hope others will dip their cups. On some mountain height I have moved aside so that others may also share the view of a mind-expanding horizon.

CHARLES L. WALLIS

Keuka College
Keuka Park, New York

ACHIEVEMENT

Success is to be measured
not so much by the position that one has reached in life
as by the obstacles
which he has overcome while trying to succeed.

BOOKER T. WASHINGTON

ACHIEVEMENT

That man is a success who has lived well, laughed often and loved much; who has gained the respect of intelligent men and the love of children; who has filled his niche and accomplished his task; who leaves the world better than he found it, whether by an improved poppy, a perfect poem or a rescued soul; who never lacked appreciation of earth's beauty or failed to express it; who looked for the best in others and gave the best he had.

ROBERT LOUIS STEVENSON

&§&

If one advances confidently in the direction of his dreams, and endeavors to live the life which he has imagined, he will meet with a success unexpected in common hours.

HENRY DAVID THOREAU

&§&

LINCOLN'S ROAD
TO THE WHITE HOUSE

Failed in business in 1831.
Defeated for Legislature in 1832.
Second failure in business in 1833.
Suffers nervous breakdown in 1836.
Defeated for Speaker in 1838.
Defeated for Elector in 1840.
Defeated for Congress in 1843.
Defeated for Congress in 1848.
Defeated for Senate in 1855.
Defeated for Vice President in 1856.
Defeated for Senate in 1858.
Elected President in 1860.

&§&

GRADATIM

Heaven is not reached at a single bound;
But we build the ladder by which we rise
From the lowly earth to the vaulted skies,
And we mount to its summit round by round.

JOSIAH GILBERT HOLLAND

&§&

GOD'S COUNTRY

Who shares his life's pure pleasures,
And walks the honest road,
Who trades with heaping measures,
And lifts his brother's load,
Who turns the wrong down bluntly,
And lends the right a hand,
He dwells in God's own country,
He tills the Holy Land.

LOUIS F. BENSON

&§&

The measure of success is not whether you have a tough problem to deal with, but whether it's the same problem you had last year.

JOHN FOSTER DULLES

&§&

THE DREAM

Ah, great it is to believe the dream
As we stand in youth by the starry stream;
But a greater thing is to fight life through,
And say at the end, "The dream is true!"

EDWIN MARKHAM

&§&

APPRECIATION

All human beings have failings, all human beings have needs and temptations and stresses. Men and women who live together through long years get to know one another's failings; but they also come to know what is worthy of respect and admiration in those they live with and in themselves. If at the end one can say, "This man used to the limit the powers that God granted him; he was worthy of love and respect and of the sacrifices of many people, made in order that he might achieve what he deemed to be his task," then that life has been lived well and there are no regrets.

ELEANOR ROOSEVELT

3

ROAD TO SUCCESS

Throw away all ambition beyond that of doing the day's work well. The travelers on the road to success live in the present, heedless of taking thought for the morrow. Live neither in the past nor in the future, but let each day's work absorb your entire energies, and satisfy your widest ambition.

WILLIAM OSLER

Show me a thoroughly satisfied man, and I will show you a failure.

THOMAS A. EDISON

BUILT TOGETHER

There are parts of a ship which taken by themselves would sink. The engine would sink. The propeller would sink. But when the parts of a ship are built together, they float. So with the events of my life. Some have been tragic. Some have been happy. But when they are built together, they form a craft that floats and is going someplace. And I am comforted.

RALPH W. SOCKMAN

SUCCESS

Before God's footstool to confess
    A poor soul knelt and bowed his head.
"I failed," he wailed. The Master said,
"Thou didst thy best—that is success."

EFFICIENCY

The right man in the right place at the right time doing the right thing in the right way.

RECIPE FOR GREATNESS

To bear up under loss;
To fight the bitterness of defeat and the weakness of grief;
To be victor over anger;
To smile when tears are close;
To resist disease and evil men and base instincts;
To hate hate and to love love;
To go on when it would seem good to die;
To look up with unquenchable faith in something ever more about to be.
That is what any man can do, and be great.

ZANE GREY

Even the woodpecker owes his success to the fact that he uses his head and keeps pecking away until he finishes the job he starts.

COLEMAN COX

The secret of success is consistency of purpose.

BENJAMIN DISRAELI

LADDER OF ACHIEVEMENT

100% — I did.
90% — I will.
80% — I can.
70% — I think I can.
60% — I might.
50% — I think I might.
40% — What is it?
30% — I wish I could.
20% — I don't know how.
10% — I can't.
0% — I won't.

Doing little things with a strong desire to please God makes them really great.

ST. FRANCIS DE SALES

ACTION

All the beautiful sentiments in the world
weigh less than a single lovely action.

JAMES RUSSELL LOWELL

THE AIM OF LIFE

We live in deeds, not years; in thoughts, not
   breaths;
In feelings, not in figures on a dial.
We should count time by heart-throbs. He
   most lives
Who thinks most, feels the noblest, acts the
   best.

PHILIP JAMES BAILEY

Life is not made up of great
      sacrifices and duties,
But of little things; in
      which smiles
And kindness and small
      obligations,
Given habitually, are
      what win and
Preserve the heart and
      secure comfort.

HUMPHRY DAVY

WHAT AN IDEAL CAN DO

A strong ideal can capture an imagination and
control a life. Just one clear picture planted
in the mind and heart of youth is all it takes
to change an apathetic man to acts of consecration that kindle strife or call for peace,
depending on the kind of passioned truth the
picture makes.

WILLIAM K. WEBB

WRITTEN IN ACTIONS

No one can write his real religious life with
pen or pencil. It is written only in actions,
and its seal is our character, not our orthodoxy.
Whether we, our neighbor, or God is the
judge, absolutely the only value of our religious life to ourselves or to anyone is what
it fits us for and enables us to do.

WILFRED T. GRENFELL

Beautiful thoughts hardly bring us to God until
they are acted upon. No one can have a true
idea of right until he does it.

WILLIAM R. INGE

ALUMNUS FOOTBALL

For when the One Great Scorer comes
To write against your name,
He writes—not that you won or lost—
But how you played the game.

GRANTLAND RICE

Man's actions are the picture book of his creeds.

RALPH WALDO EMERSON

All our actions take their hue from the com-
plexion of the heart, as landscapes their variety
from light.

FRANCIS BACON

All that is essential for the triumph of evil is
that good men do nothing.

EDMUND BURKE

THE WAYS

To every man there openeth
A Way, and Ways, and a Way.
And the High Soul climbs the High Way,
And the Low Soul gropes the Low,
And in between, on the misty flats,
The rest drift to and fro.
But to every man there openeth
A High Way, and a Low.
And every man decideth
The way his soul shall go.

JOHN OXENHAM

7

❧

I count this thing to be grandly true:
That a noble deed is a step toward God.

JOSIAH GILBERT HOLLAND

❧

OUR UNFINISHED WORLD

God gave us a world unfinished, so that we might share in the joys and satisfactions of creation.

He left oil in Trenton rock.

He left electricity in the clouds.

He left the rivers unbridged—and the mountains untrailed.

He left the forests unfelled and the cities unbuilt.

He left the laboratories unopened.

He left the diamonds uncut.

He gave us the challenge of raw materials, not the satisfaction of perfect, finished things.

He left the music unsung and the dramas unplayed.

He left the poetry undreamed, in order that men and women might not become bored, but engage in stimulating, exciting, creative activities that keep them thinking, working, experimenting, and experiencing all the joys and durable satisfactions of achievement.

ALLEN A. STOCKDALE

❧

AS A MAN SOWETH

We must not hope to be mowers,
    And to gather the ripe gold ears,
Unless we have first been sowers
    And watered the furrows with tears.

It is not just as we take it,
    This mystical world of ours,
Life's field will yield as we make it
    A harvest of thorns or of flowers.

JOHANN WOLFGANG VON GOETHE

❧

SERMON WITHOUT WORDS

Saint Francis came to preach. With smiles he met
The friendless, fed the poor, freed a trapped bird,
Led home a child. Although he spoke no word,
His test, God's love, the town did not forget.

ELIZABETH PATTON MOSS

❧

MY HAND

God knows the secret plan
Of the things he will do for the world,
Using my hand.

TOYOHIKO KAGAWA

❧

It is well with me only when I have a chisel in my hand.

MICHELANGELO

❧

DREAMS AND DEEDS

Dear Master, in whose life I see
All that I long and fail to be;
Let thy clear light for ever shine.
To shame and guide this life of mine.

Though what I dream and what I do
In my poor days are always two,
Help me, oppressed by things undone,
O thou, whose dreams and deeds were one.

JOHN HUNTER

❧

CONDITIONAL FREEDOM

God frees our souls, not from service, not from duty, but into service and into duty, and he who mistakes the purpose of his freedom mistakes the character of his freedom. He who thinks that he is being released from the work, and not set free in order that he may accomplish that work, mistakes the condition into which his soul is invited to enter.

PHILLIPS BROOKS

8

AGE

I shall grow old, but never lose life's zest,
Because the road's last turn will be the best.

HENRY VAN DYKE

WHAT IT MEANS TO BE YOUNG

Youth is not a time of life; it is a state of mind; it is not a matter of rosy cheeks, red lips and supple knees; it is a matter of the will, a quality of the imagination, a vigor of the emotions; it is the freshness of the deep springs of life.

Youth means the predominance of courage over timidity, of adventure over the love of ease. This often exists in a man of sixty more than in a boy of twenty. Nobody grows old merely by a number of years. We grow old by deserting our ideals.

Years may wrinkle the skin, but to give up enthusiasm wrinkles the soul. Worry, doubt, self-distrust, fear and despair—these bow the heart and turn the spirit back to dust.

Whether sixty or sixteen, there is in every human being's heart the love of wonder, the sweet amazement at the stars and the starlike things, the undaunted challenge of events, the unfailing childlike appetite for what-next, and the joy of the game of living.

You are as young as your faith, as old as your doubt; as young as your self-confidence, as old as your fear; as young as your hope, as old as your despair.

SAMUEL ULLMAN

&

RESPONSE OF YOUTH

Alexander the Great ascended the throne at twenty and conquered the known world by thirty-three. Julius Caesar at a young age captured eight hundred cities, conquered three hundred nations, defeated three million men, became a great orator and one of the greatest statesman known. Washington was appointed adjutant general at nineteen, was sent at twenty-one as an ambassador to treat with the French, and won his first battle as a colonel at twenty-two. Lafayette was made general of the whole French army at the age of twenty. Charlemagne was master of France and of

Germany at thirty. Galileo was but eighteen when he saw the principle of the pendulum in the swinging lamp in the cathedral at Pisa. Peel was in Parliament at twenty-one. Gladstone was in Parliament before he was twenty-two and at twenty-four was Lord of the Treasury. Luther was but twenty-nine when he nailed his famous theses to the door of the cathedral at Wittenberg. Shakespeare wrote masterpieces at thirty-six.

ANDERSON M. BATEN

&

GROWING INWARDLY

We are put here to grow, and we ought to grow, and to use all the means of growth according to the laws of our being. The only real satisfaction there is, is to be growing up inwardly all the time, becoming more just, true, generous, simple, manly, womanly, kind, active. And this can we all do, by doing each day the day's work as well as we can.

JAMES FREEMAN CLARKE

&

HOW TO LIVE A HUNDRED YEARS HAPPILY

1. Do not be on the lookout for ill health.
2. Keep usefully at work.
3. Have a hobby.
4. Learn to be satisfied.
5. Keep on liking people.
6. Meet adversity valiantly.
7. Meet the little problems of life with decision.
8. Above all, maintain a good sense of humor, best done by saying something pleasant every time you get a chance.
9. Live and make the present hour pleasant and cheerful. Keep your mind out of the past, and keep it out of the future.

JOHN A. SCHINDLER

&

INSPIRATION

It is said that hope goes with youth; but I fancy that hope is the last gift given to man, and the only gift not given to youth. For youth the end of every episode is the end of the world. But the power of hoping through everything, the knowledge that the soul survives its adventures—that great inspiration comes to the middle-aged.

GILBERT KEITH CHESTERTON

❧

DIAGNOSIS

On his eightieth birthday, John Quincy Adams responded to a query concerning his well-being by saying: "John Quincy Adams is well. But the house in which he lives at present is becoming dilapidated. It is tottering upon its foundation. Time and the seasons have nearly destroyed it. Its roof is pretty well worn out. Its walls are much shattered and it trembles with every wind. I think John Quincy Adams will have to move out of it soon. But he himself is quite well, quite well."

❧

LET US GO FORTH

The torch has been passed to a new generation . . . born in this century, tempered by war, disciplined by a hard and bitter peace, proud of our ancient heritage—and unwilling to witness or permit the slow undoing of those human rights to which this nation has always been committed. . . .

With a good conscience our only sure reward, with history the final judge of our deeds, let us go forth to lead the land we love, asking His blessing and His help, but knowing that here on earth God's work must truly be our own.

JOHN F. KENNEDY

❧

LIFE BEGINS AT SEVENTY

Psalm 90:10: "Threescore years and ten."

Between the ages of 70 and 83 Commodore Vanderbilt added about 100 millions of his fortune.

Kant at 74 wrote his *Anthropology, Metaphysics of Ethics,* and *Strife of the Faculties.*

Tintoretto at 74 painted the vast *Paradise,* a canvas 74 feet by 30.

Verdi at 74 produced his masterpiece, *Othello;* at 80, *Falstaff,* and at 85, the famous *Ave Maria, Stabet Mater,* and *Te Deum.*

Lamarck at 78 completed his great zoological work, *The Natural History of the Invertebrates.*

Oliver Wendell Holmes at 79 wrote *Over the Teacups.*

Cato at 80 began the study of Greek.

Goethe at 80 completed *Faust.*

Tennyson at 83 wrote "Crossing the Bar."

Titian at 98 painted his historic picture of the Battle of Lepanto.

THE GOLDEN BOOK

❧

MELLOWNESS

I like spring, but it is too young. I like summer, but it is too proud. So I like best of all autumn, because its leaves are a little yellow, its tone mellower, its colors richer, and it is tinged a little with sorrow. Its golden richness speaks not of the innocence of spring, nor of the power of summer, but of the mellowness and kindly wisdom of approaching age. It knows the limitations of life and is content.

LIN YUTANG

❧

To be seventy years young is sometimes far more cheerful and hopeful than to be forty years old.

OLIVER WENDELL HOLMES

From ULYSSES

We are not now that strength which in old days
Moved earth and heaven; that which we are, we
    are;
One equal temper of heroic hearts
Made weak by time and fate, but strong in will
To strive, to seek, to find and not to yield.

ALFRED TENNYSON

HIS WORDS AT NINETY

The riders in a race do not stop short when
they reach the goal. There is a little finishing
canter before they come to a standstill. There
is time to hear the kind voice of friends and to
say to one's self: "The work is done." But just
as one says that, the answer comes: "The race is
over, but the work never is done while the
power to work remains." The canter that brings
you to a standstill need not be only coming to
rest. It cannot be while you still live. For to live
is to function. That is all there is in living.

OLIVER WENDELL HOLMES, JR.

TIME BUDGETING

As you grow older, more than ever before you
need to spend part of each day alone in peace,
quiet, and meditation; and in prayer that you
may be shown how to continue to live each day
with courage, kindness, wisdom, laughter, interest, and understanding. You should take
time to absorb and enjoy the lovely world in
which you live and come to know its inhabitants
with affectionate amusement. You would do
well to budget your time as follows: one-half in
work, taking care of personal belongings, etc.;
one-fourth in social pastimes with others, both
young and old; and one-fourth as an interested,
pleased observer of life.

WILLIAM B. TERHUNE

AS I GROW OLD

God keep my heart attuned to' laughter
    When youth is done;
When all the days are gray days, coming after
    The warmth, the sun.
God keep me then from bitterness, from
      grieving,
    When life seems cold;
God keep me always loving and believing
    As I grow old.

Growing old is no more than a bad habit which
a busy man has no time to form.

ANDRÉ MAUROIS

Youth is the time for the adventures of the
body, but age for the triumphs of the mind.

LOGAN PEARSALL SMITH

So long as enthusiasm lasts, so long is youth
still with us.

DAVID STARR JORDAN

THE BEST IS YET TO COME

Though I am growing old, I maintain that the
best part is yet to come—the time when one
may see things more dispassionately and know
oneself and others more truly, and perhaps be
able to do more, and in religion rest centered
in a few simple truths. I do not want to ignore
the other side, that one will not be able to see so
well or walk so far or read so much. But there
may be more peace within more communion
with God, more real light instead of distraction
about many things, better relations with others,
fewer mistakes.

BENJAMIN JOWETT

13

From RABBI BEN EZRA

Grow old along with me!
The best is yet to be,
The last of life, for which the first was made:
Our times are in his hand
Who saith, "A whole I planned,
Youth shows but half; trust God:
  see all, nor be afraid!"

ROBERT BROWNING

RESILIENCY

Youth has the resilience to absorb disaster and weave it into the pattern of its life, no matter how anguishing the thorn that penetrates its flesh.

SHOLEM ASCH

AT EIGHTY-THREE

Thank God for life, with all its endless store
Of great experiences, of hill and dale,
Of cloud and sunshine, tempest, snow and hail.
Thank God for straining sinews, panting breast,
No less for weary slumber, peaceful rest;
Thank God for home and parents, children,
  friends,
For sweet companionship that never ends:
Thank God for all the splendor of the earth,
For nature teeming with prolific birth:
Thank God for sea and sky, for changing hours,
For trees and singing birds and fragrant flowers.
And so in looking back at eighty-three
My final word to you, my friends, shall be:
Thank God for life; and when the gift's with-
  drawn,
Thank God for twilight bell, and coming dawn.

THOMAS DURLEY LANDELS

LESSONS I HAVE LEARNED

When a man surveys his past from middle age he must surely ask himself what those bygone years have taught him. If I have learned any-thing in the swift unrolling of the web of time, it is the virtue of tolerance, of moderation in thought and deed, of forbearance toward one's fellowmen.

I have come also to acknowledge the great illusion which lies in the pursuit of a purely material goal. What slight satisfaction lies in temporal honor and worldly grandeur! All the material possessions for which I strove so strenuously mean less to me now than a glance of love from those who are dear to me.

Above all am I convinced of the need, irre-vocable and inescapable, of every human heart, for God. No matter how we try to escape, to lose ourselves in restless seeking, we cannot separate ourselves from our divine source. There is no substitute for God.

A. J. CRONIN

FULFILMENT

To fulfil the dreams of one's youth; that is the best that can happen to a man. No worldly success can take the place of that.

WILLA CATHER

LET ME GROW LOVELY

Let me grow lovely, growing old—
  So many fine things do:
Laces, and ivory, and gold,
  And silks need not be new;
And there is healing in old trees,
  Old streets a glamour hold;
Why may not I, as well as these,
  Grow lovely, growing old?

KARLE WILSON BAKER

ASPIRATION

Only God can fully satisfy
the hungry heart of man.

HUGH BLACK

GOD THE ARCHITECT

Who Thou art I know not,
   But this much I know:
Thou hast set the Pleiades
   In a silver row;

Thou hast sent the trackless winds
   Loose upon their way;
Thou hast reared a colored wall
   'Twixt the night and day;

Thou hast made the flowers to bloom
   And the stars to shine;
Hid rare gems of richest ore
   In the tunneled mine;

But chief of all thy wondrous works,
   Supreme of all thy plan,
Thou hast put an upward reach
   In the heart of Man.

HARRY KEMP

❧

Reach high, for stars lie hidden in your soul.
Dream deep, for every dream precedes the goal.

PAMELA VAULL STARR

❧

YOU CAN TOUCH STARS

Stars have too long been symbols of the un-
attainable. They should not be so. For although our physical hands cannot reach them,
we can touch them in other ways.

Let stars stand for those things which are ideal
and radiant in life; if we seek sincerely and
strive hard enough, it is not impossible to
reach them, even though the goals seem
distant at the onset.

And how often do we touch stars when we find
them close by in the shining lives of great
souls, in the sparkling universe of humanity
around us!

ESTHER BALDWIN YORK

❧

Ah, but a man's reach should exceed his grasp,
Or what's a heaven for?

ROBERT BROWNING

❧

God hides some ideal in every human soul. At
some time in our life we feel a trembling, fearful longing to do some good thing. Life finds
its noblest spring of excellence in this hidden
impulse to do our best.

ROBERT COLLYER

❧

SKYLIGHTS

There are one-story intellects, two-story intellects, and three-story intellects with sky-
lights. All fact collectors, who have no aim
beyond their facts, are one-story men. Two-
story men compare, reason, generalize, using
the labors of the fact collectors as well as their
own. Three-story men idealize, imagine, pre-
dict; their best illumination comes from above,
through the skylight.

OLIVER WENDELL HOLMES

❧

Without the Way there is no going; without the
Truth there is no knowing; without the Life
there is no living.

THOMAS A KEMPIS

❧

We must, despite ourselves, turn heavenward
our eyes.

ALFRED DE MUSSET

17

A POET'S PROVERB

God's road is all uphill,
　But do not tire,
Rejoice that we may still
　Keep climbing higher.

ARTHUR GUITERMAN

❧

Keep thou thy dreams—the tissue of all wings
　Is woven first of them; from dreams are
　　made
The precious and imperishable things,
　Whose loveliness lives on, and does not fade.

VIRNA SHEARD

❧

HIGH FLIGHT

Oh! I have slipped the surly bonds of earth
　And danced the skies on laughter-silvered
　　wings;
Sunward I've climbed, and joined the tumbling
　　mirth
　Of sun-split clouds—and done a hundred
　　things
You have not dreamed of—wheeled and soared
　　and swung
　High in the sunlit silence. Hov'ring there,
I've chased the shouting wind along, and flung
　My eager craft through footless halls of air.

Up, up the long, delirious, burning blue
　I've topped the wind-swept heights with easy
　　grace
Where never lark, or even eagle flew—
And, while with silent lifting mind I've trod
　The high untrespassed sanctity of space,
Put out my hand and touched the face of God.

JOHN GILLESPIE MAGEE, JR.

❧

There are three ingredients in the good life:
learning, earning, and yearning.

CHRISTOPHER MORLEY

❧

Our daily thoughts should be elevated above
the ceiling.

W. W. LOFLIN

❧

If a man constantly aspires, is he not elevated?

HENRY DAVID THOREAU

❧

They build too low who build beneath the skies.

INSCRIPTION ON A BUILDING
IN WASHINGTON, D. C.

❧

WINGS

Be like the bird
That, pausing in her flight
Awhile on boughs too slight,
　Feels them give way
Beneath her and yet sings,
Knowing that she hath wings.

VICTOR HUGO

❧

ALADDIN

When I was a beggarly boy,
　And lived in a cellar damp,
I had not a friend nor a toy,
　But I had Aladdin's lamp.
When I could not sleep for cold,
　I had fire enough in my brain,
And builded, with roofs of gold,
　My beautiful castles in Spain!

JAMES RUSSELL LOWELL

❦

There is never an expectant aspiration toward God which does not bring forth a revelation from God.

RICHARD ROBERTS

❦

Ideals are like stars. You will not succeed in touching them with your hands; but, like the seafaring man, you choose them as your guides, and, following them, you will reach your destiny.

CARL SCHURZ

❦

He wakes desires you never may forget;
  He shows you stars you never saw before;
  He makes you share with Him forevermore
The burden of the world's divine regret.

ALFRED TENNYSON

❦

BUOYANCY

The way to God has properly been described as "letting oneself fall," and has been compared with the first flight of a baby eagle, pushed out of the nest by its parents, and then discovering to its amazement that the invisible ocean of light in which it is dropping is capable of bearing it up. The presence of God which surrounds everyone is like this invisible ocean which bears us up more surely than do all visible means of security.

KARL HEIM

❦

And ah for a man to arise in me,
That the man I am may cease to be!

ALFRED TENNYSON

❦

A NOISELESS PATIENT SPIDER

A noiseless patient spider,
I mark'd where on a little promontory it stood isolated,
Mark'd how to explore the vacant vast surrounding,
It launch'd forth filament, filament, filament, out of itself,
Ever unreeling them, ever tirelessly speeding them.

And you O my soul where you stand,
Surrounded, detached, in measureless oceans of space,
Ceaselessly musing, venturing, throwing, seeking the spheres to connect them,
Till the bridge you will need be form'd, till the ductile anchor hold,
Till the gossamer thread you fling catch somewhere, O my soul.

WALT WHITMAN

The eagle was once nothing but an egg, but what would we know about the nature, the meaning, the possibilities of that egg had we never seen the eagle soaring in splendor against the sky?

The poor man is not he who is without a cent, but he who is without a dream.

HARRY KEMP

19

HEROISM
Whether we climb, whether we plod,
  Space for one task the scant years lend—
To choose some path that leads to God,
  And keep it to the end.

LIZETTE WOODWORTH REESE

If a man does not keep pace with his companions, perhaps it is because he hears a different drummer. Let him step to the music he hears, however measured or far away.

HENRY DAVID THOREAU

Where our duty's task is wrought
In unison with God's great tho't,
The near and future blend in one,
And whatsoe'er is willed, is done.

JOHN GREENLEAF WHITTIER

THE ALMIGHTY WILL
The child, the seed, the grain of corn,
  The acorn on the hill,
Each for some separate end is born
  In season fit, and still
Each must in strength arise to work
  The Almighty Will.

ROBERT LOUIS STEVENSON

If you have anything really valuable to contribute to the world, it will come through the expression of your own personality—that single spark of divinity that sets you off and makes you different from every other living creature.

BRUCE BARTON

THE PASSIONATE SWORD
Temper my spirit, O Lord,
  Burn out its alloy,
And make it a pliant steel for Thy wielding,
  Not a clumsy toy;
A blunt, iron thing in my hands
  That blunder and destroy.

Temper my spirit, O Lord,
  Keep it long in the fire;
Make it one with the flame. Let it share
  That up-reaching desire.
Grasp it, Thyself, O my God;
  Swing it straighter and higher!

JEAN STARR UNTERMEYER

Hitch your wagon to a star.

RALPH WALDO EMERSON

MORE WORK
Success slips away from you like sand through the fingers, like water through a leaky pail, unless success is held tightly by hard work, day by day, night by night, year in and year out. Everyone who is not looking forward to going to seed looks forward to working harder and harder and more fruitfully as long as he lasts.

STUART PRATT SHERMAN

The soul of art is beauty,
  The heart of love is youth;
The soul of courage, duty;
  The heart of science, truth;
And so man struggles upward,
  To find beyond the sod
The heart and soul of the universe,
  The Infinite, his God.

M. GRACE HOUSEMAN

AWARENESS

The world
will never starve
for want of wonders.
GILBERT KEITH CHESTERTON

AWARENESS

God—let me be aware.
Let me not stumble blindly down the ways,
Just getting somehow safely through the days,
Not even groping for another hand,
Not even wondering why it all was planned,
Eyes to the ground unseeking for the light,
Soul never aching for a wild-winged flight,
Please, keep me eager just to do my share.
God—let me be aware.

God—let me be aware.
Stab my soul fiercely with others' pain,
Let me walk seeing horror and stain.
Let my hands, groping, find other hands.
Give me the heart that divines, understands.
Give me the courage, wounded, to fight.
Flood me with knowledge, drench me in light.
Please, keep me eager just to do my share.
God—let me be aware.

MIRIAM TEICHNER

❧

THE ART OF AWARENESS

Thoreau wrote: "Only that day dawns to which we are awake." The art of awareness is the art of learning how to wake up to the eternal miracle of life with its limitless possibilities.

It is rising to the challenge of the stirring old hymn: "Awake my soul, stretch every nerve."

It is developing the deep sensitivity through which you may suffer and know tragedy, and die a little, but through which you will also experience the grandeur of human life.

It is following the philosophy of Albert Schweitzer who teaches "reverence for life," from ants to men; it is developing a sense of oneness with all life.

It is identifying yourself with the hopes, dreams, fears, and longings of others, that you may understand them and help them.

It is learning to interpret the thoughts, feelings, and moods of others through their words, tones, inflections, facial expressions, and movements.

It is keeping mentally alert to all that goes on around you; it is being curious, observant, imaginative that you may build an ever increasing fund of knowledge of the universe.

It is striving to stretch the range of eye and ear; it is taking time to look and listen and comprehend.

It is searching for beauty everywhere, in a flower, a mountain, a machine, a sonnet, and a symphony.

It is knowing wonder, awe, and humility in the face of life's unexplained mysteries.

It is discovering the mystic power of the silence and coming to know the secret inner voice of intuition.

It is avoiding blind spots in considering problems and situations; it is striving "to see life steadily and see it whole."

It is enlarging the scope of your life through the expansion of your personality.

It is through a growing awareness that you stock and enrich your memory . . . and as a great philosopher has said: "A man thinks with his memory."

WILFERD A. PETERSON

❧

GOD'S EXPRESSIONS

Look without!
Behold the beauty of the day,
The shout
Of color to glad color,
Rocks and trees,
And sun and seas,
And wind and sky:
All these
Are God's expression,
Art work of His hand,
Which men must love
Ere they can understand.

RICHARD HOVEY

❧

NOT BY BREAD ALONE

Man does not live by bread alone, but by beauty and harmony, truth and goodness, work and recreation, affection and friendship, aspiration and worship.

Not by bread alone, but by the splendor of the firmament at night, the glory of the heavens at dawn, the blending of colors at sunset, the loveliness of magnolia trees, the magnificence of mountains.

Not by bread alone, but by the majesty of ocean breakers, the shimmer of moonlight on a calm lake, the flashing silver of a mountain torrent, the exquisite patterns of snow crystals, the creations of artists.

Not by bread alone, but by the sweet song of a mockingbird, the rustle of the wind in the trees, the magic of a violin, the sublimity of a softly lighted cathedral.

Not by bread alone, but by the fragrance of roses, the scent of orange blossoms, the smell of new-mown hay, the clasp of a friend's hand, the tenderness of a mother's kiss.

Not by bread alone, but by the lyrics of poets, the wisdom of sages, the holiness of saints, the biographies of great souls.

Not by bread alone, but by comradeship and high adventure, seeking and finding, serving and sharing, loving and being loved.

Man does not live by bread alone, but by being faithful in prayer, responding to the guidance of the Holy Spirit, finding and doing the loving will of God now and eternally.

THE UNIVERSITY PRESBYTERIAN

❦

AUGURIES OF INNOCENCE

To see a World in a grain of sand,
And a Heaven in a wild flower,
Hold Infinity in the palm of your hand,
And Eternity in an hour.

WILLIAM BLAKE

❦

To me, every hour of the day and night is an unspeakably perfect miracle.

WALT WHITMAN

❦

ANTIDOTE

If I had influence with the good fairy who is supposed to preside over the christening of all children I should ask that her gift to each child be a sense of wonder so indestructible that it would last throughout life, an unfailing antidote against the boredom and disenchantment of later years, the sterile preoccupation with things that are artificial, the alienation from the sources of our strength.

RACHEL CARSON

❦

THE MYSTERIOUS

The most beautiful thing we can experience is the mysterious. It is the source of all true art and science. He to whom this emotion is a stranger, who can no longer pause to wonder and stand rapt in awe, is as good as dead: his eyes are closed.

ALBERT EINSTEIN

❦

VOYAGE OF DISCOVERY

The first intelligent expression of the infant is wonder; this quickly develops into active curiosity, until life becomes an enthralling and breathless voyage of discovery. Its possession is the great distinction between youth and age. Youth is past when the sensation of adventure is ended, when instead of boundless expectation and of curiosity that penetrates into all the corners of existence, a man is content to take things as they are, when eagerness gives way to complacency and questioning to the cynicism of experience. The man devoid of curiosity is the man who in the end attains to nothing.

THE LIVING AGE

KINSHIP

I am aware of the splendor that ties
All the things of the earth with the things of
    the skies,
Here in my body the heavenly heat,
Here in my flesh the melodious beat
Of the planets that circle Divinity's feet.

ANGELA MORGAN

I have no fear that the candle lighted in Palestine years ago will ever be put out.

WILLIAM R. INGE

From THE CATHEDRAL

This life were brutish did we not sometimes
Have intimations clear of wider scope,
Hints of occasion infinite, to keep
The soul alert with noble discontent
And onward yearnings of unstilled desire;
Fruitless, except we now and then divined
A mystery of Purpose, gleaming through
The secular confusions of the world,
Whose will we darkly accomplish, doing ours.

JAMES RUSSELL LOWELL

ALIVE TO LIFE

Life is what we are alive to. It is not length but breadth. To be alive only to appetite, pleasure, pride, money-making, and not to goodness, kindness, purity, love, history, poetry, music, flowers, stars, God, and eternal hope is to be all but dead.

MALTBIE D. BABCOCK

REVELATION

I made a pilgrimage to find the God:
I listened for his voice at holy tombs,
Searched for the print of his immortal feet
In dust of broken altars; yet turned back
With empty heart. But on the homeward road,
A great light came upon me, and I heard
The God's voice singing in a nestling lark;
Felt his sweet wonder in a swaying rose;
Received his blessing from a wayside well;
Looked on his beauty in a lover's face;
Saw his bright hand send signal from the sun.

EDWIN MARKHAM

EARTH'S COMMON THINGS

In wonder-workings, or some bush aflame,
    Men look for God and fancy him concealed;
    But in earth's common things he stands revealed,
While grass and flowers and stars spell out his
    name.

MINOT J. SAVAGE

EYES FOR INVISIBLES

I have walked with people whose eyes are full of light but who see nothing in sea or sky, nothing in city streets, nothing in books. It were far better to sail forever in the night of blindness with sense, and feeling, and mind, than to be content with the mere act of seeing. The only lightless dark is the night of darkness in ignorance and insensibility.

HELEN KELLER

Two things fill me with constantly increasing admiration and awe, the longer and more earnestly I reflect on them: the starry heavens without and the moral law within.

IMMANUEL KANT

REFLECTIONS

In a puddle by the roadside
Left by the warm, spring rain,
Its waters dark and muddy
With the brown earth stain,
I saw a glorious mountain
That stood up bold and high
Reflected in the water,
With a patch of cloud-decked sky.

Sometimes in folk around me
With burdens, hurts and fears:
Through joyful, happy hours
And often through their tears:
In some loving acts of kindness
As they show how much they care—
In the lives of folk around me
I find God reflected there.

CYRUS E. ALBERTSON

I *am*—the power of self-knowledge

I *think*—the power to investigate

I *know*—the power to master facts

I *feel*—the power to appreciate, to value, to love

I *wonder*—the spirit of reverence, curiosity, worship

I *see*—the power of insight, imagination, vision

I *believe*—the power of adventurous faith

I *can*—the power to act and the skill to accomplish

I *ought*—the power of conscience, the moral imperative

I *will*—will power, loyalty to duty, consecration

I *serve*—the power to be useful, devotion to a cause.

GEORGE WALTER FISKE

BLIND

"Show me your God!" the doubter cries.
I point him to the smiling skies;
I show him all the woodland greens;
I show him peaceful sylvan scenes;
I show him winter snows and frost;
I show him waters tempest-tossed;
I show him hills rock-ribbed and strong;
I bid him hear the thrush's song;
I show him flowers in the close—
The lily, violet and rose;
I show him rivers, babbling streams;
I show him youthful hopes and dreams;
I show him maids with eager hearts;
I show him toilers in the marts;
I show him stars, the moon, the sun;
I show him deeds of kindness done;
I show him joy; I show him care,
And still he holds his doubting air,
And faithless goes his way, for he
Is blind of soul, and cannot see!

JOHN KENDRICK BANGS

The man who cannot wonder is but a pair of spectacles behind which there is no eye.

THOMAS CARLYLE

THE EXTRAVAGANCE OF GOD

More sky than man can see,
More seas that he can sail,
More sun than he can bear to watch,
More stars than he can scale.

More breath than he can breathe,
More yield than he can sow,
More grace than he can comprehend,
More love than he can know.

RALPH W. SEAGER

26

BEAUTY

Beauty is God's handwriting.

CHARLES KINGSLEY

GOD'S WORLD

O World, I cannot hold thee close enough!
　　Thy winds, thy wide grey skies!
　　Thy mists that roll and rise!
Thy woods, this autumn day, that ache and sag
And all but cry with colour! That gaunt crag
To crush! To lift the lean of that black bluff!
World, World, I cannot get thee close enough!
Long have I known a glory in it all,
　　But never knew I this;
　　Here such a passion is
As stretcheth me apart. Lord, I do fear
Thou'st made the world too beautiful this year,
My soul is all but out of me—let fall
No burning leaf; prithee, let no bird call.

　　　　　　EDNA ST. VINCENT MILLAY

❧

THE FACT OF BEAUTY

Definitions of beauty are many and varied. For example, beauty has been defined as "truth," "the expression of an ideal," "an assemblage of properties satisfying the aesthetic sense," "harmony in diversity," and "an intrinsic quality of things themselves." While definitions do not agree, there is no uncertainty concerning the fact of beauty. A formula cannot contain and explain it, but, fortunately for most of us, beauty in some form is almost continuously present. Even those who are forced to live in comparatively drab and unpleasant surroundings find frequent opportunity to experience the delights of beauty: an expression, a face, a garment or some trinket, a bit of cloud or sky, the sunset or the landscape. While men differ widely in their capacity for appreciation of beauty, some enjoyment of beauty is possible for all.

　　　　　　HAROLD H. TITUS

❧

"Beauty is truth, truth beauty,"—that is all
Ye know on earth, and all ye need to know.

　　　　　　JOHN KEATS

❧

The mountains are God's majestic thoughts.
The stars are God's brilliant thoughts.
The flowers are God's beautiful thoughts.

　　　　　　ROBERT STUART MAC ARTHUR

❧

Beauty is like the surf that never ceases,
Beauty is like the night that never dies,
Beauty is like a forest pool where peace is
And a recurrent waning planet lies.

　　　　　　STRUTHERS BURT

❧

Music is the only language in which you cannot say a mean or sarcastic thing.

　　　　　　JOHN ERSKINE

❧

In every man's heart there is a secret nerve that answers to the vibrations of beauty.

　　　　　　CHRISTOPHER MORLEY

❧

NEW WORLDS

Goethe wrote of "the Americas of the mind." In the artist's life of the imagination there is vision and adventure and the discovery of new worlds. An artist's masterpiece is such an America of the mind: a new world of meaning expressed in terms of abiding beauty, be it in marble or paint or words or musical tone. And in this great vision we are privileged to share. To see eye to eye with a great artist is to expand and enrich the world in which we live.

　　　　　　RADOSLAV A. TSANOFF

❧

29

BARTER

Life has loveliness to sell,
　　All beautiful and splendid things,
Blue waves whitened on a cliff,
　　Soaring fire that sways and sings,
And children's faces looking up
Holding wonder like a cup.

Life has loveliness to sell,
　　Music like a curve of gold,
Scent of pine trees in the rain,
　　Eyes that love you, arms that hold,
And for your spirit's still delight,
Holy thoughts that star the night.

Spend all you have for loveliness,
　　Buy it and never count the cost;
For one white singing hour of peace
　　Count many a year of strife well lost,
And for a breath of ecstasy
Give all you have been, or could be.

　　　　　　　　　　　SARA TEASDALE

❧⬥☙

We ought to hear at least one little song every day, read a good poem, see a first-rate painting, and if possible speak a few sensible words.

　　　　JOHANN WOLFGANG VON GOETHE

❧⬥☙

I AM MUSIC

Servant and master am I; servant of those dead and master of those living. Through me spirits immortal speak the message that makes the world weep, and laugh, and wonder, and worship. I tell the story of love, the story of hate, the story that saves, and the story that damns. I am the incense upon which prayers float to heaven. I am the smoke which palls over the field of battle where men lie dying with me on their lips. I am close to the marriage altar, and when the graves open I stand near by. I call the wanderer home, I rescue the soul from the depths, I open the lips of lovers, and through me the dead whisper to the living. One I serve as I serve all; and the king I make my slave as easily as I subject his slave. I speak through the birds of the air, the insects of the field, the crash of waters on rock-ribbed shores, the sighing of wind in the trees, and I am even heard by the soul that knows me in the clatter of wheels on city streets. I know no brother, yet all men are my brothers; I am the father of the best that is in them, and they are fathers of the best that is in me; I am of them, and they are of me. For I am the instrument of God.

❧⬥☙

POETRY

If I read a book and it makes my whole body so cold no fire can ever warm me, I know that is poetry. If I feel physically as if the top of my head were taken off, I know that is poetry. These are the only ways I know it. Is there any other way?

　　　　　　　　　　EMILY DICKINSON

❧⬥☙

THE THINGS I PRIZE

These are the things I prize
　　And hold of dearest worth:
Light of the sapphire skies,
Peace of the silent hills,
Shelter of the forest, comfort of the grass,
Music of birds, murmur of little rills,
Shadows of clouds that swiftly pass,
　　And, after showers,
　　The smell of flowers
And of the good brown earth—
And best of all, along the way, friendship
　　and mirth.

　　　　　　　　　HENRY VAN DYKE

❧⬥☙

God scatters beauty as he scatters flowers
O'er the wide earth, and tells us all are ours.
A hundred lights in every temple burn,
And at each shrine I bend my knee in turn.

WALTER SAVAGE LANDOR

❦

TOO LITTLE TIME

I still find each day too short for all the thoughts
I want to think, all the walks I want to take, all
the books I want to read, and all the friends I
want to see. The longer I live the more my
mind dwells upon the beauty and the wonder
of the world.

JOHN BURROUGHS

❦

LOVELIEST OF TREES

Loveliest of trees, the cherry now
Is hung with bloom along the bough,
And stands about the woodland ride
Wearing white for Eastertide.

Now, of my threescore years and ten,
Twenty will not come again,
And take from seventy springs a score,
It only leaves me fifty more.

And since to look at things in bloom
Fifty springs are little room,
About the woodlands I will go
To see the cherry hung with snow.

ALFRED EDWARD HOUSMAN

❦

A thing of beauty is a joy forever:
Its loveliness increases; it will never
Pass into nothingness; but still will keep
A bower quiet for us, and a sleep
Full of sweet dreams, and health, and quiet
    breathing.

JOHN KEATS

❦

The beauty of the sunbeam lies partly in the
fact that God does not keep it; he gives it away
to us all.

DAVID SWING

❦

A SONG OF THE ROAD

I lift my cap to Beauty,
    I lift my cap to Love;
I bow before my Duty,
    And know that God's above!
My heart through shining arches
    Of leaf and blossom goes;
My soul, triumphant, marches
    Through life to life's repose.
And I, through all this glory,
    Nor know, nor fear my fate—
The great things are so simple,
    The simple are so great!

FRED G. BOWLES

❦

BREAD

Be gentle when you touch bread. Let it not lie
uncared for and unwanted. So often bread is
taken for granted. There is so much beauty in
bread: beauty of sun and soil, beauty of patient
toil. Winds and rains have caressed it, Christ
often blessed it. Be gentle when you touch
bread.

❦

GOD IS HERE

God is here! I hear his voice
While thrushes make the woods rejoice.

I touch his robe each time I place
My hand against a pansy's face.

I breathe his breath if I but pass
Verbenas trailing through the grass.

God is here! From every tree
His leafy fingers beckon me.

MADELEINE AARON

❦

WORLD AFLAME

Friendships, family ties, the companionship of little children, an autumn forest flung in prodigality against a deep blue sky, the intricate design and haunting fragrance of a flower, the counterpoint of a Bach fugue or the melodic line of a Beethoven sonata, the fluted note of bird song, the glowing glory of a sunset: the world is aflame with things of eternal moment.

E. MARGARET CLARKSON

MIRACLE

Who is in love with loveliness,
    Need not shake with cold;
For he may tear a star in two,
    And frock himself in gold.

Who holds her first within his heart,
    In certain favor goes;
If his roof tumbles, he may find
    Harbor in a rose.

LIZETTE WOODWORTH REESE

NATURE'S CREED

I believe in the brook as it wanders
    From hillside into glade;
I believe in the breeze as it whispers
    When evening's shadows fade.
I believe in the roar of the river
    As it dashes from high cascade;
I believe in the cry of the tempest
    'Mid the thunder's cannonade.
I believe in the light of shining stars,
    I believe in the sun and the moon;
I believe in the flash of lightning,
    I believe in the night-bird's croon.
I believe in the faith of the flowers,
    I believe in the rock and sod,
For in all of these appeareth clear
    The handiwork of God.

VOICE OF THE PETALS

The exceeding beauty of the earth, in her splendor of life, yields a new thought with every petal. The hours when the mind is absorbed by beauty are the only hours when we really live, so that the longer we can stay among these things so much the more is snatched from inevitable Time.

RICHARD JEFFERIES

BEAUTY ON PARADE

Fragile as a flower stem,
Fragrant as a rose,
Flaming as a fiery gem,
Beauty comes and goes.

LAWRENCE E. NELSON

THE OLD WOMAN

As a white candle
In a holy place,
So is the beauty
Of an aged face.

JOSEPH CAMPBELL

PRAYER

O God, we thank thee for the world in which thou hast placed us, for the universe whose vastness is revealed in the blue depths of the sky, whose immensities are lit by shining stars beyond the strength of mind to follow. We thank thee for every sacrament of beauty; for the sweetness of flowers, the solemnity of the stars; the sound of streams and swelling seas; for far-reaching lands and mighty mountains which rest and satisfy the soul, the purity of dawn which calls to holy dedication, the peace of evening which speaks of everlasting rest.

WILLIAM E. ORCHARD

BIBLE

Its light is like the body
of heaven in its clearness;
Its vastness like the bosom
of the sea;
Its variety like scenes
of nature.

JOHN HENRY NEWMAN

EVER-FLOWING RIVER

The Bible is a great river of spiritual reality rising out of Israel's remote past and continuing to flow more deeply and powerfully through succeeding centuries. It is fed by many rushing streams and mighty torrents and into it has flowed the spiritual wisdom and insight of twelve centuries.

The long river of the Bible is broad and very deep, and the Spirit of God moves upon the face of its waters. Here men that thirst come to drink of the water of life. The power of its onrushing current turns many a wheel. It gives direction and continuity to our individual understanding of spiritual things. Following the shores of this river, no man need lose his way in jungles of speculation nor deserts of spiritual dryness. It is like the ancient river that "went out of Eden to water the garden," for it is a river that enriches the soil of our civilization.

ALICE PARMELEE

❧❧

UNIVERSAL BOOK

The Bible is not only many books. It is a literature. History, poetry, prophecy, philosophy, theology, oratory, humor, sarcasm, irony, music, drama, tragedy, strategy, love tales, war tales, travelogues, laws, jurisprudence, songs, sermons, warnings, prayers, all are here. Was there ever such a literature? The Bible begins with a garden and ends with a city. It starts with a morning followed by a night and ends with a day that shall know no night. It breaks the silence with "In the beginning" and it hushes the universe to sleep with "The grace of our Lord Jesus Christ be with you all."

JOHN SNIDER

❧❧

RECEPTIVITY

There is a very large part of the Bible which can be received by us only when we come into the places for which the words were given.

There are promises for weakness which we can never get while we are strong. There are words for times of danger which we can never know while we need no protection. There are consolations for sickness whose comfort we can never get while we are in robust health. There are promises for times of loneliness, when men walk in solitary ways, which never can come with real meaning to us while loving companions are by our side. There are words for old age which we never can appropriate for ourselves along the years of youth, when the arm is strong, the blood warm, the heart brave. God cannot show us the stars while the sun shines in the heavens.

J. R. MILLER

❧❧

MORE THAN A DEAD LETTER

The Bible is like a telescope. If a man looks *through* his telescope, then he sees worlds beyond; but if he looks *at* his telescope, then he does not see anything but that. The Bible is a thing to be looked through, to see that which is beyond; but most people only look at it; and so they see only the dead letter.

PHILLIPS BROOKS

❧❧

What you bring away from the Bible depends to some extent on what you carry to it.

OLIVER WENDELL HOLMES

❧❧

I thoroughly believe in a university education for both men and women; but I believe a knowledge of the Bible without a college course is more valuable than a college course without the Bible.

WILLIAM LYON PHELPS

❧❧

KNOWLEDGE AGAINST IGNORANCE

No person can be considered well educated who has not some knowledge of the Old and the New Testament. Here it is not a question of vocabulary, though the infinite riches of the English language are nowhere so gloriously displayed. It is not a question of history, though the development of man may be profitably studied in the chronicles of a powerful and intellectual people. It is a question of knowledge against ignorance. The language, the episodes, the personages of the Bible are so interwoven with our daily speech, with the books we read, with every human utterance throughout Christendom, that our children cannot afford to be ignorant of it.

LAURA B. RICHARDS

❧

HOW TO GET THE MOST OUT OF THE BIBLE

1. Come to the Word expectantly.
2. Come surrendering to the truths here revealed.
3. Come expecting to use the truths here revealed.
4. Come unhurriedly.
5. Come with a proper emphasis.
6. Come to it even if nothing apparently comes from your coming.

E. STANLEY JONES

❧

BIBLE WITHIN THE BIBLE

The world of the Bible is a great world. I have wandered through it all, but I have never made it all my own. But some friendly hills and valleys in it are mine by right of experience. Some chapters have comforted me; some have made me homesick; some have braced me like a bugle call; and some always enlarge me within by a sense of unutterable fellowship with a great, quiet Power that pervades all things and fills me. Such passages make up for each of us his Bible within the Bible, and the extent and variety of these claims he has staked out in it measure how much of the great Book has really entered into the substance of his life.

WALTER RAUSCHENBUSCH

❧

WHAT THE BIBLE CAN DO FOR US

The Bible can give us the wholesome pleasure of reading good literature.

The Bible can help us to understand human nature in ourselves and in others.

The Bible can help us to understand many practices and ideals of our present social order by showing us their roots and how they came to be.

The Bible can correct and elevate our ideals and our faith by its strong and noble expression of the noblest faith and ideals ever given to man.

The Bible can help us to live worthily through the inspiration of the great examples it sets before us.

AMERICAN BIBLE SOCIETY

❧

WAY OF LIGHT

The Bible is a great and responsible book, not a sad book. The last thing about it that one can say justly is that it is a sad book. The Bible is a brave, strong book. It seldom speaks easily about life, but it never speaks desperately about it. If it has to admit, as it has to admit, that things at one time or another—and it may even be for the most part—are full of difficulty, the Bible never locks us up in a cell, leaving us to mere anger or despair or remorse. In the Bible there is always a way out. It may not be an easy way; it may not be the way that we should have chosen; but a way out there always is.

JOHN A. HUTTON

❧

BIBLE BE'S

"Be ye therefore perfect." Matthew 5:48.

"Be ye holy in all manner of conversation; . . . be ye holy; for I am holy." 1 Peter 1:15, 16.

"Be patient." James 5:7.

"Be at peace." Job 22:21.

"Be of good cheer; it is I; be not afraid." Matthew 14:27.

"Be diligent that ye may be found of him in peace, without spot, and blameless." 2 Peter 3:14.

"Be subject one to another." 1 Peter 5:5.

"Be clothed with humility." 1 Peter 5:5.

"Be sober, be vigilant." 1 Peter 5:8.

"Be ye kind one to another, tenderhearted, forgiving one another." Ephesians 4:32.

"Be strong and of a good courage." Joshua 1:6.

WORD OF LIFE

The Bible is the Word of Life. I beg you will read it and find this out for yourself—read, not little snatches here and there, but long passages that will really be the road to the heart of it.

You will not only find it full of real men and women, but also of things you have wondered about and been troubled about all your life, as men have been always, and the more you read, the more will it become plain to you what things are worthwhile and what are not; what things make men happy—loyalty, right dealing, speaking the truth, readiness to give everything for what they think their duty, and, most of all, the wish that they may have the real approval of the Christ, who gave everything for them; and the things that are guaranteed to make men unhappy—selfishness, cowardice, greed, and everything that is low and mean.

When you have read the Bible, you will know that it is the Word of God, because you will have found it the key to your own heart, your own happiness, and your own duty.

WOODROW WILSON

HOW TO READ THE BIBLE

It shall greatly helpe ye to understande
  Scripture,
If thou mark
Not only what is spoken or wrytten,
But of whom,
And to whom,
With what words,
At what time,
Where,
To what intent,
With what circumstances,
Considering what goeth before
And what followeth.

JOHN WYCLIFFE

WHY I READ MY BIBLE

1. Within its pages I find power for the ordering of my inner life.

2. It offers a way of escape from those inner perils which threaten our modern life.

3. In its pages are found the secrets by which men walk the pathways of light and hope and freedom.

4. It assures me that man is supremely dear to God.

5. It points the way to world brotherhood.

6. It tells me whither I am bound and why.

7. It offers me sound social philosophy.

8. It teaches me, in the words of Emerson, that "the lesson of life is to believe what the years and the centuries say, as against the hours."

PAUL B. KERN

What is home without a Bible?
  'Tis a home where daily bread
For the body is provided,
  But the soul is never fed.

C. D. MEIGS

MEDICINE CHEST

For the blues, read Psalm 27.
For an empty purse, read Psalm 37.
If discouraged about work, Psalm 128.
If people seem unkind to you, John 15.
If you are losing confidence in people,
  I Corinthians 13.
If you cannot have your own way, James 3.
If you are all out of sorts, Hebrews 12.
For a traveling companion, Psalm 121.

❦

THE ANVIL

Last eve I passed beside a blacksmith's door,
And heard the anvil ring the vesper chime;
Then looking in, I saw upon the floor
Old hammers, worn with beating years of time.

"How many anvils have you had," I said,
"To wear and batter all these hammers so?"
"Just one," said he, and then with twinkling
  eye,
"The anvil wears the hammers out, you know."

And so, thought I, the anvil of God's word,
For ages skeptic blows have beat upon;
Yet though the noise of falling blows was
  heard,
The anvil is unharmed . . . the hammers gone.

❦

FLAME

The spiritual life of the world has burned
during all these centuries with the pure flame
first kindled by the sublime mystic of the
Galilean Hills.

JOHN MORLEY

THE UNIVERSAL BOOK

How many ages and generations
Have brooded and wept and agonized
Over this Book!
What untellable joys and ecstasies,
What support to martyrs at the stake!
To what myriads has it been
The shore and rock of safety—
The refuge from the driving tempest
  and wreck.
Translated into all languages,
How it has united this diverse world!
Of its thousands there is not a verse,
Not a word but is thick-studded
With human emotion.

WORSHIP RESOURCES FOR
THE CHRISTIAN YEAR

❦

TRIBUTE

This book is the hive of all sweetness, the
armory of all well-tempered weapons, the tower
containing the crown jewels of the universe,
the lamp that kindles all other lights, the home
of all majesties and splendors, the stepping-
stone on which heaven stoops to kiss the earth
with its glories, the marriage-ring that unites
the celestial and the terrestrial, while all the
clustering white-robed multitudes of the sky
stand round to rejoice at the nuptials. This book
is the wreath into which are twisted all gar-
lands, the song into which hath struck all
harmonies, the river of light into which hath
poured all the great tides of hallelujahs, the
firmament in which all suns and moons and
stars and constellations and galaxies and immensities and universes and eternities wheel
and blaze and triumph.

T. DE WITT TALMAGE

BROTHERHOOD

Grant us brotherhood, not only for this day but for all our years—
a brotherhood not of words but of acts and deeds.

STEPHEN VINCENT BENÉT

WHAT IS BROTHERHOOD?

What is brotherhood? It is the wisdom of Lincoln and the warmth of Gandhi. It is the humility of Jesus, the humbleness of Mohammed, and the humanitarianism of Confucius. It is Catholic and Protestant and Jew living together in peacefulness and harmony. It is Italian and Dane and Bulgarian and Pole working side by side on the job and sitting shoulder to shoulder in the union hall searching for ways to advance the common good. It is the Ten Commandments and the Sermon on the Mount. It is the Bible, the Talmud, and the Koran. It is the essence of all wisdom of all the ages distilled into a single word. But equally it is the understanding of neighbors and friends who sorrow at your misfortunes and rejoice at your triumphs. You cannot see brotherhood; neither can you hear it nor taste it. But you can feel it a hundred times a day. It is the pat on the back when things look gloomy. It is the smile of encouragement when the way seems hard. It is the helping hand when the burden becomes unbearable.

PETER E. TERZICK

❧❦❧

I sought my soul,
    But my soul I could not see.
I sought my God,
    But my God eluded me.
I sought my brother,
    And I found all three.

❧❦❧

TRUE BROTHERHOOD

God, what a world, if men in street and mart
Felt that same kinship of the human heart
Which makes them, in the face of fire and
    flood,
Rise to the meaning of True Brotherhood.

ELLA WHEELER WILCOX

❧❦❧

FOR WHOM THE BELL TOLLS

No man is an island entire of itself. Every man is a piece of the continent, a part of the main. If a clod be washed away by the sea, Europe is the less, as well as if a promontory were, as well as if a manor of thy friends or of thine own were. Any man's death diminishes me, because I am involved in mankind. Therefore never send to know for whom the bell tolls. It tolls for thee.

JOHN DONNE

❧❦❧

PRAYER

Blessed is the servant who loves his brother as much when he is sick and useless as when he is well and can be of service to him. And blessed is he who loves his brother as well when he is afar off as when he is by his side, and who would say nothing behind his back he might not, in love, say before his face.

ST. FRANCIS OF ASSISI

❧❦❧

Have Love. Not love alone for one,
    But man as man thy brother call;
And scatter like the circling sun
    Thy charities on all.

JOHANN VON SCHILLER

❧❦❧

IN THE BEGINNING

God, the Master Sculptor, chiseled out the hills,
Hung great mountain-curtains at his window
    sills.
God the Artist painted murals in the sky,
Tinted all the landscape with ecstatic dye,
Cleft the dark and light, and named them night
    and day,
Set the circling seasons on their purposed way,
Looked upon his work, and pronounced it good,
Fashioned creatures like himself, and ordained
    brotherhood!

ELINOR LENNEN

✿

PRAYER

Give us, Lord, a bit o' sun,
A bit o' work, and a bit o' fun;
Give us all in the struggle and splutter,
Our daily bread and a bit o' butter.

Give us, Lord, a chance to be
Our goodly best, brave, wise, and free,
Our goodly best for ourselves and others,
Till all men learn to live as brothers.

FROM AN OLD ENGLISH INN

✿

Let's remember that it takes both the white and black keys of the piano to play "The Star-Spangled Banner."

✿

OUTWITTED

He drew a circle that shut me out—
Heretic, rebel, a thing to flout.
But Love and I had the wit to win;
We drew a circle that took him in!

EDWIN MARKHAM

✿

Jesus was the only teacher tall enough to see over the fences that divide the human race into compartments.

FRANK CRANE

✿

Partnership is not a principle, but a relationship between persons who share in a common enterprise, involving common risks, common privileges, and common responsibilities. Everything depends on the reality of our partnership with one another and of each of us with God.

GEORGE CRAIG STEWART

✿

And a thousand million lives are his
Who carries the world in his sympathies.

JAMES RUSSELL LOWELL

✿

Then let us pray that come it may,—
As come it will for a' that,—
That man to man, the world o'er,
Shall brothers be for a' that.

ROBERT BURNS

✿

If civilization is to survive, we must cultivate the science of human relationships—the ability of all peoples, of all kinds, to live together, in the same world at peace.

FRANKLIN D. ROOSEVELT

✿

A great many people think they are thinking when they are merely rearranging their prejudices.

WILLIAM JAMES

✿

No one can be wrong with man and right with God.

HARRY EMERSON FOSDICK

✿

To have courage without pugnacity,
to have conviction without bigotry,
to have charity without condescension,
to have faith without credulity,
to have love of humanity without
    mere sentimentality,
to have meekness with power
and emotion with sanity—
that is brotherhood.

CHARLES EVANS HUGHES

CHARACTER

It is not what he has, nor even what he does,
which directly expresses the worth of a man, but what he is.

HENRI FREDERIC AMIEL

This above all: to thine own self be true,
And it must follow, as the night the day,
Thou canst not then be false to any man.

WILLIAM SHAKESPEARE

❧§❧

The finest qualities of our characters do not come from trying but from that mysterious and yet most effective capacity to be inspired.

HARRY EMERSON FOSDICK

❧§❧

Education lays hold of what is best in a person, but character lays hold of what is worst. It takes hold of a failing and by very skillful manipulation and training turns it into a perfection.

FULTON J. SHEEN

❧§❧

Good habits are not made on birthdays, nor Christian character at the new year. The workshop of character is everyday life. The uneventful and commonplace hour is where the battle is lost or won.

MALTBIE D. BABCOCK

❧§❧

THE CHRISTIAN GENTLEMAN

A Christian gentleman will be slow to lose patience—a Christian grace.

A Christian gentleman will look for a way to be constructive, even when provoked.

A Christian gentleman will not envy the good fortune of others.

A Christian gentleman will refrain from trying to impress others with his own importance.

A Christian gentleman will have good manners.

A Christian gentleman will not be "touchy," even when he feels the right of resentment.

A Christian gentleman will think the best, not the worst, of others; he will try to be as wise as the serpent and harmless as a dove in handling others.

A Christian gentleman will not gloat over the wickedness of other people.

Above all else, a Christian gentleman will exhibit the love of Christ in his heart and life.

L. NELSON BELL

❧§❧

REPUTATION AND CHARACTER

The circumstances amid which you live determine your reputation; the truth you believe determines your character.

Reputation is what you are supposed to be; character is what you are.

Reputation is the photograph; character is the face.

Reputation comes over one from without; character grows up from within.

Reputation is what you have when you come to a new community; character is what you have when you go away.

Your reputation is learned in an hour; your character does not come to light for a year.

Reputation is made in a moment; character is built in a lifetime.

Reputation grows like a mushroom; character grows like the oak.

A single newspaper report gives you your reputation; a life of toil gives you your character.

Reputation makes you rich or makes you poor; character makes you happy or makes you miserable.

Reputation is what men say about you on your tombstone; character is what angels say about you before the throne of God.

WILLIAM HERSEY DAVIS

❧§❧

I will hew great windows, wonderful windows, measureless windows for my soul.

ANGELA MORGAN

❧❦❧

You should remember that though another may have more money, beauty, and brains than you, yet when it comes to the rarer spiritual values such as charity, self-sacrifice, honor, nobility of heart, you have an equal chance with everyone to be the most beloved and honored of all people.

ARCHIBALD RUTLEDGE

❧❦❧

Spiritual maturity begins when we realize that we are God's guests in this world. We are not householders, but pilgrims; not landlords, but tenants; not owners, but guests.

C. WILLARD FETTER

❧❦❧

Whatever the world thinks, he who hath not much meditated upon God, the human mind, and the *summum bonum,* may possibly make a thriving earthworm, but will most indubitably make a sorry patriot and a sorry statesman.

GEORGE BERKELEY

❧❦❧

GRACE OF GOD

We have need of patience with ourselves and with others; with those below and those above us, and with our own equals; with those who love and those who love us not; for the greatest things and for the least; against sudden inroads of trouble, and under our daily burdens; for disappointments as to the weather, or the breaking of the heart; in the weariness of the body, or the wearing of the soul; in our own failure of duty, or others' failure toward us; in everyday wants, or in the aching of sickness or the decay of age; in disappointment, bereavement, losses, injuries, reproaches; in heaviness of the heart or in sickness amid delayed hopes. In all these things, from childhood's little troubles to the martyr's sufferings, patience is the grace of God, whereby we endure evil for the love of God.

EDWARD B. PUSEY

❧❦❧

You must become something more than "mere man" on pain of becoming otherwise something less.

A. E. TAYLOR

❧❦❧

BE A PERSON

What Jesus Christ would say to us if he should speak to us in audible voice now would be something like this: Be a person. Be a real person. Stand on your own feet. Do not be pushed about by passing fads. Live by an inward light. Be true to an inward loyalty. If skepticism divides the church, vulgarity discolors social living, the profit motive makes industry often cruel, and nationalism blockades the way to peace, do not yes, yes the situation. Have a conscience of your own and, when in private life the clamor of public custom grows very loud, do you grow quiet, quiet enough to hear the beat and catch the rhythm of that inward drum.

HARRY EMERSON FOSDICK

❧❦❧

Character is what you are in the dark.

DWIGHT L. MOODY

❧❦❧

The measure of a man's real character is what he would do if he knew he would never be found out.

THOMAS MACAULAY

SPLENDID GIFT

Live your life while you have it. Life is a splendid gift. There is nothing small in it. For the greatest things grow by God's Law out of the smallest. But to live your life you must discipline it. You must not fritter it away in "fair purpose, erring act, inconstant will" but make your thoughts, your acts, all work to the same end and that end, not self but God. That is what we call character.

FLORENCE NIGHTINGALE

LINCOLN

There is no new thing to be said of Lincoln. There is no new thing to be said of the mountains, or of the sea, or of the stars. The years may go their way, but the same old mountains lift their granite shoulders above the drifting clouds, the same mysterious seas beat upon the shore, and the same silent stars keep holy vigil above a tired world. But to mountains and seas and stars men turn forever in unwearied homage. And thus with Lincoln. For he was mountain in grandeur of soul; he was sea in deep undervoice of mystic loneliness; he was star in steadfast purity of purpose and of service. And he abides.

HOMER HOCK

The toys and blocks with which we play
Are houses, lands, and gold.
Their values quickly pass away,
As does a tale that's told.

But kindly, gracious deeds abide,
Their wealth will not depart;
Their flowers of joy are multiplied
In gardens of the heart.

CHARLES RUSSELL WAKELEY

There are two freedoms, the false where one is free to do what he likes, and the true where he is free to do what he ought.

CHARLES KINGSLEY

WEST POINT CADET PRAYER

O God, our Father, thou Searcher of men's hearts, help us to draw near to thee in sincerity and truth. May our religion be filled with gladness and may our worship of thee be natural. Strengthen and increase our admiration for honest dealing and clean thinking, and suffer not our hatred of hypocrisy and pretense ever to diminish. Encourage us in our endeavor to live above the common level of life. Make us to choose the harder right instead of the easier wrong, and never to be content with a half truth when the whole can be won. Endow us with courage that is born of loyalty to all that is noble and worthy, that scorns to compromise with vice and injustice and knows no fear when truth and right are in jeopardy. Guard us against flippancy and irreverence in the sacred things of life. Grant us new ties of friendship and new opportunities of service. Kindle our hearts in fellowship with those of a cheerful countenance, and soften our hearts with sympathy for those who sorrow and suffer

CLAYTON E. WHEAR

The tragedy of the world is that men have given first class loyalty to second class causes and these causes have betrayed them.

LYNN HAROLD HOUGH

Better keep yourself clean and bright; you are the window through which you must see the world.

GEORGE BERNARD SHAW

A half century of living should put a good deal into a woman's face besides a few wrinkles and some unwelcome folds around the chin.

FRANCES PARKINSON KEYES

The most consummately beautiful thing in the universe is the rightly fashioned life of a good person.

GEORGE HERBERT PALMER

The tissue of the Life to be
  We weave with colors all our own,
And in the field of Destiny
  We reap as we have sown.

JOHN GREENLEAF WHITTIER

BE THE BEST OF WHATEVER YOU ARE

If you can't be a pine on the top of the hill,
  Be a scrub in the valley—but be
The best little scrub by the side of the rill;
  Be a bush if you can't be a tree.

If you can't be a bush, be a bit of the grass,
  Some highway happier make;
If you can't be a muskie, then just be a bass—
  But the liveliest bass in the lake!

We can't all be captains, we've got to be crew,
  There's something for all of us here,
There's big work to do, and there's lesser to do,
  And the task we must do is the near.

If you can't be a highway, then just be a trail,
  If you can't be the sun, be a star;
It isn't by size that you win or you fail—
  Be the best of whatever you are!

DOUGLAS MALLOCH

Thank God that I can trust,
That tho' a thousand times I feel the thrust
Of Faith betrayed, I still have faith in man,
Believe him pure and good since time began,
Thy child forever, tho' he may forget
The perfect mold in which his soul was set.

ANGELA MORGAN

The farther a man knows himself to be from perfection, the nearer he is to it.

GERARD GROOTE

WHOSE SHOES?

Shoes divide men into three classes. Some men wear their father's shoes. They make no decisions of their own. Some are unthinkingly shod by the crowd. The strong man is his own cobbler. He insists on making his own choices. He walks in his own shoes.

S. D. GORDON

CAST YOUR VOTE

Never be afraid to stand with the minority when the minority is right, for the minority which is right will one day be the majority; always be afraid to stand with the majority which is wrong, for the majority which is wrong will one day be the minority.

WILLIAM JENNINGS BRYAN

It would not be easy, even now, even for an unbeliever, to find a better translation of virtue from the abstract into the concrete than so to live that Christ would approve his life.

JOHN STUART MILL

CHILDREN

Every child comes with the message
that God is not yet discouraged of man.

RABINDRANATH TAGORE

I BELIEVE IN CHILDREN

I believe in children—little ones, big ones, chubby and thin ones. There is faith in their eyes, love in their touch, hope in their attitude. I thrill with them at life's joys, run with them through tall grasses, bow with them in worship, and hold them close in tragedy. I believe in children—the fragile dream of yesterday, life's radiant reality today, and the vibrant stuff of tomorrow. Yes, I believe in children, for wherever I go, to mountain village, industrial center, or open country, I find yesterday's children who were nurtured in the things of Christ at work in the building of the Kingdom of God.

❦

Children are the anchors that hold a mother to life.

SOPHOCLES

❦

Babies are bits of stardust blown from the hand of God. Lucky the woman who knows the pangs of birth, for she has held a star.

LARRY BARRETTO

❦

PETITION

I have a boy to bring up. Help me to perform my task with wisdom, kindness, and good cheer. Help me always to see him clearly, as he is. Let not my pride hide his faults. Let not my fear for him magnify my doubts and fears until I make him doubting and fearful in his turn. Quicken my judgment so that I shall know how to train him to think as a child, to be in all things pure and simple as a child.

I have a boy to bring up. Give me great patience and a long memory. Let me remember the hard places of my own youth, so that I may help when I see him struggling as I struggled then. Let me remember the things that made me glad, lest I, sweating in the toil and strain of life, forget that a child's laughter is the light of life.

I have a boy to bring up. Teach me that love understandeth all things, knows no weakness, tolerates no selfishness. Keep me from weakening my son through granting him pleasures that end in pain, ease of body that brings sickness of soul, and a vision of life that ends in death. Grant that I may love my son wisely and myself not at all.

I have a son to bring up. Give him the values and beauty and just rewards of industry. Give him an understanding brain and hands that are cunning that he may work out his own happiness.

I have a boy to bring up. Help me to send him into the world with a mission of service. Strengthen my mind and heart that I may teach him that he is his brother's keeper. Grant that he may serve those who know not the need of service, and not knowing, need it the most.

I have a boy to bring up. So guide and direct me that I may do this service to the glory of God, the service of my country, and to my son's happiness.

ANGELO PATRI

❦

WONDER OF LIFE

Children are the most wholesome part of the race, the sweetest, for they are freshest from the hand of God. Whimsical, ingenious, mischievous, they fill the world with joy and good humor. We adults live a life of apprehension as to what they will think of us; a life of defense against their terrifying energy; a life of hard work to live up to their great expectations. We put them to bed with a sense of relief—and greet them in the morning with delight and anticipation. We envy them the freshness of adventure and the discovery of life. In all these ways, children add to the wonder of being alive. In all these ways, they help to keep us young.

HERBERT HOOVER

51

WHAT IS A BOY?

Between the innocence of babyhood and the dignity of manhood we find a delightful creature called a boy. Boys come in assorted sizes, weights, and colors, but all boys have the same creed: to enjoy every second of every minute of every hour of every day and to protest with noise (their only weapon) when their last minute is finished and the adult males pack them off to bed at night.

Boys are found everywhere—on top of, underneath, inside of, climbing on, swinging from, running around, or jumping to. Mothers love them, little girls hate them, older sisters and brothers tolerate them, adults ignore them, and Heaven protects them. A boy is Truth with dirt on its face, Beauty with a cut on its finger, Wisdom with bubble gum in its hair, and the Hope of the future with a frog in its pocket.

When you are busy, a boy is an inconsiderate, bothersome, intruding jangle of noise. When you want him to make a good impression, his brain turns to jelly or else he becomes a savage, sadistic, jungle creature bent on destroying the world and himself with it.

A boy is a composite—he has the appetite of a horse, the digestion of a sword swallower, the energy of a pocket-sized atomic bomb, the curiosity of a cat, the lungs of a dictator, the imagination of a Paul Bunyan, the shyness of a violet, the audacity of a steel trap, the enthusiasm of a firecracker, and when he makes something he has five thumbs on each hand.

He likes ice cream, knives, saws, Christmas, comic books, the boy across the street, woods, water (in its natural habitat), large animals, Dad, trains, Saturday mornings, and fire engines. He is not much for Sunday School, company, schools, books without pictures, music lessons, neckties, barbers, girls, overcoats, adults, or bedtime.

Nobody else is so early to rise, or so late to supper. Nobody else gets so much fun out of trees, dogs, and breezes. Nobody else can cram into one pocket a rusty knife, a half-eaten apple, three feet of string, an empty Bull Durham sack, two gum drops, six cents, a slingshot, a chunk of unknown substance, and a genuine supersonic code ring with a secret compartment.

A boy is a magical creature—you can lock him out of your workshop, but you can't lock him out of your heart. You can get him out of your study, but you can't get him out of your mind. Might as well give up—he is your captor, your jailor, your boss, and your master—a freckled-faced, pint-sized, cat-chasing, bundle of noise. But when you come home at night with only the shattered pieces of your hopes and dreams, he can mend them like new with the two magic words, "Hi Dad!"

ALAN BECK

❧

You may give them your love but not your thoughts,
For they have their own thoughts.
You may house their bodies but not their souls,
For their souls dwell in the house of tomorrow, which you cannot visit, not even in your dreams.
You may strive to be like them, but seek not to make them like you.
For life goes not backward nor tarries with yesterday.
You are the bows from which your children as living arrows are sent forth.

KAHLIL GIBRAN

❧

God sends children to enlarge our hearts, and to make us unselfish and full of kindly sympathies and affections.

MARY HOWITT

❧

WHAT IS A GIRL?

Little girls are the nicest things that happen to people. They are born with a little bit of angel-shine about them, and though it wears thin sometimes, there is always enough left to lasso your heart—even when they are sitting in the mud, or crying temperamental tears, or parading up the street in Mother's best clothes.

A little girl can be sweeter (and badder) oftener than anyone else in the world. She can jitter around, and stomp, and make funny noises that frazzle your nerves, yet just when you open your mouth, she stands there demure with that special look in her eyes. A girl is Innocence playing in the mud, Beauty standing on its head, and Motherhood dragging a doll by the foot.

Girls are available in five colors—black, white, red, yellow, or brown—yet Mother Nature always manages to select your favorite color when you place your order. They disprove the law of supply and demand—there are millions of little girls, but each is as precious as rubies.

God borrows from many creatures to make a little girl. He uses the song of a bird, the squeal of a pig, the stubbornness of a mule, the antics of a monkey, the spryness of a grasshopper, the curiosity of a cat, the speed of a gazelle, the slyness of a fox, the softness of a kitten, and to top it all off He adds the mysterious mind of a woman.

A little girl likes new shoes, party dresses, small animals, first grade, noisemakers, the girl next door, dolls, make-believe, dancing lessons, ice cream, kitchens, coloring books, make-up, cans of water, going visiting, tea parties, and one boy. She doesn't care so much for visitors, boys in general, large dogs, hand-me-downs, straight chairs, vegetables, snowsuits, or staying in the front yard. She is loudest when you are thinking, the prettiest when she has provoked you, the busiest at bedtime, the quietest when you want to show her off, and the most flirtatious when she absolutely must not get the best of you again.

Who else can cause you more grief, joy, irritation, satisfaction, embarrassment, and genuine delight than this combination of Eve, Salome, and Florence Nightingale? She can muss up your home, your hair, and your dignity—spend your money, your time, and your patience—and just when your temper is ready to crack, her sunshine peeks through and you've lost again.

Yes, she is a nerve-racking nuisance, just a noisy bundle of mischief. But when your dreams tumble down and the world is a mess—when it seems you are pretty much of a fool after all—she can make you a king when she climbs on your knee and whispers, "I love you best of all!"

ALAN BECK

❦

GOD'S WAY

When God wants a great work done in the world or a great wrong righted, he goes about it in a very unusual way. He doesn't stir up his earthquakes or send forth his thunderbolts. Instead, he has a helpless baby born, perhaps in a simple home and of some obscure mother. And then God puts the idea into the mother's heart, and she puts it into the baby's mind. And then God waits. The greatest forces in the world are not the earthquakes and the thunderbolts. The greatest forces in the world are babies.

E. T. SULLIVAN

❦

Life is a flame that is always burning itself out, but it catches fire again every time a child is born.

GEORGE BERNARD SHAW

❦

53

TO MY CHILD

You are the trip I did not take;
You are the pearls I cannot buy;
You are my blue Italian lake;
You are my piece of foreign sky.

ANNE CAMPBELL

IF . . .

If a child lives with criticism, he learns to condemn.

If a child lives with hostility, he learns to fight.

If a child lives with fears, he learns to be apprehensive.

If a child lives with pity, he learns to feel sorry for himself.

If a child lives with jealousy, he learns to feel guilty.

If a child lives with encouragement, he learns to be confident.

If a child lives with tolerance, he learns to be patient.

If a child lives with praise, he learns to be appreciative.

If a child lives with acceptance, he learns to love.

If a child lives with approval, he learns to like himself.

If a child lives with recognition, he learns to have a goal.

If a child lives with fairness, he learns what justice is.

If a child lives with honesty, he learns what truth is.

If a child lives with security, he learns to have faith in himself and in those about him.

If a child lives with friendliness, he learns that the world is a good place in which to live.

THE WATCHMAN-EXAMINER

The great man is he who does not lose his child's heart.

MENCIUS

A LITTLE CHILD SHALL LEAD US

You, little child, with your shining eyes and dimpled cheeks, you can lead us along the pathway to the more abundant life:

We blundering grownups need in our lives the virtues that you have in yours:

The joy and enthusiasm of looking forward to each new day with glorious expectations of wonderful things to come.

The vision that sees the world as a splendid place with good fairies, brave knights, and glistening castles reaching toward the sky.

The radiant curiosity that finds adventure in simple things: the mystery of billowy clouds, the miracle of snowflakes, the magic of growing flowers.

The tolerance that forgets differences as quickly as your childish quarrels are spent, that holds no grudges, that hates never, that loves people for what they are.

The genuineness of being oneself; to be done with sham, pretense, and empty show; to be simple, natural, and sincere.

The courage that rises from defeat and tries again, as you with laughing face rebuild the house of blocks that topples to the floor.

The believing heart that trusts others, knows no fear, and has faith in a Divine Father who watches over his children from the sky.

The contented, trusting mind that at the close of day woos the blessing of childlike slumber.

Little child, we would become like you, that we may find again the Kingdom of Heaven within our hearts.

We need love's tender lessons taught
As only weakness can;
God hath his small interpreters;
The child must teach the man.

JOHN GREENLEAF WHITTIER

Happy the child that has for friend an old, sympathetic, encouraging mind, one eager to develop, slow to rebuke or discourage.

ARTHUR BRISBANE

THE HEART OF A CHILD

Our religion is one which challenges the ordinary human standards by holding that the ideal of life is the spirit of a little child. We tend to glorify adulthood and wisdom and worldly prudence, but the Gospel reverses all this. The Gospel says that the inescapable condition of entrance into the divine fellowship is that we turn and become as a little child. As against our natural judgment we must become tender and full of wonder and unspoiled by the hard skepticism on which we so often pride ourselves. But when we really look into the heart of a child, willful as he may be, we are often ashamed. God has sent children into the world, not only to replenish it, but to serve as sacred reminders of something ineffably precious which we are always in danger of losing. The sacrament of childhood is thus a continuing revelation.

ELTON TRUEBLOOD

THE CHILD'S APPEAL

I am the Child.
All the world waits for my coming.
All the earth watches with interest to see
 what I shall become.
Civilization hangs in the balance,
For what I am, the world of tomorrow will be.

I am the Child.
I have come into your world, about which I
 know nothing.

Why I came I know not;
How I came I know not.
I am curious; I am interested.

I am the Child.
You hold in your hand my destiny.
You determine, largely, whether I shall
 succeed or fail.
Give me, I pray you, those things that make
 for happiness.
Train me, I beg you, that I may be a blessing
 to the world.

MAMIE GENE COLE

CHILDHOOD

To be Himself a star most bright
To bring the wise men to His sight,
To be Himself a voice most sweet
To call the shepherds to His feet,
To be a child—it was His will,
That folk like us might find Him still.

JOHN ERSKINE

TWO PRAYERS

Last night my little boy confessed to me
Some childish wrong;
And kneeling at my knee,
He prayed with tears—
"Dear God, make me a man
Like Daddy—wise and strong;
I know you can."

Then while he slept
I knelt beside his bed,
Confessed my sins,
And prayed with low-bowed head—
"O God, make me a child
Like my child here—
Pure, guileless,
Trusting Thee with faith sincere."

ANDREW GILLIES

THE CHOIR BOY

In his white surplice there he stands,
A hymnal in his boyish hands;
The morning sun upon his hair
Suggests a halo circling there.

His voice as sweet and fresh to hear
As feathered songbird singing clear;
His eyes as innocent and blue
As skies with heaven shining through.

Is this the boy who all the week
Brought worried lines to father's cheek?
Is this the mischievous small lad
Whom teacher found so very bad?

It cannot be! but mother, who
Serenely listens from her pew,
Feels truly what the others miss—
At heart he always is like this!

ANNE CAMPBELL

GOD'S OPINION

A baby is God's opinion that life should go on. Never will a time come when the most marvelous recent invention is as marvelous as a newborn baby. The finest of our precision watches, the most supercolossal of our supercargo planes, don't compare with a newborn baby in the number and ingenuity of coils and springs, in the flow and change of chemical solutions, in timing devices and interrelated parts that are irreplaceable.

CARL SANDBURG

What gift has Providence bestowed on man that is so dear to him as his children?

CICERO

SOMEWHERE THE CHILD

Among the thousands of tiny things growing up all over the land, some of them under my very wing—watched and tended, unwatched and untended, loved, unloved, protected from danger, thrust into temptation—among them somewhere is the child who will write the novel that will stir men's hearts to nobler issues and incite them to better deeds.

There is the child who will paint the greatest picture or carve the greatest statue of the age; another who will deliver his country in an hour of peril; another who will give his life for a great principle; and another, born more of the spirit than of the flesh, who will live continually on the heights of moral being, and dying, draw men after him.

It may be that I shall preserve one of these children to the race. It is a peg big enough on which to hang a hope, for every child born into the world is a new incarnate thought of God, an ever fresh and radiant possibility.

KATE DOUGLAS WIGGIN

INEXHAUSTIBLE TREASURY

Once you've loved a child, you love all children. You give away your love to one, and you find that by the giving you have made yourself an inexhaustible treasury.

MARGARET LEE RUNBECK

THE UNSEEN GUEST

We had from childhood not only the experience of love and truth common to all family life, but the idea of them embodied in the person of Jesus, a picture always present to our imagination as well as our feelings.

JOYCE CARY

CHURCH

There is a little plant called reverence
in the corner of my soul's garden,
which I love to have watered once a week.

OLIVER WENDELL HOLMES

THE CHURCH OF MY DREAMS

This is the church of my dreams:
The church of the warm heart,
Of the open mind,
Of the adventurous spirit;
The church that cares,
That heals hurt lives,
That comforts old people,
That challenges youth;
That knows no divisions of culture or class,
No frontiers, geographical or social;
The church that inquires as well as avers,
That looks forward as well as backward;
The church of the Master,
The church of the people,
High as the ideals of Jesus,
Low as the humblest human;
A working church,
A worshipping church,
A winsome church,
A church that interprets the truth
    in terms of truth,
That inspires courage for this life and hope
    for the life to come;
A church of courage
A church of all good men,
A church of the living God.

JOHN MILTON MOORE

BENEDICTION

Go on your way in peace.
Be of good courage.
Hold fast that which is good.
Render to no man evil for evil.
Strengthen the fainthearted.
Support the weak.
Help and cheer the sick.
Honor all men.
Love and serve the Lord.
May the blessing of God be upon you
    and remain with you forever.

GLOUCESTER CATHEDRAL

ON ENTERING CHURCH

Pause ere thou enter, traveler, and bethink thee
How holy, yet how homelike, is this place;
Time that thou spendest humbly here shall
    link thee
With men unknown who once were of thy race.

PLAQUE IN AN ENGLISH CHURCH

Enter expectantly,
Breathe prayerfully,
Worship reverently,
Relax restfully,
Greet others cordially,
Leave thoughtfully,
Come again soon.

SONNET

Oft have I seen at some cathedral door
    A laborer, pausing in the dust and heat,
    Lay down his burden, and with reverent
        feet
    Enter, and cross himself, and on the floor
Kneel to repeat his paternoster o'er;
    Far off the noises of the world retreat;
    The loud vociferations of the street
    Become an undistinguishable roar.
So, as I enter here from day to day,
    And leave my burden at this minster gate,
    Kneeling in prayer, and not ashamed to pray,
The tumult of the time disconsolate
    To inarticulate murmurs dies away,
    While the eternal ages watch and wait.

HENRY WADSWORTH LONGFELLOW

The church exists to train its members through
the practice of the presence of God to be
servants of others, to the end that Christlike-
ness may become common property.

WILLIAM ADAMS BROWN

59

WHAT IS THE CHURCH?

The church is man when his awed soul goes out,
In reverence to a mystery that swathes him all
   about.
When any living man in awe gropes Godward
   in his search;
Then in that hour, that living man becomes
   the living church,
Then, though in wilderness or in waste, his
   soul is swept along
Down naves of prayer, through aisles of praise,
   up altar-stairs of song.
And where man fronts the Mystery with spirit
   bowed in prayer,
There is the universal church—the church of
   God is there.

SAM WALTER FOSS

GREETING

Friend, you have come to this Church; leave
   it not without a prayer. No man entering a
   house ignores him who dwells in it. This is
   the House of God and He is here.
Pray then to Him who loves you and bids you
   welcome and awaits your greeting.
Give thanks for those who in past ages built
   this place to His glory and for those who,
   dying that we might live, have preserved
   for us our heritage.
Praise God for His gifts of beauty in painting
   and architecture, handicraft and music.
Ask that we who now live may build the
   spiritual fabric of the nation in truth, beauty,
   and goodness, and that as we draw near to
   the one Father through our Lord and Savior
   Jesus Christ we may draw nearer to one
   another in perfect brotherhood.
The Lord preserve thy going out and thy coming in.

CANTERBURY CATHEDRAL

THE CHURCH UNIVERSAL

I believe in the church universal, all denom-
inations of it, Catholic and Protestant and
Jewish. I believe in it because it is the only
institution, faulty as it is, which has been
created to keep God and Jesus alive in the
world, to hold up God's picture, and to propa-
gate God's words and teaching. It has failed
time and again to be faithful to its tasks; it
has gone off into side issues; it has emphasized
wrong angles of vision; it has been guilty of
wrong action and utterly twisted and perverted
aims; nevertheless with all its faults I love it
and believe in it still, because it is the chief
dwelling place on earth of my Master and my
Savior.

BURRIS A. JENKINS

CALL TO UNITY

The call to unity is like the flow of a river:
it never ceases. It has been sounding with
varying accent through the successive generations since the beginning. To us it has of late
come with new force through the voice of God's
Spirit speaking to the many divided com-
munions of our day, as the call of a shepherd
to his scattered flock. We have responded to
His call. He presides over us. In proportion
to our obedience to His guidance we shall be
able to promote His will and embrace it as our
own. He appeals to us to hush our prejudices,
to sit lightly to our opinions, to look on the
things of others as though they were our very
own—all this without slighting the convictions
of our hearts or our loyalty to God.

CHARLES H. BRENT

To be unknown of God is altogether too much
privacy.

THOMAS MERTON

❧

You go to your church, and I'll go to mine,
    But let's walk along together;
Our Father has built them side by side,
    So let's walk along together.

PHILLIPS H. LORD

❧

LOVE AND POWER

There are two ways of being united—one is by being frozen together, and the other is by being melted together. What Christians need is to be united in brotherly love, and then they may expect to have power.

DWIGHT L. MOODY

❧

WHY BELONG?

1. I should belong to the church because I ought to be better than I am. Henry Ward Beecher once said: "The church is not a gallery for the exhibition of eminent Christians, but a school for the education of imperfect ones."

2. I should belong to the church because of what I can give to it and do through it, as well as because of what I may get out of it. The church is not a dormitory for sleepers; it is an institution of workers. It is not only a rest camp; it is a front-line trench.

3. I should belong to the church because every man should pay his debts and do his share toward discharging the obligation of society. Not only has the church been the bearer of the good news of personal salvation; it has been and is the supreme uplifting and conserving agency, without which "civilization would lapse into barbarism and press its way to perdition."

4. I should belong to the church because of memories—memories of things I can never forget, memories of faces that will never fade, memories of vows that are the glory of youth.

5. I should belong to the church because of hope—hope that lives when promises are dead, hope that paves the way for progress, hope that visions peace and social justice, hope for all time to come—and hope for eternity, the great hope that casts its anchor behind Jesus Christ.

6. I should belong to the church because of the strong men in it who need reinforcing, the weak men in it who need encouraging, the rascals in it who need rebuking. If I say that I am not good enough, my humility recommends me. If I sit in the seat of the scornful, by inactivity condemns me.

7. I should belong to the church—but not until I am ready to join a going concern; not until I am willing to become an active partner with Jesus Christ.

DANIEL A. POLING

❧

We should think of the church as an orchestra in which the different churches play on different instruments while a Divine Conductor calls the tune.

WILLIAM R. INGE

❧

My church helps me
    to keep a sky in my life and to look up,
    to keep my hand in God's and hold on to
        him,
    to see the eternal values above the material,
    to lift life above self to service for Christ,
    to see the good in others and praise it,
    to keep sweet and to keep busy for him,
    to have a seeing eye, a feeling heart,
        a helping hand,
    to test the motive of life and choose the best,
    to do justly, love mercy, and walk humbly.

THE WATCHMAN-EXAMINER

SUNDAY

The repose of the one day in seven is essential for all men, and for more than health reasons. The modern world seems to have forgotten this divine law; even when the necessity for a weekly "day of rest" is admitted, the reason for it has usually been forgotten, and so people waste the time which might have been spent in true re-creation; of spirit as well as of body and mind. The Christian Sunday should be a festival, gathering up all the life of the week and offering it to God in worship, and then spending the day in a way which most truly promotes joy and happiness and refreshment for oneself and for other people.

OLIVE WYON

Worship is the highest act of which man is capable. It not only stretches him beyond all the limits of his finite self to affirm the divine depth of mystery and holiness in the living and eternal God, but it opens him at the deepest level of his being to an act which unites him most realistically with his fellow man.

SAMUEL H. MILLER

WORSHIP

It is the soul searching for its counterpart.
It is a thirsty land crying out for rain.
It is a candle in the act of being kindled.
It is a drop in quest of the ocean.
It is a man listening through a tornado for the Still Small Voice.
It is a voice in the night calling for help.
It is a sheep lost in the wilderness pleading for rescue by the Good Shepherd.
It is the same sheep nestling in the arms of the rescuer.
It is the Prodigal Son running to his Father.
It is a soul standing in awe before the mystery of the Universe.
It is a poet enthralled by the beauty of a sunrise.
It is a workman pausing a moment to listen to a strain of music.
It is a hungry heart seeking for love.
It is a heart of love consecrating herself to her lover.
It is Time flowing into Eternity.
It is my little self engulfed in the Universal Self.
It is a man climbing the altar stairs to God.

DWIGHT BRADLEY

THE CHURCH IN THE HEART

Who builds a church within his heart
And takes it with him everywhere
Is holier far than he whose church
Is but a one-day house of prayer.

MORRIS ABEL BEER

THIS IS MY CHURCH

A door
    into an opportunity for service,
    into the most useful life,
    into the best experience,
    into the most hopeful future—
    my church gives me a start.

An armory
    to get power to fight evil,
    to get inspiration to keep going right,
    to get an uplifting influence,
    to learn how to use spiritual weapons,
    to get a vision of Christ—
    my church keeps me moving.

An anchor
    to steady me in the storm,
    to keep me from the breakers,
    to guide me in the strenuous life,
    to hold me lest I drift away from God,
    to save me in the hour of temptation—
    and lead me into the harbor.

CONFIDENCE

I can see how it might be possible for a man
to look down upon the earth
and be an atheist,
but I cannot conceive how
he could look up into the heavens
and say there is no God.

ABRAHAM LINCOLN

UNDERGIRDING

Faith is a living, daring confidence in God's grace, so sure and certain that a man would stake his life on it a thousand times. This confidence in God's grace and knowledge of it makes men glad and bold and happy in dealing with God and with all his creatures; and this is the work of the Holy Ghost in faith. Hence a man is ready and glad, without compulsion, to do good to everyone, to serve everyone, to suffer everything, in love and praise of God, who has shown him this grace.

MARTIN LUTHER

Let nothing disturb thee,
Nothing affright thee;
All things are passing;
God never changeth;
Patient endurance
Attaineth to all things.
Whom God possesseth
In nothing is wanting:
Alone God sufficeth.

ST. TERESA

THE CROSS

Because the cross alone measures "the breadth, and length, and depth, and height" of the love of God, it is beyond the comprehension of man. The love of Christ "passeth knowledge." Its "breadth" is wide enough to comprehend the whole world, including all races. Its "length" reaches down through all the ages from the beginning to the end of the reign of sin. Its "depth" reaches down to the lowest deeps of man's degradation and saves even "to the uttermost." Its "height" includes the highest heaven to which it will eventually lift those who know its power.

TAYLOR G. BUNCH

I see the rainbow in the sky, the dew upon
the grass;
I see them, and I ask not why they glimmer
or they pass.
With folded arms I linger not to call them
back; 'twere vain:
In this, or in some other spot, I know they'll
shine again.

WALTER SAVAGE LANDOR

OVERTONES

I heard a bird at break of day
Sing from the autumn trees
A song so mystical and calm,
So full of certainties,
No man, I think, could listen long
Except upon his knees.
Yet this was but a simple bird,
Alone, among the trees.

WILLIAM ALEXANDER PERCY

There is but one way to tranquillity of mind and happiness. Let this therefore be always ready at hand with thee, both when thou wakest early in the morning, and when thou goest late to sleep, to account no external thing thine own, but commit all these to God.

EPICTETUS

Every great discovery I ever made, I gambled that the truth was there, and then I acted on it in faith until I could prove its existence.

ARTHUR H. COMPTON
(*Nobel Prize physicist*)

Communion with God is a great sea that fits every bend in the shore of human need.

HARRY EMERSON FOSDICK

✦❧

Our belief at the beginning of a doubtful undertaking is the one thing that insures the successful outcome of our venture.

WILLIAM JAMES

✦❧

PARTNER

The Lord is my partner. I shall not be troubled about temporal prosperity. He maketh me to live upon the fat of the land; he leadeth me away from bad investments; he restoreth my confidence in him; he leadeth me to know the blessings of scriptural giving. Yea, though I pass through a season of business depression, I will not fear for the outcome, for thou, O Lord, wilt not permit our enterprise to fail. Thou preparest a way and a will to enjoy spiritual blessings more than ever I have known before in all my Christian experience. Thou causeth thy fund to contain enough money and still some for every work of thine. Surely real prosperity—of the heart as well as of the purse —shall continue with me as long as I confidently do my part and let him prove what he can do; and together we build up his kingdom unto everlasting day.

E. A. STANISTREET

✦❧

Tell him about the heartache,
And tell him the longings, too.
Tell him the baffled purpose
When we scarce know what to do.

Then leaving all our weakness
With the One divinely strong,
Forget that we bore a burden
And carry away a song.

PHILLIPS BROOKS

✦❧

Forgive me if too close I lean
My human heart on thee.

JOHN GREENLEAF WHITTIER

✦❧

My bark is wafted to the strand
By breath divine;
And on the helm there rests a hand
Other than mine.

WASHINGTON GLADDEN

✦❧

He paints the lily of the field,
Perfumes each lily bell;
If he so loves the little flowers,
I know he loves me well.

MARIA STRAUS

✦❧

I believe in God, in the same way in which I believe in my friends, because I feel the breath of his love and his invisible, intangible hand, bringing me here, carrying me there, pressing upon me.

MIGUEL DE UNAMUNO

✦❧

PRAYER

Son of Man, whenever I doubt of life, I think of thee. Nothing is so impossible as that thou shouldst be dead. I can imagine the hills to dissolve in vapour, and the stars to melt in smoke, and the rivers to empty themselves in sheer exhaustion, but I feel no limit in thee. Thou never growest old to me. Last century is old, last year is old, last season is an obsolete fashion, but thou are not obsolete. Thou are abreast of all the centuries, nay, thou goest before them like the star. I have never come up with thee, modern as I am.

GEORGE MATHESON

COURAGE

*Courage is the first of human qualities because
it is the quality which guarantees all the others.*

WINSTON CHURCHILL

COURAGE

Courage is armor
A blind man wears;
The calloused scar
Of outlived despairs:
Courage is fear
That has said its prayers.

KARLE WILSON BAKER

Courage is the price
that life extracts
for granting peace.
The soul
that knows it not,
knows no release
from little things.

AMELIA EARHART

MIRACLE

Do not pray for easy lives; pray to be stronger
men. Do not pray for tasks equal to your
powers; pray for powers equal to your tasks.
Then the doing of your work shall be no
miracle, but you shall be a miracle. Every day
you shall wonder at yourself, at the richness
of life which has come to you by the grace of
God.

PHILLIPS BROOKS

Keep your fears to yourself, but share your
courage with others.

ROBERT LOUIS STEVENSON

As the essence of courage is to stake one's life
on a possibility, so the essence of faith is to
believe that the possibility exists.

WILLIAM SALTER

PROFILE IN COURAGE

To be courageous requires no exceptional quali-
fications, no magic formula, no special combination of time, place, and circumstance. It is an
opportunity that sooner or later is presented to
us all. Politics merely furnish one arena which
imposes special tests of courage. In whatever
arena of life one may meet the challenge of
courage, whatever may be the sacrifices he
faces if he follows his conscience—the loss
of his friends, his fortune, his contentment,
even the esteem of his fellow men—each man
must decide for himself the course he will
follow. The stories of past courage can define
that ingredient—they can teach, they can offer
hope, they can provide inspiration. But they
cannot supply courage itself. For this each man
must look into his own soul.

JOHN F. KENNEDY

There is a Light where'er I go,
    There is a Splendor where I wait.
Though all around be desolate,
    Warm on my eyes I feel the glow.

The fight is long, the triumph slow,
    Yet shall my soul stand strong and straight;
There is a Light where'er I go,
    There is a Splendor where I wait.

From COURAGE

Courage isn't a brilliant dash,
A daring deed in a moment's flash;
It isn't an instantaneous thing
Born of despair with a sudden spring.

But it's something deep in the soul of man
That is working always to serve some plan.

EDGAR A. GUEST

CHALLENGE

I marvel at the courage of the shrub or little
    tree
That struggles 'mongst the rocks, well know-
    ing it can never be
Much more than just a scrawny scrub, yet
    serving in God's plot
To add a little beauty to a useless barren spot.
I've seen them cling tenaciously to sides of
    rocky bluff,
As if in pure defiance of those elements so
    rough;
Or else to strive to justify audacity to choose
Such most unlikely habitat with odds so great
    to lose.
They send their eager tendons out along thin
    veins of soil,
Extracting meager sustenance for their per-
    sistent toil;
Thus serving as a challenge to us mortals who
    complain
About the petty hardships that we often en-
    tertain.

                                      CARL D. ROLLINS

Men grow when inspired by a high purpose,
when contemplating vast horizons. The sacrifice of oneself is not very difficult for one burning with the passion for a great adventure.

                                      ALEXIS CARREL

The hero is no braver than an ordinary man,
but he is brave five minutes longer.

                              RALPH WALDO EMERSON

To fight aloud is very brave,
But gallanter, I know,
Who charge within the bosom
The cavalry of woe.

                              EMILY DICKINSON

DYKES OF COURAGE

Courage and cowardice are antithetical.
Courage is an inner resolution to go forward
    in spite of obstacles and frightening situa-
    tions; cowardice is a submissive surrender
    to circumstance.
Courage breeds creative self-affirmation; cow-
    ardice produces destructive self-abnegation.
Courage faces fear and thereby masters it;
    cowardice represses fear and is thereby mas-
    tered by it.
Courageous men never lose the zest for living
    even though their life situation is zestless;
    cowardly men, overwhelmed by the uncer-
    tainties of life, lose the will to live.
We must constantly build dykes of courage to
    hold back the flood of fear.

                          MARTIN LUTHER KING, JR.

The world has no room for cowards, We must
all be ready somehow to toil, to suffer, to die.
And yours is not the less noble because no drum
beats before you when you go out to your
daily battlefields, and no crowds shout your
coming when you return from your daily victory
and defeat.

                        ROBERT LOUIS STEVENSON

PRAYER

I do not ask to walk smooth paths
Nor bear an easy load.
I pray for strength and fortitude
To climb the rock-strewn road.

Give me such courage I can scale
The hardest peaks alone,
And transform every stumbling block
Into a steppingstone.

                        GAIL BROOK BURKET

CREED

Faithfully faithful to every trust,
Honestly honest in every deed,
Righteously righteous and justly just:
This is the whole of the good man's creed.

MY SYMPHONY

To live content with small means;

To seek elegance rather than luxury, and refinement rather than fashion;

To be worthy, not respectable, and wealthy, not rich;

To study hard, think quietly, talk gently, act frankly;

To listen to stars and birds, to babes and sages, with open heart;

To bear all cheerfully, do all bravely, await occasions, hurry never.

In a word, to let the spiritual, unbidden and unconscious, grow up through the common.

This is to be my symphony.

WILLIAM ELLERY CHANNING

God never gave a man a thing to do concerning which it would be irreverent to ponder how the Son of God would have done it.

GEORGE MACDONALD

MY TASK

To be honest, to be kind;

To earn a little and to spend a little less;

To make upon the whole a family happier for his presence;

To renounce when that shall be necessary and not to be embittered;

To keep a few friends, but those without capitulation;

Above all, on the same grim conditions, to keep friends with himself—

Here is a task for all that man has of fortitude and delicacy.

ROBERT LOUIS STEVENSON

RESOLUTION

Let then our first act every morning be to make the following resolve for the day:

I shall not fear anyone on earth.

I shall fear only God.

I shall not bear ill will toward anyone.

I shall not submit to injustice from anyone.

I shall conquer untruth by truth.

And in resisting untruth I shall put up with all suffering.

MAHATMA GANDHI

MY PURPOSE

To awaken each morning with a smile brightening my face;

To greet the day with reverence for the opportunities it contains;

To approach my work with a clean mind;

To hold ever before me, even in the doing of little things, the Ultimate Purpose toward which I am working;

To meet men and women with laughter on my lips and love in my heart;

To be gentle, kind, and courteous through all the hours;

To approach the night with weariness that ever woos sleep, and the joy that comes from work well done—

This is how I desire to waste wisely my days.

THOMAS DEKKER

WHAT I LIVE FOR

I live for those who love me, for those who know me true;

For the heaven that smiles above me, and awaits my spirit too;

For the cause that lacks assistance, for the wrong that needs resistance,

For the future in the distance, and the good that I can do.

GEORGE LINNAEUS BANKS

WINDOWS OF THE SOUL

Let there be many windows in your soul,
That all the glory of the universe
May beautify it. Not the narrow pane
Of one poor creed can catch the radiant rays
That shine from countless sources. Tear away
The blinds of superstition. Let the light
Pour through fair windows, broad as
    truth itself,
And high as heaven . . . Tune your ear
To all the wordless music of the stars,
And to the voice of Nature; and your heart
Shall turn to truth and goodness as the plant
Turns to the sun. A thousand unseen hands
Reach down to help you to their peace-
    crowned heights;
And all the forces of the firmament
Shall fortify your strength. Be not afraid
To thrust aside half-truths and grasp the whole.

ELLA WHEELER WILCOX

Every human being has a work to carry on within, duties to perform abroad, influence to exert, which are peculiarly his, and which no conscience but his own can teach.

WILLIAM ELLERY CHANNING

TEN SPIRITUAL TONICS

1. *Stop worrying.* Worry kills life.
2. *Begin each day with a prayer.* It will arm your soul.
3. *Control appetite.* Over-indulgence clogs body and mind.
4. *Accept your limitations.* All of us can't be great.
5. *Don't envy.* It wastes time and energy.
6. *Have faith in people.* Cynicism sours the disposition.
7. *Find a hobby.* It will relax your nerves.
8. *Read a book a week* to stimulate imagination and broaden your view.
9. *Spend some time alone,* for the peace of solitude and silence.
10. *Try to want what you have,* instead of spending your strength trying to get what you want.

ABRAHAM L. FEINBERG

Most people are willing to take the Sermon on the Mount as a flag to sail under, but few will use it as a rudder by which to steer.

OLIVER WENDELL HOLMES

MY CREED

To live as gently as I can;
To be, no matter where, a man;
To take what comes of good or ill
And cling to faith and honor still;
To do my best, and let that stand
The record of my brain and hand;
And then, should failure come to me,
Still work and hope for victory.

To have no secret place wherein
I stoop unseen to shame or sin;
To be the same when I'm alone
As when my every deed is known;
To live undaunted, unafraid
Of any step that I have made;
To be without pretense or sham
Exactly what men think I am.

To leave some simple mark behind
To keep my having lived in mind;
If enmity to aught I show,
To be an honest, generous foe,
To play my little part, nor whine
That greater honors are not mine.
This, I believe, is all I need
For my philosophy and creed.

EDGAR A. GUEST

Give the best you have received from the past to the best that you may come to know in the future.

Accept life daily not as a cup to be drained but as a chalice to be filled with whatsoever things are honest, pure, lovely, and of good report.

Making a living is best undertaken as a part of the more important business of making a life.

Every now and again take a good look at something not made with hands—a mountain, a star, the turn of a stream. There will come to you wisdom and patience and solace and, above all, the assurance that you are not alone in the world.

SIDNEY LOVETT

TWELVE THINGS TO REMEMBER

1. The value of time
2. The success of perseverance
3. The pleasure of working
4. The dignity of simplicity
5. The worth of character
6. The power of kindness
7. The influence of example
8. The obligation of duty
9. The wisdom of economy
10. The virtue of patience
11. The improvement of talent
12. The joy of originating.

WHATSOEVER THINGS

The only social security any able man needs is a good place to work, a good place to worship, and a good home to love.

JAMES J. O'REILLY

THOMAS JEFFERSON'S DECALOGUE

I. Never put off till tomorrow what you can do today.

II. Never trouble another for what you can do yourself.

III. Never spend your money before you have it.

IV. Never buy what you do not want, because it is cheap; it will be dear to you.

V. Pride costs us more than hunger, thirst, and cold.

VI. We never repent of having eaten too little.

VII. Nothing is troublesome that we do willingly.

VIII. How much pain have cost us the evils which have never happened.

IX. Take things always by their smooth handle.

X. When angry, count ten, before you speak; if very angry, an hundred.

The human heart is all I need,
For I have found God ever there—
Love is the one sufficient creed,
And comradeship the purest prayer.

ROBERT NORWOOD

MY CREED

I would be true, for there are those
who trust me;
I would be pure, for there are those who care.
I would be strong, for there is much to suffer,
I would be brave, for there is much to dare.
I would be friend to all—the foe,
the friendless;
I would be giving, and forget the gift.
I would be humble, for I know my weakness;
I would look up—and laugh—and love—and lift.

HOWARD ARNOLD WALTER

PROMISE YOURSELF—

1. To be so strong that nothing can disturb your peace of mind.
2. To talk health, happiness, and prosperity to every person you meet.
3. To make all your friends feel that there is something in them.
4. To look at the sunny side of everything and make your optimism come true.
5. To think only of the best, to work only for the best, and to expect only the best.
6. To be just as enthusiastic about the success of others as you are about your own.
7. To forget the mistakes of the past and press on to the greater achievements of the future.
8. To wear a cheerful countenance at all times and give every living creature you meet a smile.
9. To give so much time to the improvement of yourself that you have no time to criticize others.
10. To be too large for worry, too noble for anger, too strong for fear, and too happy to permit trouble.

OPTIMIST INTERNATIONAL

I BELIEVE

I believe in the supreme worth of the individual and in his right to life, liberty, and the pursuit of happiness.

I believe that every right implies a responsibility; every opportunity, an obligation; every possession, a duty.

I believe that the law was made for man and not man for the law; that government is the servant of the people and not their master.

I believe in the dignity of labor, whether with head or hand; that the world owes no man a living but that it owes every man an opportunity to make a living.

I believe that thrift is essential to well-ordered living and that economy is a prime requisite of a sound financial structure, whether in government, business, or personal affairs.

I believe that truth and justice are fundamental to an enduring social order.

I believe in the sacredness of a promise, that a man's word should be as good as his bond; that character—not wealth or power or position—is of supreme worth.

I believe that the rendering of useful service is the common duty of mankind and that only in the purifying fire of sacrifice is the dross of selfishness consumed and the greatness of the human soul set free.

I believe in an all-wise and all-loving God, named by whatever name, and that the individual's highest fulfillment, greatest happiness, and widest usefulness are to be found in living in harmony with His will.

I believe that love is the greatest thing in the world; that it alone can overcome hate; that right can and will triumph over might.

JOHN D. ROCKEFELLER, JR.

ABRAHAM LINCOLN'S CREED

I believe in God, the Almighty Ruler of nations, our great and good and merciful Maker, our Father in heaven, who notes the fall of a sparrow and numbers the hairs on our heads. I recognize the sublime truth announced in the Holy Scriptures and proved by all history that those nations are blessed whose God is the Lord. I believe that the will of God prevails. Without him, all human reliance is vain. With that assistance I cannot fail. I have a solemn vow registered in heaven to finish the work I am in, in full view of my responsibility to my God, with malice toward none; with charity for all; with firmness in the right, as God gives me to see the right.

COMPILED BY WILLIAM E. BARTON

CRITICISM

The question is not what a man can scorn,
or disparage, or find fault with,
but what he can love, and value, and appreciate.

JOHN RUSKIN

SQUATTER'S RIGHTS

If you forgive people enough you belong to them, and they to you, whether either person likes it or not—squatter's rights of the heart.

JAMES HILTON

VARIETY

We are not hen's eggs, or bananas, or clothespins, to be counted off by the dozen. Down to the last detail we are all different. Everyone has his own fingerprints. Recognize and rejoice in that endless variety. The white light of the divine purpose streams down from heaven to be broken up by these human prisms into all the colors of the rainbow. Take your own color in the pattern and be just that.

CHARLES R. BROWN

A CREED

There is a destiny that makes us brothers;
    None goes his way alone:
All that we send into the lives of others
    Comes back into our own.

I care not what his temples or his creeds,
    One thing holds firm and fast—
That into his fateful heap of days and deeds
    The soul of man is cast.

EDWIN MARKHAM

I ought to reflect again and again, and yet again, that the beings among whom I have to steer are just as inevitable in the scheme of evolution as I am myself; have just as much right to be themselves as I am entitled to; and they all deserve from me as much sympathy as I give to myself.

ARNOLD BENNETT

He who cannot forgive breaks the bridge over which he himself must pass.

GEORGE HERBERT

THREE GATES

If you are tempted to reveal
A tale to you someone has told
About another, make it pass,
Before you speak, three gates of gold.
These narrow gates: First, "Is it true?"
Then, "Is it needful?" In your mind
Give truthful answer. And the next
Is last and narrowest, "Is it kind?"
And if to reach your lips at last
It passes through these gateways three,
Then you may tell the tale, nor fear
What the result of speech may be.

FROM THE ARABIAN

I have made a ceaseless effort not to ridicule, not to bewail, not to scorn human actions, but to understand them.

BARUCH SPINOZA

In men whom men condemn as ill
I find so much of goodness still,
In men whom men pronounce divine
I find so much of sin and blot,
I do not dare to draw a line
Between the two, where God has not.

JOAQUIN MILLER

He has the right to criticize who has the heart to help.

ABRAHAM LINCOLN

Consider the hammer—
It keeps its head.
It doesn't fly off the handle.
It keeps pounding away.
It finds the point and then drives it home.
It looks at the other side, too, and thus
often clinches the matter.
It makes mistakes, but when it does
it starts all over.
It is the only knocker in the world
that does any good.

SUNRISES AND CYCLONES

It seems to be a general belief that the will of
God is to make things distasteful for us, like
taking bad-tasting medicine when we are sick,
or going to the dentist. Somebody needs to tell
us that sunrise is also God's will. There is the
time of harvest, the harvest which will provide food and clothes for us, without which
life could not be sustained on earth. God
ordered the seasons—they are his will. In fact,
the good things in life far outweigh the bad.
There are more sunrises than cyclones.

CHARLES L. ALLEN

How seldom we weigh our neighbor in the
same balance with ourselves.

THOMAS A KEMPIS

Be not angry that you cannot make others as
you wish them to be, since you cannot make
yourself as you wish to be.

THOMAS A KEMPIS

CRITICS

What one approves, another scorns,
And thus his nature each discloses;
You find the rosebush full of thorns,
I find the thornbush full of roses.

ARTHUR GUITERMAN

The touch of human hands—
Not vain, unthinking words,
Not that cold charity
Which shuns our misery;
We seek a loyal friend
Who understands,
And the warmth, the pulsing warmth
Of human hands.

THOMAS CURTIS CLARK

WANTED: MORE PRAISE

I cannot help believing that the world will be
a better and a happier place when people are
praised more and blamed less; when we utter
in their hearing the good we think and also
gently intimate the criticisms we hope may be
of service. For the world grows smaller every
day. It will be but a family circle after a while.

FRANCIS E. WILLARD

PRAYER

Dear Lord of gracious mind and heart, forgive
me for the unbearable ways of my arrogance
and snobbishness. How unkind of me to think
poorly without cause of those about me! Help
me realize that a song can be lovely even though
I neither wrote nor sang it. Make clear to me
that all worthy thoughts did not originate in
my mind; that other folk have good manners;
and that when I pass away the world will not
be bereft of grace and good breeding.

ALLEN A. STOCKDALE

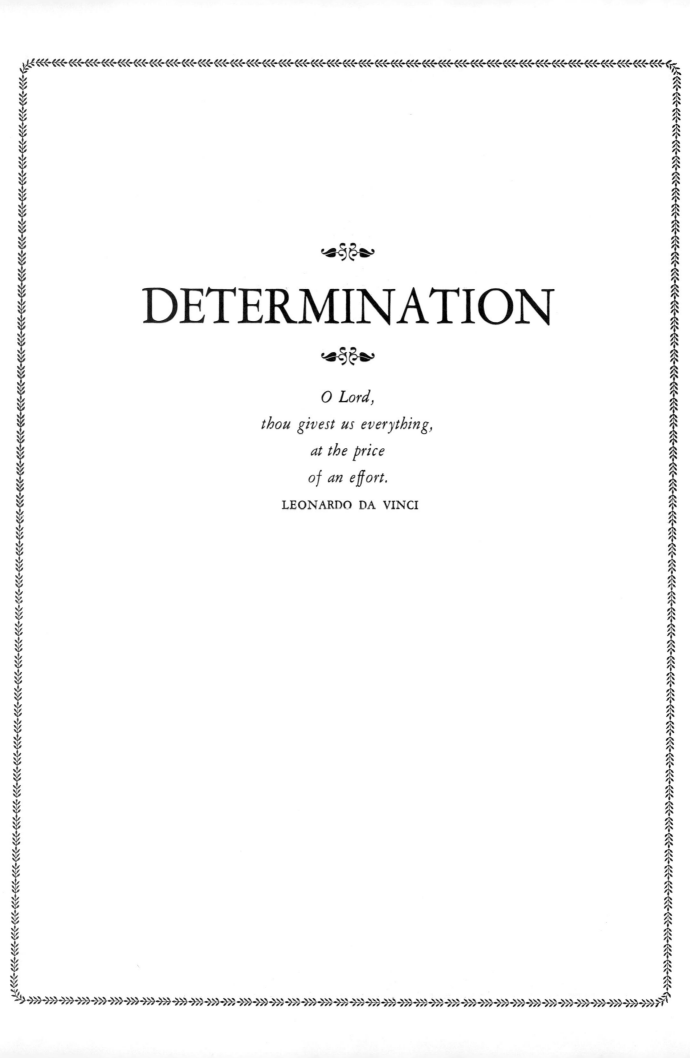

DETERMINATION

O Lord,
thou givest us everything,
at the price
of an effort.
LEONARDO DA VINCI

STUBBORN OUNCES
To one who doubts the worth of doing anything if you can't do everything.

You say the little efforts that I make
will do no good: they never will prevail
to tip the hovering scale
where Justice hangs in balance.
                    I don't think
I ever thought they would.
But I am prejudiced beyond debate
in favor of my right to choose which side
shall feel the stubborn ounces of my weight.

BONARO W. OVERSTREET

The rung of a ladder was never meant to rest upon, but only to hold a man's foot long enough to enable him to put the other somewhat higher.

THOMAS HENRY HUXLEY

Dear God,
The little plans I tried to carry through
Have failed.
I will not sorrow.
I'll pause a little while,
Dear God,
And try, again, tomorrow.

JOHN FICO

With all the infinite possibilities of spiritual life before you, do not settle down on a little patch of dusty ground at the mountain's foot in restful content. Be not content until you reach the mountain's summit.

J. R. MILLER

What we are is God's gift to us. What we become is our gift to God.

LOUIS NIZER

As the sculptor devotes himself to wood and stone, I would devote myself to my soul.

TOYOHIKO KAGAWA

A KNIGHT'S PRAYER
My Lord, I am ready on the threshold of this new day to go forth armed with thy power, seeking adventure on the high road, to right wrong, to overcome evil, to suffer wounds and endure pain if need be, but in all things to serve thee bravely, faithfully, joyfully, that at the end of the day's labor, kneeling for thy blessing, thou mayst find no blot upon my shield.

CHESTER CATHEDRAL

I held it truth, with him who sings
    To one clear harp in divers tones,
    That men may rise on stepping-stones
Of their dead selves to higher things.

ALFRED TENNYSON

The difficult we do immediately; the impossible takes a little longer.

AN AIR FORCE MOTTO

To reach the port of heaven we must sail, sometimes with the wind and sometimes against it —but we must sail, not drift or lie at anchor.

OLIVER WENDELL HOLMES

PRAYER FOR STRENGTH

This is my prayer to thee, my Lord—
Strike, strike at the root of penury in my heart.
Give me the strength lightly to bear my joys
    and sorrows.
Give me the strength to make my love fruitful
    in service.
Give me the strength never to disown the poor
    or bend my knees before insolent might.
Give me the strength to raise my mind high
    above daily trifles.
And give me the strength to surrender my
    strength to thy will with love.

RABINDRANATH TAGORE

PRAYER

Great God, I ask thee for no meaner pelf
Than that I may not disappoint myself.
That in my action I may soar as high
As I can now discern with this clear eye.

HENRY DAVID THOREAU

THE ADVENTUROUS LIFE

The only life worth living is the adventurous
life. Of such a life the dominant characteristic
is that it is unafraid. It is unafraid of what other
people think. Like Columbus, it dares not only
to assert a belief but to live it in the face of
contrary opinion. It does not adapt either its
pace or its objectives to the pace and objectives
of its neighbors. It thinks its own thoughts, it
reads its own books, it develops its own
hobbies, and it is governed by its own conscience. The herd may graze where it pleases or
stampede where it pleases, but he who lives
the adventurous life will remain unafraid when
he finds himself alone.

RAYMOND B. FOSDICK

Make no little plans; they have no magic to stir
men's blood and probably themselves will not
be realized. Make big plans; aim high in hope
and work, remembering that a noble, logical
diagram once recorded will never die, but long
after we are gone will be a living thing, as-
serting itself with ever-growing insistency.

DANIEL H. BURNHAM

TRUE GREATNESS

A man is as great as the dreams he dreams,
    As great as the love he bears;
As great as the values he redeems,
    And the happiness he shares.
A man is as great as the thoughts he thinks,
    As the worth he has attained;
As the fountains at which his spirit drinks
    And the insight he has gained.
A man is as great as the truth he speaks,
    As great as the help he gives,
As great as the destiny he seeks,
    As great as the life he lives.

C. E. FLYNN

Weak men are the slaves of what happens.
Strong men are masters of what happens. Weak
men are victims of their environment. Strong
men are victors in any environment. Strong
men may not change the circumstances, but
they will use them, compel them to serve, and
bend them to their purposes. They may not
be able to change the direction of the wind, but
somehow they will coerce the wind to fill their
sails while they drive the tiller over to keep
their course.

GEORGE CRAIG STEWART

Great things are done when men and mountains meet.

WILLIAM BLAKE

EDUCATION

If you have knowledge,
let others light their candles at it.

THOMAS FULLER

THE BUILDER

A builder builded a temple,
He wrought it with grace and skill;
Pillars and groins and arches
All fashioned to work his will.
Men said, as they saw its beauty,
"It shall never know decay;
Great is thy skill, O Builder!
Thy fame shall endure for aye."

A Teacher builded a temple
With loving and infinite care,
Planning each arch with patience,
Laying each stone with prayer.
None praised her unceasing efforts,
None knew of her wondrous plan,
For the temple the Teacher builded
Was unseen by the eyes of man.

Gone is the Builder's temple,
Crumpled into the dust;
Low lies each stately pillar,
Food for consuming rust.
But the temple the Teacher builded
Will last while the ages roll,
For that beautiful unseen temple
Was a child's immortal soul.

❧

FRONTIERS

We often think of ourselves as living in a world which no longer has any unexplored frontiers. We speak of pioneering as a thing of the past. But in doing so we forget that the greatest adventure of all still challenges us—what Mr. Justice Holmes called "the adventure of the human mind." Men may be hemmed in geographically, but every generation stands on the frontiers of the mind. In the world of ideas, there is always pioneering to be done, and it can be done by anyone who will use the equipment with which he is endowed. The great ideas belong to everyone.

MORTIMER J. ADLER

❧

The entire object of true education is to make people not merely to do the right things, but enjoy them; not merely industrious, but to love industry; not merely learned, but to love knowledge; not merely pure, but to love purity; not merely just, but to hunger and thirst after justice.

JOHN RUSKIN

❧

I have four things to learn in life:
   To think clearly without hurry or confusion;
   To love everybody sincerely;
   To act in everything with the highest motives;
   To trust in God unhesitatingly.

HELEN KELLER

❧

Perhaps the most valuable result of all education is the ability to make yourself do the thing you have to do, when it ought to be done, whether you like it or not. This is the first lesson to be learned.

THOMAS HENRY HUXLEY

❧

RELIGION IN THE CURRICULUM

We teach it in arithmetic by accuracy.
We teach it in language by learning to say what we mean—"yea, yea" or "nay, nay."
We teach it in history by humanity.
We teach it in geography by breadth of mind.
We teach it in handicraft by thoroughness.
We teach it in astronomy by reverence.
We teach it by good manners to one another and by truthfulness in all things.

L. P. JACKS

LIBERAL EDUCATION

In a democracy, liberal education should be of value to men and women both as private individuals and as free, self-reliant, and responsible members of the community to which they belong. It should help them, as individuals, to grow in self-mastery and personal depth, to develop wider and deeper appreciations, to acquire an enthusiasm for hard work, to love good talk and good books, to delight in the adventures of intellectual curiosity, to become fair-minded, open-minded, and generous in all their human responses.

ASSOCIATION OF AMERICAN COLLEGES

God stands as it were a handbreadth off, leaving his creatures room to grow in.

ROBERT BROWNING

The great difficulty in education is to get experience out of ideas.

GEORGE SANTAYANA

RELEASE

Every piece of marble has a statue in it waiting to be released by a man of sufficient skill to chip away the unnecessary parts. Just as the sculptor is to the marble, so is education to the soul. It releases it. For only educated men are free men. You cannot create a statue by smashing the marble with a hammer, and you cannot by force of arms release the spirit or the soul of man.

CONFUCIUS

PSALM

The Lord is my teacher. I shall not want. He maketh me to learn in God's out-of-doors. He teacheth me by his written word. He instructeth my soul. He guideth me in the paths of true knowledge for his name's sake. Yea, when the day's task is done, and life's lessons have been learned, I will fear no evil, for thou wilt be with me, my Teacher and my Comforter still. Thou teachest even my enemies to become pupils of the Great Teacher. Thou leadest me gently from the known to the unknown. Thou givest me satisfaction in my day's work. Surely goodness and mercy shall follow me all the days of my life, and I shall be a learner in the school of the Great Teacher forever.

FREDERIC S. GOODRICH

THE TEACHER

Lord, who am I to teach the way
To little children day by day,
So prone myself to go astray?

I teach them KNOWLEDGE, but I know
How faint they flicker and how low
The candles of my knowledge glow.

I teach them POWER to will and do,
But only now to learn anew
My own great weakness through and through.

I teach them LOVE for all mankind
And all God's creatures, but I find
My love comes lagging far behind.

Lord, if their guide I still must be,
Oh, let the little children see
The teacher leaning hard on thee.

LESLIE PINCKNEY HILL

Education does not mean teaching people to know what they do not know; it means teaching them to behave as they do not behave.

JOHN RUSKIN

EDUCATION AND INSTRUCTION

Education consists in preparing the moral character of a child, in teaching him the few fundamental and invariable principles accepted in all the countries of the world. It consists in giving him, from tenderest childhood, the notion of human dignity. On the other hand, instruction consists in making him absorb the accumulated knowledge of man in every realm. Education directs his actions, inspires his behavior in all his contacts with mankind, and helps him to master himself. Instruction gives him the elements of his intellectual activity and informs him of the actual state of his civilization. Education gives him the unalterable foundations of his life; instruction enables him to adapt himself to the variations of his environment and to link these variations to past and future events.

LECOMTE DU NOÜY

A SUCCESSFUL TEACHER NEEDS

The education of a college president,
The executive ability of a financier,
The humility of a deacon,
The adaptability of a chameleon,
The hope of an optimist,
The courage of a hero,
The wisdom of a serpent,
The gentleness of a dove,
The patience of Job,
The grace of God, and
The persistence of the devil.

Life is like playing a violin solo in public and learning the instrument as one goes on.

SAMUEL BUTLER

A LEARNER

Each day I learn more
Than I teach;
I learn that half knowledge of another's life
Leads to false judgment;
I learn that there is a surprising kinship
In human nature;
I learn that it's a wise father who knows his
own son;
I learn that what we expect we get;
I learn that there's more good than evil in this
world;
That age is a question of spirit;
That youth is the best of life
No matter how numerous its years;
I learn how much there is to learn.

VIRGINIA CHURCH

SEVEN PURPOSES OF RELIGIOUS EDUCATION

1. To lead the pupil into a personal relationship with God.
2. To give the pupil an understanding and appreciation of the life and teachings of Jesus, to lead him to accept Christ as Savior, Friend, Companion, and Lord, and to lead him into loyalty to Christ and his cause.
3. To lead to a progressive development of Christian character.
4. To lead into enthusiastic and intelligent participation of the building of a Christian community and world.
5. To develop the ability and desire to participate in the life and work of the church.
6. To give a Christian interpretation of life and the universe.
7. To give a knowledge, understanding, and love of the Bible.

CYCLOPEDIA OF BIBLE ILLUSTRATIONS

I am not a teacher, but an awakener.

ROBERT FROST

The secret of education lies in respecting the pupil.

RALPH WALDO EMERSON

❧

THE TEACHER'S PRAYER

My Lord, I do not ask to stand
  As king or prince of high degree.
I only pray that, hand in hand,
  A child and I may come to thee.

Help me to share what thou dost give
  And be a friend, a trusted guide.
As in thy sight, oh, let me live.
  May selfishness be crucified.

Thou art the life, the truth, the way
  That leads to God, that saves from sin.
Oh, may my teaching, day by day,
  Help those in need, thy life to win.

Oh, grant thy patience, Lord, to share
  Thy holy purpose, life to bring.
May I the inexperience bear
  Of those who need love's fostering.

NORMAN E. RICHARDSON

❧

ABSOLUTE TRUST

All a child's life depends on the ideal it has of its parents. Destroy that and everything goes— morals, behavior, everything. Absolute trust in someone else is the essence of education.

E. M. FORSTER

❧

FOCUS ON DISCIPLINE

No horse gets anywhere until he is harnessed. No steam or gas ever drives anything until it is confined. No Niagara is ever turned into light and power until it is tunneled. No life ever grows great until it is focused, dedicated, disciplined.

HARRY EMERSON FOSDICK

❧

Man is obviously made to think. It is his whole dignity and his whole merit; and his whole duty is to think as he ought.

BLAISE PASCAL

❧

MARKS OF AN EDUCATED MAN

1. Has your education made you a friend of all good causes?
2. Has your education made you a brother to the weak?
3. Do you see anything to love in a little child?
4. Would a lost dog follow you in the street?
5. Do you enjoy being alone?
6. Do you believe in the dignity of labor?
7. Can you look into a mud puddle and see the blue sky?
8. Can you go out in the night, look up in the sky, and see beyond the stars?
9. Is your life linked with the Infinite?

❧

The person who limits his interests to the means of living without consideration of the content or meaning of his life is defeating God's great purpose when he brought into existence a creature with the intelligence and godlike powers that are found in man.

ARTHUR H. COMPTON

❧

Life is neither a banquet nor a dreary pilgrimage; it is neither a trading concern where all dividends that are fairly earned are punctually paid, nor a lotus-eater's paradise; it is a school of manhood.

BURNETT H. STREETER

FAITH

Whoso draws nigh to God one step through doubtings dim,
God will advance a mile in blazing light to him.

O world, thou choosest not the better part!
It is not wisdom to be only wise,
And on the inward vision close the eyes;
But it is wisdom to believe the heart.
Columbus found a world, and had no chart
Save one that faith deciphered in the skies;
To trust the soul's invincible surmise
Was all his science and his only art.
Our knowledge is a torch of smoky pine
That lights the pathway but one step ahead
Across a void of mystery and dread.
Bid, then, the tender light of faith to shine
By which alone the mortal heart is led
Unto the thinking of the thought divine.

GEORGE SANTAYANA

❧❦❧

CAPACITY TO BELIEVE

This capacity to believe is the most significant and fundamental human faculty, and the most important thing about a man is what he believes in the depth of his being. This is the thing that makes him what he is; the thing that organizes him and feeds him; the thing that keeps him going in the face of untoward circumstances; the thing that gives him resistance and drive. Let neutrality, confusion, indifference, or skepticism enter this inner place, and the very springs of life will cease to flow.

HUGH STEVENSON TIGNER

❧❦❧

FAITH-LADDER

A conception of the world arises in you somehow, no matter how. Is it true or not? you ask.

It *might* be true somewhere, you say, for it is not self-contradictory.

It *may* be true, you continue, even here and now.

It is *fit* to be true, it would be *well if it were true*, it *ought* to be true, you presently feel.

It *must* be true, something persuasive in you whispers next; and then—as a final result—

It shall be *held for true,* you decide; it *shall be* as if true, for *you.*

And your acting thus may in certain special cases be a means of making it securely true in the end.

WILLIAM JAMES

❧❦❧

Faith is an act of rational choice which determines us to act as if certain things were true and in the confident expectation that they will prove to be true.

WILLIAM R. INGE

❧❦❧

Faith is not belief without proof, but trust without reservations.

ELTON TRUEBLOOD

❧❦❧

Faith is not belief in spite of evidence, but life in scorn of consequences.

KIRSOPP LAKE

❧❦❧

Faith is like a boomerang; begin using what you have and it comes back to you in greater measure.

CHARLES L. ALLEN

❧❦❧

It is no unworthy thing to wish to count for something and to do a great work in the world; but we shall count in the final audit not by the measure of our capacity, our business, our energy, but of the tenacity and vitality of our faith and our love.

RICHARD ROBERTS

❧❦❧

93

FAITH

Faith is not merely praying
    Upon your knees at night;
Faith is not merely straying
    Through darkness to the light.

Faith is not merely waiting
    For glory that may be.
Faith is not merely hating
    The sinful ecstasy.

Faith is the brave endeavor,
    The splendid enterprise,
The strength to serve, whatever
    Conditions may arise.

S. E. KISER

❧❦❧

The person who has a firm trust in the Supreme Being is powerful in his power, wise by his wisdom, happy by his happiness.

JOSEPH ADDISON

❧❦❧

FAITH'S RESPONSE

The world answers back to our faith. It trusts when we trust it. It responds to our confidence. It says to the farmer, "Sow your seed"; to the aviator, "Spread your wings"; to the miner, "Sink your shaft"; to the sailor, "Hoist your sail"; to the engineer, "Swing your bridge"; to the scientist, "Trust your hypothesis"; to the financier, "Make your investment"; to the explorer, "Follow the gleam." Faith is man's highest venture. The poet Whitman puts it thus: "The steps of faith fall on the seeming void and find the rock beneath." It is a "seeming void" on which we set our faith; beneath us, however, is the unseen reality, and faith gives it substance.

HUGH THOMPSON KERR

❧❦❧

THE ROSE

If you doubt there is a God, look deep into a
    rose;
See the velvet petals from the folded bud un-
    close;
Note the tint and texture and the lovely color-
    ing;
Could blind Nature of itself evolve so fair a
    thing?

Feel the softness of the petal, breathe the fra-
    grant scent;
Need you waste another thought on further
    argument?
Here is proof of a Creator: God made manifest;
In this little rose we see divinity expressed.

PATIENCE STRONG

❧❦❧

FEAR AND FAITH

Fear imprisons, faith liberates; fear paralyzes, faith empowers; fear disheartens, faith encourages; fear sickens, faith heals; fear makes useless, faith makes serviceable—and, most of all, fear puts hopelessness at the heart of life, while faith rejoices in its God.

HARRY EMERSON FOSDICK

❧❦❧

To believe that this terrible machine world is really from God, in God, and unto God, and through it and in spite of its blind fatality all works for good—that is faith in long trousers.

GEORGE TYRRELL

❧❦❧

We shall be made truly wise if we be made content; content, too, not only with what we can understand, but content with what we do not understand—the habit of mind which theologians call, and rightly, faith in God.

CHARLES KINGSLEY

WHAT CHRIST ASKS

The best definition of faith that I know is that it is reason grown courageous. Moreover, that is all that Christ ever asked us for, and the reason that he asked us for that was because he wants to use us. He needs our help. It is almost impossible to believe it, but God Almighty wants our help, so Christ tells us. Theoretically or mathematically this is unintelligible, that God should want human help. But this is the bottom of all Christ's teaching. The faith he asks for is not to understand him but to follow him. By that and that alone can man convert the tragedy of human life, full of disappointments, disillusionments, and with so-called death ever looming ahead, into the most glorious field of honor, worthy of the dignity of a son of God. What Christ asks is that we shall try it out. He actually dares us to follow him. In that way, he says, you shall win that prize in life, for which any man can with perfect reason afford to give everything else.

WILFRED T. GRENFELL

THE SONG OF A HEATHEN

If Jesus Christ is a man,—
 And only a man—I say
That of all mankind I cleave to him,
 And to him will I cleave alway.

If Jesus Christ is a God,—
 And the only God,—I swear
I will follow him through heaven and hell,
 The earth, the sea, and the air!

RICHARD WATSON GILDER

My soul is like unto a cup which can be filled only with Eternity.

AMADO NERVO

THIS IS FAITH

The anchored trust that at the core of things
Health, goodness, animating strength flow from
 exhaustless springs;
That no star rolls unguided down the rings of
 endless maze,
That no feet tread an aimless path through
 wastes of empty days;
That trusts the everlasting voice, the glad calm
 voice that saith
That order grows from chaos, and that life is
 born from death;
That from the wreck of rending stars behind
 the storm and scathe,
There dwells a heart of central calm;—and this,
 and this is faith!

ACT OF FAITH

I have always believed that the long view of man's history will show that his destiny on earth is progress toward the good life, even though that progress is based on sacrifices and sufferings which taken by themselves seem to constitute a hideous melange of evils. This is an act of faith. We must not let ourselves be engulfed in the passing waves which obscure the current of progress. The sinfulness and weakness of man are evident to anyone who lives in the active world. But men are also great, kind, and wise. Honor begets honor; trust begets trust; faith begets faith; and hope is the mainspring of life.

HENRY L. STIMSON

THE LOOM OF TIME

Man's life is laid in the loom of time
 To a pattern he does not see,
While the weavers work and shuttles fly
 'Til the dawn of eternity.

LOST AND FOUND

I missed him when the sun began to bend;
I found him not when I had lost his rim;
With many tears I went in search of him,
Climbing high mountains which did still ascend,
And gave me echoes when I called my friend;
Through cities vast and charnel-houses grim,
And high cathedrals where the light was dim,
Through books and arts and works without
   an end,
But found him not—the friend whom I had
   lost.
And yet I found him—as I found the lark,
A sound in fields I heard but could not mark;
I found him in my heart, a life in frost,
A light I knew not till my soul was dark.

GEORGE MACDONALD

I do not want merely to possess a faith; I want
a faith that possesses me.

CHARLES KINGSLEY

ON TRIAL

A living faith is always on trial; we call it faith
for that reason. When I read in some alarmist
book that the Christian faith is now on trial,
or "at the crossroads," my impulse is to answer,
Why not? Does anybody know of a time when
the Christian faith was not on its trial, or when
the Christian life was a simple walkover, with
neither principalities nor powers to dispute its
advance?

J. EDGAR PARK

To lose faith in our fellow men is the unforgiv-
able sin.

JOHN DEWEY

REQUESTS

I asked for Peace—
   My sins arose,
   And bound me close,
I could not find release.

I asked for Truth—
   My doubts came in,
   And with their din
They wearied all my youth.

I asked for Love—
   My lovers failed,
   And griefs assailed
Around, beneath, above.

I asked for Thee—
   And thou didst come
   To take me home
Within thy Heart to be.

DIGBY M. DOLBEN

DIVINE FOOTSTEPS

Christ has come, the Light of the world. Long
ages may yet elapse before his beams have re-
duced the world to order and beauty, and
clothed a purified humanity with light as with a
garment. But he has come: the Revealer of the
snares and chasms that lurk in darkness, the
Rebuker of every evil thing that prowls by
night, the Stiller of the storm-winds of passion,
the Quickener of all that is wholesome, the
Adorner of all that is beautiful, the Reconciler
of contradictions, the Harmonizer of discords,
the Healer of diseases, the Savior from sin.

He has come: the Torch of truth, the Anchor
of hope, the Pillar of faith, the Rock for
strength, the Refuge for security, the Fountain
for refreshment, the Vine for gladness, the
Rose for beauty, the Lamb for tenderness, the
Friend for counsel, the Brother for love. Jesus
Christ has trod the world. The trace of the
divine footsteps will never be obliterated.

PETER BAYNE

FRIENDSHIP

I didn't find my friends;
the good God gave them to me.
RALPH WALDO EMERSON

TO A FRIEND

I love you not only for what you are, but for what I am when I am with you.

I love you not only for what you have made of yourself, but for what you are making of me.

I love you for the part of me that you bring out.

I love you for putting your hand into my heaped-up heart and passing over all the foolish and frivolous and weak things that you can't help dimly seeing there, and for drawing out into the light all the beautiful radiant belongings that no one else had looked quite far enough to find.

I love you for ignoring the possibilities of the fool and weakling in me, and for laying firm hold on the possibilities of the good in me.

I love you for closing your ears to the discords in me, and for adding to the music in me by worshipful listening.

I love you because you are helping me to make of the timber of my life not a tavern, but a temple, and of the words of my every day not a reproach, but a song.

I love you because you have done more than any creed could have done to make me happy.

You have done it without a touch, without a word, without a sign.

You have done it first by being yourself.

After all, perhaps this is what being a friend means.

❦

A PRAYER

It is my joy in life to find
At every turning of the road
The strong arm of a comrade kind
To help me onward with my load.

And since I have no gold to give,
And love alone must make amends,
My only prayer is, while I live—
God make me worthy of my friends.

FRANK DEMPSTER SHERMAN

❦

WHAT IS A FRIEND?

An English publication offered a prize for the best definition of a friend, and among the thousands of answers received were the following:

"One who multiplies joys, divides grief, and whose honesty is inviolable."

"One who understands our silence."

"A volume of sympathy bound in cloth."

"A watch which beats true for all time and never runs down."

Here is the definition that won the prize: "A friend is the one who comes in when the whole world has gone out."

❦

Am I united with my friend in heart,
What matters if our place be wide apart?
ANWAR-I-SUHEILI (*Persian poet*)

❦

Friends are necessary to a happy life. When friendship deserts us we are as lonely and helpless as a ship, left by the tide high upon the shore. When friendship returns to us, it is as though the tide came back, gave us buoyancy and freedom, and opened to us the wide places of the world.

HARRY EMERSON FOSDICK

❦

The love of humanity as such is mitigated by violent dislike of the next-door neighbor.

ALFRED NORTH WHITEHEAD

❦

"Stay" is a charming word in a friend's vocabulary.

AMOS BRONSON ALCOTT

❦

99

Silences make the real conversations between friends. Not the saying but the never needing to say is what counts.

MARGARET LEE RUNBECK

❧

TO OUR GUESTS

In ancient times there was a prayer for "The Stranger within our gates." Because this hotel is a human institution to serve people, and not solely a money-making organization, we hope that God will grant you peace and rest while you are under our roof.

May this room and hotel be your "second" home. May those you love be near you in thoughts and dreams. Even though we may not get to know you, we hope that you will be as comfortable and happy as if you were in your own house.

May the business that brought you our way prosper. May every call you make and every message you receive add to your joy. When you leave, may your journey be safe.

We are all travelers. From "birth till death" we travel between the eternities. May these days be pleasant for you, profitable for society, helpful for those you meet, and a joy to those who know and love you best.

FROM A WASHINGTON, D.C., HOTEL

❧

BORROWING

Someone has said, "If you want your friends to remember you, borrow something from them." I want to turn this around and say, if you want to remember your friends, be sure to borrow from them. Borrow faith, hope, and love. Borrow courage, humility, and integrity. Borrow their Christian example of the unseen values of the soul. Borrow their confidence in the living God and their loyalty to the triumphant Christ. Then indeed your days will be filled with strength.

JOHN W. MC KELVEY

❧

NEW FRIENDS AND OLD FRIENDS
Make new friends, but keep the old;
Those are silver, these are gold.
New-made friendships, like new wine,
Age will mellow and refine.
Friendships that have stood the test—
Time and change—are surely best;
Brow may wrinkle, hair grow gray;
Friendship never knows decay.
For 'mid old friends, tried and true,
Once more we reach and youth renew.
But old friends, alas! may die;
New friends must their place supply;
Cherish friendships in your breast—
New is good, but old is best;
Make new friends, but keep the old;
Those are silver, these are gold.

JOSEPH PARRY

❧

The first general rule for friendship is to be a friend, to be open, natural, interested; the second rule is to take time for friendship. Friendship, after all, is what life is finally about. Everything material and professional exists in the end for persons.

NELS F. S. FERRÉ

❧

ONLY THE HUMAN HEART
The robin never looks
At last year's brittle nest,
Hushes his song, and feels
Grief tear his breast.

Only the human heart
Holds close its dearest things,
And bears the wounds, the scars,
Their going brings.

IDA NORTON MUNSON

❧

Few delights can equal the mere presence of one whom we trust utterly.

GEORGE MACDONALD

❧

YOUR TEARS

I dare not ask your very all:
    I only ask a part.
Bring me—when dancers leave the hall—
    Your aching heart.

Give other friends your lighted face,
    The laughter of the years:
I come to crave a greater grace—
    Bring me your tears!

EDWIN MARKHAM

❧

We cannot tell the precise moment when friendship is formed. As in filling a vessel drop by drop, there is at last a drop which makes it run over; so in a series of kindnesses there is at last one which makes the heart run over.

SAMUEL JOHNSON

❧

THE ARROW AND THE SONG

I shot an arrow into the air,
It fell to earth, I knew not where;
For, so swiftly it flew, the sight
Could not follow it in its flight.

I breathed a song into the air,
It fell to earth, I knew not where;
For who has sight so keen and strong,
That it can follow the flight of song?

Long, long afterward, in an oak
I found the arrow, still unbroke;
And the song, from beginning to end,
I found again in the heart of a friend.

HENRY WADSWORTH LONGFELLOW

❧

A true friend unbosoms freely, advises justly, assists readily, adventures boldly, takes all patiently, defends courageously, and continues a friend unchangeably.

WILLIAM PENN

❧

So long as we love, we serve; so long as we are loved by others, I should say that we are almost indispensable; and no man is useless while he has a friend.

ROBERT LOUIS STEVENSON

❧

UNDERSTANDING

If I knew you and you knew me,
If both of us could clearly see,
And with an inner sight divine
The meaning of your heart and mine,
I'm sure that we would differ less,
And clasp our hands in friendliness;
Our thoughts would pleasantly agree
If I knew you and you knew me.

NIXON WATERMAN

❧

If a man does not make new acquaintances, as he advances through life, he will soon find himself left alone. A man should keep his friendship in constant repair.

SAMUEL JOHNSON

❧

Don't flatter yourself that friendship authorizes you to say disagreeable things to your intimates. The nearer you come into relation with a person, the more necessary do tact and courtesy become.

OLIVER WENDELL HOLMES

MENDING WALL

Something there is that doesn't love a wall,
That sends the frozen-ground-swell under it,
And spills the upper boulders in the sun;
And makes gaps even two can pass abreast.
The work of hunters is another thing:
I have come after them and made repair
Where they have left not one stone on a stone,
But they would have the rabbit out of hiding,
To please the yelping dogs. The gaps I mean,
No one has seen them made or heard them
   made,
But at spring mending-time we find them there.
I let my neighbor know beyond the hill;
And on a day we meet to walk the line
And set the wall between us once again.
We keep the wall between us as we go.
To each the boulders that have fallen to each.
And some are loaves and some so nearly balls
We have to use a spell to make them balance:
"Stay where you are until our backs are turned!"
We wear our fingers rough with handling them.
Oh, just another kind of outdoor game,
One on a side. It comes to little more:
There where it is we do not need the wall:
He is all pine and I am apple-orchard.
My apple trees will never get across
And eat the cones under his pines, I tell him.
He only says, "Good fences make good neigh-
   bors."
Spring is the mischief in me, and I wonder
If I could put a notion in his head:
"*Why* do they make good neighbors? Isn't it
Where there are cows? But here there are no
   cows.
Before I built a wall I'd ask to know
What I was walling in or walling out,
And to whom I was like to give offense.
Something there is that doesn't love a wall,
That wants it down!" I could say "Elves" to
   him,
But it's not elves exactly, and I'd rather
He said it for himself. I see him there

Bringing a stone grasped firmly by the top
In each hand, like an old-stone savage armed.
He moves in darkness, as it seems to me,
Not of woods only and the shade of trees.
He will not go behind his father's saying,
And he likes having thought of it so well
He says again, "Good fences make good neigh-
   bors."

ROBERT FROST

People are lonely because they build walls instead of bridges.

JOSEPH FORT NEWTON

WHO IS MY NEIGHBOR?

Our friends are the people whom we choose;
usually friends are the same sort of people
as ourselves. My neighbor is the man whom I
do not choose; he is the man whom God gives
to me. He is the man who happens to live in
the house next to mine; he is the man who
happens to sit opposite to me in the train; he
is the clerk who works at the desk next to
mine. I have no right to say that he is no concern of mine, because, if I am a Christian, I
know that he is the man whom God has given
to me.

STEPHEN C. NEILL

Oh, the comfort, the inexpressible comfort of
feeling safe with a person; having neither to
weigh thoughts nor measure words, but to pour
them all out, just as they are, chaff and grain
together, knowing that a faithful hand will take
and sift them, keep what is worth keeping, and
then, with the breath of kindness, blow the rest
away.

GEORGE ELIOT

GIFTS

Blessed are those who can give without remembering
and take without forgetting.

ELIZABETH BIBESCO

A man has made at least a start on discovering the meaning of human life when he plants shade trees under which he knows full well he will never sit.

ELTON TRUEBLOOD

❧❧❧

MAGIC

It costs so little, I wonder why
We give it so little thought;
A smile, kind words, a glance, a touch—
What magic by them is wrought.

❧❧❧

True generosity requires more of us than kindly impulse. Above all it requires imagination— the capacity to see people in all their perplexities and needs, and to know how to expend ourselves effectively for them.

I. A. R. WYLIE

❧❧❧

From THE PROPHET

There are those who give little of the much they have—and they give it for recognition and their hidden desire makes their gifts unwholesome.

And there are those who have little and give it all.

These are the believers in life and the bounty of life, and their coffer is never empty.

There are those who give with joy, and that joy is their reward.

And there are those who give with pain, and that pain is their baptism.

And there are those who give and know not pain in giving, nor do they seek joy, nor give with mindfulness of virtue;

They give as in yonder valley the myrtle breathes its fragrance into space.

Through the hands of such as these God speaks, and from behind their eyes He smiles upon the earth.

GIBRAN KAHLIL

❧❧❧

PARADOX

It is in loving—not in being loved,—
The heart is blest;
It is in giving—not in seeking gifts,—
We find our quest.

If thou art hungry, lacking heavenly food,—
Give hope and cheer.
If thou art sad and wouldst be comforted,—
Stay sorrow's tear.

Whatever be thy longing and thy need,—
That do thou give;
So shall thy soul be fed, and thou indeed,
Shalt truly live.

❧❧❧

THE GOLDEN LADDER OF GIVING

1. To give reluctantly, the gift of the hand, but not of the heart.
2. To give cheerfully, but not in proportion to need.
3. To give cheerfully and proportionately, but not until solicited.
4. To give cheerfully, proportionately, and un-solicited, but to put the gift into the poor man's hand, thus creating shame.
5. To give in such a way that the distressed may know their benefactor, without being known to him.
6. To know the objects of our bounty, but re-main unknown to them.
7. To give so that the benefactor may not know those whom he has relieved, and they shall not know him.
8. To prevent poverty by teaching a trade, set-ting a man up in business, or in some other way preventing the need of charity.

MAIMONIDES

❧❧❧

Give what you have. To some one, it may be better than you dare to think.

HENRY WADSWORTH LONGFELLOW

I have held many things in my hands, and I have lost them all; but whatever I have placed in God's hands, that I still possess.

MARTIN LUTHER

LAST WILL AND TESTAMENT

I, Charles Lounsbury, being of sound mind and disposing memory, do hereby make and publish this, my last will and testament, in order, as justly as I may, to distribute my interests in the world among succeeding men.

That part of my interests which is known in the law and recognized in the sheep-bound volumes as my property, being inconsiderable and of no account, I make no disposal of it in my will.

My right to live, being but a life estate, is not at my disposal, but, these excepted, all else in the world I now proceed to devise and bequeath.

Item: I give to good fathers and mothers, but in trust for their children all and every, the flowers of the fields and the blossoms of the woods, with the right to play among them freely, according to the custom of children, warning them at the same time against the thistles. And I devise to children the banks of the brooks, and the golden sands beneath the waters thereof, and the odors of the willows that dip therein, and the white clouds that float high over the giant trees. And I leave the children the long, long days to be merry in, in a thousand ways, and the night, and the moon, and the train of the Milky Way to wonder at, but subject, nevertheless, to the rights hereinafter given to lovers.

Item: I devise to boys jointly all the useful idle fields and commons where ball may be played; all pleasant waters where one may swim; all snow-clad hills where one may coast; and all streams and ponds where one may fish, or where, when grim winter comes, one may skate; to have and to hold the same for the period of their boyhood. And all meadows with the clover blossoms and butterflies thereof, the woods and their appurtenances, the squirrels, and birds, and echoes, and strange noises, and all distant places which may be visited, together with the adventures there found. And I give to said boys each his own place at the fireside at night, with all pictures that may be seen in the burning wood, to enjoy without let or hindrance, and without incumbrance of cares.

Item: To lovers I devise their imaginary world, with whatever they may need—the stars of the sky, the red roses by the wall, the bloom of the hawthorn, the sweet strains of music, and aught else by which they may desire to figure to each other the lastingness and beauty of their love.

Item: To young men jointly, I devise and bequeath all boisterous, inspiring sports of rivalry, and I give to them the disdain of weakness and undaunted confidence in their own strength. I give them the power to make lasting friendships, and of possessing companions, and to them exclusively I give all merry songs and brave choruses to sing with lusty voices.

Item: And to those who are no longer children or youths or lovers, I leave memory, and I bequeath to them the volumes of the poems of Burns and Shakespeare and of other poets, if there be others, to the end that they may live the old days again, freely and fully, without tithe or diminution. To our loved ones with snowy crowns I bequeath the happiness of old age, and the love and gratitude of their children.

MORE HEART THROBS

Love that is hoarded moulds at last
   Until we know some day
The only thing we ever have
   Is what we give away.

LOUIS GINSBERG

MAY YOU HAVE

Enough happiness to keep you sweet,
Enough trials to keep you strong,
Enough sorrow to keep you human,
Enough hope to keep you happy;
Enough failure to keep you humble,
Enough success to keep you eager,
Enough friends to give you comfort,
Enough wealth to meet your needs;
Enough enthusiasm to look forward,
Enough faith to banish depression,
Enough determination to make each day
    better than yesterday.

A SONG OF SERVICE

If all my pain and all my tears,
And all that I have learned throughout the
    years
Could make one perfect song
To lift some fallen head
To light some darkened mind,
I should feel that not in vain
I served mankind.

MARGUERITE FEW

MIRROR

One day a rich man of a miserly disposition
visited a rabbi, who took him by the hand and
led him to a window. "Look out there," he
said. The rich man looked out into the street.
"What do you see?" I see men and women and
little children." Again the rabbi took him to
a mirror. "What do you see now?" "I see myself." "Behold, the window there is glass and
the mirror is glass also. But the glass of the
mirror is covered with silver. No sooner is silver
added than you cease to see others and see only
yourself."

THE HUMAN TOUCH

'Tis the human touch in this world that counts,
    The touch of your hand and mine,
Which means far more to the fainting heart
    Than shelter and bread and wine;
For shelter is gone when the night is o'er,
    And bread lasts only a day,
But the touch of the hand, the sound of the
    voice
    Sing on in the soul alway.

SPENCER MICHAEL FREE

GIFTS

To your enemy, forgiveness.
To an opponent, tolerance.
To a friend, your heart.
To a customer, service.
To all men, charity.
To every child, a good example.
To yourself, respect.

Lord, make me a channel of thy peace
That where there is hatred I may bring love,
That where there is wrong I may bring the
    spirit of forgiveness,
That where there is discord I may bring
    harmony,
That where there is error I may bring truth,
That where there is doubt I may bring faith,
That where there is despair I may bring hope,
That where there are shadows I may bring
    thy light,
That where there is sadness I may bring joy.

Lord, grant that I may seek rather
To comfort—than to be comforted;
To understand—than to be understood;
To love—than to be loved;
For it is by giving that one receives;
It is by self-forgetting that one finds;
It is by forgiving that one is forgiven;
It is by dying that one awakens to eternal life.

ST. FRANCIS OF ASSISI

Not what we give, but what we share,—
For the gift without the giver is bare;
Who gives himself with his alms feeds three,—
Himself, his hungering neighbor, and Me.

JAMES RUSSELL LOWELL

COMMANDMENT

Be unselfish. That is the first and final commandment for those who would be useful and happy in their usefulness. If you think of yourself only, you cannot develop because you are choking the source of development, which is spiritual expansion through thought for others.

CHARLES W. ELIOT

What can I give Him
Poor as I am?
If I were a shepherd,
I would give Him a lamb,
If I were a Wise Man,
I would do my part,—
But what I can I give Him,
Give my heart.

CHRISTINA G. ROSSETTI

Of all the dear sights in the world, nothing is so beautiful as a child when it is giving something. Any small thing it gives. A child gives the world to you. It opens the world to you as if it were a book you'd never been able to read. But when a gift must be found, it is always some absurd little thing, pasted on crooked . . . an angel looking like a clown. A child has so little that it can give, because it never knows it has given you everything.

MARGARET LEE RUNBECK

LIFE'S FINEST GIFTS

Dawn;
Silent church before service begins;
The love of a little child;
The moment just before one is sure of being loved;
The moment of rescue from danger;
The understanding between friends;
The mountains, the desert, the sea;
Two aged lovers going down the hill of life together;
First love;
The joy of existence.

THESE TIMES

God's gifts put man's best dreams to shame.

ELIZABETH BARRETT BROWNING

GIVING IS FUN

If you believe in something, you support it. If you support something, the time comes when good wishes and cordial words are not enough and your hand reaches for your pocketbook. Then the fun begins. For giving is fun. If you refuse to give, your support is wavering; and if your support wavers, it can't be that you believe in that something in any strong way. Maybe our account books, after all, offer the honest list of those things in which we really believe.

KENNETH IRVING BROWN

Thou that hast given so much to me,
Give one thing more—a grateful heart;
Not thankful when it pleaseth me,
As if thy blessings had spare days;
But such a heart, whose pulse may be
Thy praise.

GEORGE HERBERT

GOODNESS

A saint is one who makes goodness attractive.

LAURENCE HOUSMAN

VARIATIONS OF THE GOLDEN RULE

Do as you would be done by.—Persian.

Do not that to a neighbor which you shall take ill from him.—Grecian.

What you would not wish done to yourself do not do unto others.—Chinese.

One should seek for others the happiness one desires for one's self.—Buddhist.

Let none of you treat his brother in a way he himself would not like to be treated.—Mohammedan.

The true rule of life is to guard and do by the things of others as they do by their own.—Hindu.

The law imprinted on the hearts of all men is to love the members of society as themselves.—Roman.

❦

God has put something noble and good into every heart which his hand created.

MARK TWAIN

❦

We ought to do good to others as simply and as naturally as a horse runs, or a bee makes honey, or a vine bears grapes season after season without thinking of the grapes it has borne.

MARCUS AURELIUS

❦

HOLINESS

One should hallow all that one does in one's natural life. One eats in holiness, tastes the taste of food in holiness, and the table becomes an altar. One works in holiness, and he raises up the sparks which hide themselves in all tools. One walks in holiness across the fields, and the soft songs of all herbs, which they voice to God, enter into the song of our soul.

MARTIN BUBER

❦

All that is good, all that is true, all that is beautiful, all that is beneficent, be it great or small, be it perfect or fragmentary, natural as well as supernatural, moral as well as material, comes from God.

JOHN HENRY NEWMAN

❦

Conviction is worthless unless it is converted into conduct.

THOMAS CARLYLE

❦

HOW MAY WE KNOW WHAT IS RIGHT?

1. Pay reverent heed to the wisdom of the ages, more especially as it has been authenticated and glorified by the great masters of right living.
2. Live in the open. Do only what you are willing should be done "in the sight of all men."
3. Live in humanity. Do only what you are willing that all men should do as a universal rule of conduct.
4. Eliminate yourself, and act only from disinterested motives.

JOHN HAYNES HOLMES

❦

Be not simply good; be good for something.

HENRY DAVID THOREAU

❦

The essence of evil is to think of oneself and of other people simply as perishable by-products of an impersonal nature and to live accordingly. The essence of good is to think of oneself and others as children of the Father, God, and to live accordingly.

✥

God is too wise not to know all about us, and what is really best for us to be and to have. And he is too good not to desire our highest good, and too powerful, desiring, not to effect it.

H. P. LIDDON

✥

PRICELESS

Let the weakest, let the humblest remember, that in his daily course he can, if he will, shed around him almost a heaven. Kindly words, sympathizing attentions, watchfulness against wounding men's sensitiveness—these cost very little, but they are priceless in their value. Are not they almost staples of our daily happiness? From hour to hour, from moment to moment, we are supported, blest, by small kindnesses.

FREDERICK W. ROBERTSON

✥

PRAYER

Keep me, O Lord, from all pettiness. Let me be large in thought and word and deed.
Let me leave off self-seeking and have done with fault-finding.
Help me put away all pretense, that I may meet my neighbor face to face, without self-pity and without prejudice.
May I never be hasty in my judgments, but generous to all and in all things.
Make me grow calm, serene, and gentle.
Teach me to put into action my better impulses and make me straightforward and unafraid.
Grant that I may realize that it is the trifling things of life that create differences, that in the higher things we are all one.
And, O Lord, God, let me not forget to be kind!

MARY STUART

✥

Do all the good you can,
By all the means you can,
In all the ways you can,
In all the places you can,
At all the times you can,
To all the people you can,
As long as ever you can.

JOHN WESLEY

✥

Good actions are the invisible hinges on the doors of heaven.

VICTOR HUGO

✥

ABOU BEN ADHEM

Abou Ben Adhem (may his tribe increase!)
Awoke one night from a deep dream of peace,
And saw within the moonlight in his room,
Making it rich and like a lily in bloom,
An angel writing in a book of gold;
Exceeding peace had made Ben Adhem bold,
And to the Presence in the room he said,
"What writest thou?" The vision raised its head,
And with a look made of all sweet accord,
Answered, "The names of those who love the
    Lord."
"And is mine one?" said Abou. "Nay, not so,"
Replied the angel. Abou spoke more low,
But cheerily still, and said, "I pray thee, then,
Write me as one that loves his fellow-men."
The angel wrote, and vanished. The next night
It came again with a great wakening light,
And showed the names whom love of God had
    blessed;
And, lo! Ben Adhem's name led all the rest!

LEIGH HUNT

✥

No man or woman can really be strong, gentle, pure, and good without the world being better for it.

PHILLIPS BROOKS

112

SON OF MAN

Jesus of Nazareth, without money and arms, conquered more millions than Alexander, Caesar, Mohammed, and Napoleon; without science and learning, he shed more light on things human and divine than all the philosophers and scholars combined; without the eloquence of the school, he spoke words of life such as were never spoken before, nor since, and produced effects which lie beyond the reach of orator or poet; without writing a single line, he has set more pens in motion and furnished themes for more sermons, orations, discussions, works of art, learned volumes, and sweet songs of praise than the whole army of great men of ancient and modern times. Born in a manger and crucified as a malefactor, he now controls the destinies of the civilized world, and rules a spiritual empire which embraces one third of the inhabitants of the globe.

PHILIP SCHAFF

WHAT IS A SAINT?

1. His life is imbued with a deep love of the Christian religion as a way of "feeling at home" in the universe.

2. He lives with a radiance because his spirit is rooted in God's Spirit. "A saint is a person who has quit worrying about himself" because his life is centered in God. With Jakob Böhme he says, "Though my head and my hand be at labor, yet doth my heart dwell in God."

3. He starts each day with these words: "May the image of Christ radiate through me this day in each life situation."

4. He asks that God use him as an instrument of his love to bear the burdens of his fellow men. Like Francis of Assisi, the saint loves "not humanity but men."

5. He believes that before God's kingdom can arrive in society, it must first begin in him.

6. He has humility, caused by his belief that life is too much trouble unless he can live for something that is big. And most of all, his life is lost in the bigness of God.

7. He feels that every person—regardless of color, race, creed, or nation—is a person in whom lie the possibilities of becoming a saint. With Robert Southwell he says, "Not where I breathe but where I love, I live."

8. He desires to use the results of prayer and devotion to better the world.

9. He believes that the two great secrets for becoming a saint lie in "the imitation of Christ" and "the practice of the presence of God."

10. His daily preparation for sainthood is in these words:

By all means use some time to be alone.
Salute thyself; see what thy soul doth wear.
Dare to look into thy chest; for 'tis thy own.

THOMAS S. KEPLER

To live in the presence of great truths, to be dealing with eternal laws, to be led by permanent ideals—that is what keeps a man patient when the world ignores him, and calm and unspoiled when the world praises him.

FRANCIS G. PEABODY

ROOTED AND GROUNDED

Trees suspended in mid-air do not bear fruit. They are rooted. As one contemplates the endless moral struggle of mankind through the centuries, he is assured that man's moral effort is rooted and grounded in his faith in God. One feels that to lose faith in God is to deprive morality of its cosmic significance. In time it will be no longer compelling. Like the tree pulled out of the soil, it will die because it is not grounded.

HAROLD COOKE PHILLIPS

PRAYER

Lord, might I be but as a saw,
A plane, a chisel in thy hand.
No, Lord, I take it back in awe;
Such prayer for me is far too grand.
I pray thee, rather let me lie
As on thy bench the favored wood;
Thy saw, thy plane, thy chisel ply
And work me into something good.

GEORGE MACDONALD

We like people in proportion to the good we do them and not to the good they do us.

LAURENCE STERNE

JESUS AND LINCOLN

There is a striking similarity between the Man of Galilee and the man from Illinois.

Both had obscure beginnings.

Each came to his own and they received him not.

Neither allowed difficulty to turn him from his central purpose.

Both prepared for responsibility through self-sacrifice and self-denial.

Both loved little children.

Both befriended the weak.

The common people heard each of them gladly.

Neither condescended, yet both loved all men as children of God.

Both hated the things which enslaved men.

Each had a passion for justice and truth.

Each took the pains of humanity as his own so that he was a "man of sorrows . . . acquainted with grief."

Neither made room for bitterness.

Each of them knew the loneliness of following the course of the heart rather than the dictates of men.

Both marched resolutely toward death for humanity.

Each of them died to set men free.

K. MORGAN EDWARDS

You will never be sorry—
for thinking before acting,
for hearing before judging,
for forgiving your enemies,
for being candid and frank,
for helping a fallen brother,
for being honest in business,
for thinking before speaking,
for being loyal to your church,
for standing by your principles,
for stopping your ears to gossip,
for bridling a slanderous tongue,
for harboring only pure thoughts,
for sympathizing with the afflicted,
for being courteous and kind to all.

TRUE MORALITY

Morality has been conceived up to the present in a very narrow spirit, as obedience to a law, as inner struggle between opposite laws. As for me, I declare that when I do good I obey no one, I fight no battle and win no victory. The cultivated man has only to follow the delicious incline of his inner impulses. Be beautiful and then do at each moment whatever your heart may inspire you to do. This is the whole of morality.

ERNEST RENAN

HAPPINESS

Happiness comes of the capacity to feel deeply, to enjoy simply, to think freely, to risk life, to be needed.

STORM JAMESON

THE HAPPIEST PEOPLE

Every person in the world may not become a personage. But every person may become a personality. The happiest people are those who think the most interesting thoughts. Interesting thoughts can only live in cultivated minds. Those who decide to use leisure as a means of mental development, who love good music, good books, good pictures, good plays at the theater, good company, good conversation—what are they? They are the happiest people in the world; and they are not only happy in themselves, they are the cause of happiness in others.

WILLIAM LYON PHELPS

Such happiness as life is capable of comes from the full participation of all our powers in the endeavor to wrest from each changing situation of experience its own full and unique meaning.

JOHN DEWEY

TWELVE RULES FOR HAPPINESS

I. Live a simple life. Be temperate in your habits. Avoid self-seeking and selfishness. Make simplicity the keynote of your daily plans. Simple things are best.

II. Spend less than you earn. This may be difficult but it pays big dividends. Keep out of debt. Cultivate frugality, prudence, and self-denial. Avoid extravagance.

III. Think constructively. Train yourself to think clearly and accurately. Store your mind with useful thoughts. Stand porter at the door of your mind.

IV. Cultivate a yielding disposition. Resist the common tendency to want things your own way. Try to see the other person's point of view.

V. Be grateful. Begin the day with gratitude for your opportunities and blessings. Be glad for the privilege of life and work.

VI. Rule your moods. Cultivate a mental attitude of peace and good will.

VII. Give generously. There is no greater joy in life than to render happiness to others by means of intelligent giving.

VIII. Work with right motives. The highest purpose of your life should be to grow in spiritual grace and power.

IX. Be interested in others. Direct your mind from self-centeredness. In the degree that you give, serve, and help will you experience the by-product of happiness.

X. Live in a daylight compartment. This means living one day at a time. Concentrate on your immediate task. Make the most of today for it is all you have.

XI. Have a hobby. Nature study, walking, gardening, music, golfing, carpentry, stamp collecting, sketching, voice culture, foreign language, books, photography, social service, public speaking, travel, authorship are samples. Cultivate an avocation to which you can turn for diversion and relaxation.

XII. Keep close with God. True and enduring happiness depends on close alliance with him. It is your privilege to share his thoughts for your spiritual nourishment, and to have a constant assurance of Divine protection and guidance.

NATIONAL RELIGIOUS PRESS

Lord, let me give and sing and sow
  And do my best, though I
In years to come may never know
  What soul was helped thereby.

Content to feel that thou canst bless
  All things however small
To someone's lasting happiness
  So, Lord, accept my all.

PRUDENCE TASKER OLSEN

That is happiness; to be dissolved into something complete and great. When it comes to one, it comes as naturally as sleep.

WILLA CATHER

❦

DEEPLY ROOTED

The happiness which brings enduring worth to life is not the superficial happiness that is dependent on circumstances. It is the happiness and contentment that fills the soul even in the midst of the most distressing of circumstances and the most bitter environment. It is the kind of happiness that grins when things go wrong and smiles through the tears. The happiness for which our souls ache is one undisturbed by success or failure, one which will root deeply inside us and give inward relaxation, peace, and contentment, no matter what the surface problems may be. That kind of happiness stands in need of no outward stimulus.

BILLY GRAHAM

❦

It is not easy to find happiness in ourselves, and it is not possible to find it elsewhere.

AGNES REPPLIER

❦

FULL LIFE

If you observe a really happy man you will find him building a boat, writing a symphony, educating his son, growing double dahlias in his garden, or looking for dinosaur eggs in the Gobi desert. He will not be searching for happiness as if it were a collar button that has rolled under the radiator. He will not be striving for it as a goal in itself. He will have become aware that he is happy in the course of living life twenty-four crowded hours of the day.

W. BÉRAN WOLFE

❦

The inner half of every cloud
  Is bright and shining;
I therefore turn my clouds about,
And always wear them inside out
  To show the lining.

ELLEN THORNEYCROFT FOWLER

❦

HARMONY

When a man achieves a fair measure of harmony within himself and his family circle, he achieves peace; and a nation made up of such individuals and groups is a happy nation. As the harmony of a star in its course is expressed by rhythm and grace, so the harmony of a man's life-course is expressed by happiness; this, I believe, is the prime desire of mankind.

RICHARD E. BYRD

❦

RESPONSIBILITY

A little thought will show you how vastly your own happiness depends on the way other people bear themselves toward you. The looks and tones at your breakfast table, the conduct of your fellow-workers or employers, the faithful or unreliable men you deal with, what people say to you on the street, the letters you get, the friends or foes you meet—these things make up very much of the pleasure or misery of your day. Turn the idea around, and remember that just so much are you adding to the pleasure or the misery of other people's days. And this is the half of the matter which you can control. Whether any particular day shall bring to you more of happiness or of suffering is largely beyond your power to determine. Whether each day of your life shall *give* happiness or suffering rests with yourself.

GEORGE S. MERRIAM

❦

From THE FAMILY REUNION

I feel quite happy, as if happiness
Did not consist in getting what one wanted
Or in getting rid of what can't be got rid of
But in a different vision.

T. S. ELIOT

A SMILE

A smile costs nothing but gives much. It enriches those who receive, without making poorer those who give. It takes but a moment, but the memory of it sometimes lasts forever. No one is so rich or mighty that he can get along without it, and no one is so poor but that he can be made rich by it. A smile creates happiness in the home, fosters good will in business, and is the countersign of friendship. It brings rest to the weary, cheer to the discouraged, sunshine to the sad, and is nature's best antidote for trouble. Yet it cannot be bought, begged, borrowed, or stolen, for it is something that is of no value to anyone until it is given away. Some people are too tired to give a smile. Give them one of yours, as no one needs a smile so much as he who has none to give.

THESE TIMES

One of the sanest, surest, and most generous joys of life comes from being happy over the good fortune of others.

ARCHIBALD RUTLEDGE

There is an idea abroad among moral people that they should make their neighbors good. One person I have to make good: myself. But my duty to my neighbor is much more nearly expressed by saying that I must make him happy —if I may.

ROBERT LOUIS STEVENSON

The only way on earth to multiply happiness is to divide it.

PAUL SCHERER

The year's at the spring
And day's at the morn;
Morning's at seven:
The hillside's dew-pearled;
The lark's on the wing;
The snail's on the thorn;
God's in his heaven—
All's right with the world!

ROBERT BROWNING

NEW WORLD

No person probably ever made so ardent a personal appeal as Jesus. He discovered a whole new world of emotional life, a new expansion of joy. It is his distinction that he has for us permanently expanded the bounds of individuality. So that now when I open and turn over with reverent joy the leaves of the Gospels, I feel that here is enshrined the highest achievement of man the artist, a creation to which nothing can be added, from which nothing can be taken away.

HAVELOCK ELLIS

That state of life is most happy where superfluities are not required and necessities are not wanting.

PLUTARCH

Happiness is the full use of your powers along lines of excellence in a life affording scope.

JOHN F. KENNEDY

THE HAPPIEST HEART

Who drives the horses of the sun
    Shall lord it but a day.
Better the lowly deed were done
    And kept the humble way.

The rust will find the sword of fame;
    The dust will hide the crowd,
Aye, none shall nail so high his name
    Time will not tear it down.

The happiest heart that ever beat
    Was in some quiet breast
That found the common daylight sweet
    And left to heaven the rest.

JOHN VANCE CHENEY

If one only wished to be happy, this could be easily accomplished; but we wish to be happier than other people, and this is always difficult, for we believe others to be happier than they are.

MONTESQUIEU

I accept life unconditionally. Life holds so much—so much to be so happy about always. Most people ask for happiness on condition. Happiness can be felt only if you don't set conditions.

ARTUR RUBINSTEIN

If you would make a man happy, do not add to his possessions but subtract from the sum of his desires.

SENECA

Everybody really knows what to do to have his life filled with joy. What is it? Quit hating people; start loving them. Quit being mad at people; start liking them. Quit doing wrong; quit being filled with fear. Quit thinking about yourself and go out and do something for other people. Everybody knows what you have to do to be happy. But the wisdom of the test lies in the final words: "If ye know these things, *happy are ye if ye do them.*"

NORMAN VINCENT PEALE

THE CELESTIAL SURGEON

If I have faltered more or less
In my great task of happiness;
If I have moved among my race
And shown no glorious morning face;
If beams from happy human eyes
Have moved me not; if morning skies,
Books, and my food, and summer rain
Knocked on my sullen heart in vain:—
Lord, thy most pointed pleasure take
And stab my spirit broad awake;
Or, Lord, if too obdurate I,
Choose thou, before that spirit die,
A piercing pain, a killing sin,
And to my dead heart run them in!

ROBERT LOUIS STEVENSON

To be without some of the things you want is an indispensable part of happiness.

BERTRAND RUSSELL

The measure of a happy life is not from the fewer or more suns we behold, the fewer or more breaths we draw, or meals we repeat, but from having once lived well, acted our part handsomely, and made our exit cheerfully.

LORD SHAFTSBURY

HELPFULNESS

They might not need me; but they might.
I'll let my head be just in sight;
A smile as small as mine might be
Precisely their necessity.

EMILY DICKINSON

It is better to light a candle than to curse the darkness.

⋆⋆⋆

If I can stop one heart from breaking,
I shall not live in vain;
If I can ease one life the aching,
Or cool one pain,
Or help one fainting robin
Unto his nest again,
I shall not live in vain.

EMILY DICKINSON

⋆⋆⋆

When your own burden is heaviest, you can always lighten a little some other burden. At the times when you cannot see God, there is still open to you this sacred possibility, to show God; for it is the love and kindness of human hearts through which the divine reality comes home to men, whether they name it or not. Let this thought, then, stay with you: there may be times when you cannot find help, but there is no time when you cannot give help.

GEORGE S. MERRIAM

⋆⋆⋆

THE COST IS SMALL

Kindness has been described in many ways. It is the poetry of the heart, the music of the world. It is a golden chain which binds society together. It is a fountain of gladness. Kind hearts are more than coronets. Kind words produce their own beautiful image in man's soul. Everyone knows the pleasure of receiving a kind look, a warm greeting, a hand held out in time of need. And such gestures can be made at so little expense, yet they bring such dividends to the investor.

THE WAR CRY

⋆⋆⋆

After Benjamin Franklin had received a letter thanking him for having done a kindness, he replied:

"As to the kindness you mention, I wish I could have been of more service to you than I have been, but if I had, the only thanks that I should desire are that you would always be ready to serve any other person that may need your assistance, and so let good offices go around, for mankind are all of a family. As for my own part, when I am employed in serving others I do not look upon myself as conferring favors but paying debts."

⋆⋆⋆

MY DAILY PRAYER

If I can do some good today,
If I can serve along life's way,
If I can something helpful say,
  Lord, show me how.

If I can right a human wrong,
If I can help to make one strong,
If I can cheer with smile or song,
  Lord, show me how.

If I can aid one in distress,
If I can make a burden less,
If I can spread more happiness,
  Lord, show me how.

GRENVILLE KLEISER

⋆⋆⋆

A hundred times every day I remind myself that my inner and outer life depend on the labors of other men, living and dead, and that I must exert myself in order to give in the same measure as I have received and am still receiving.

ALBERT EINSTEIN

REGRET

I have wept in the night
For the shortness of sight
That to somebody's need made me blind;
But I never have yet
Felt a tinge of regret
For being a little too kind.

Die when I may, I want it said of me by those who knew me best, that I always plucked a thistle and planted a flower where I thought a flower would grow.

ABRAHAM LINCOLN

The greatest object in the universe, says a certain philosopher, is a good man struggling with adversity; yet there is a still greater, which is the good man that comes to relieve it.

OLIVER GOLDSMITH

You will find, as you look back upon your life, that the moments that stand out are the moments when you have done things for others.

HENRY DRUMMOND

That best portion of a good man's life,
His little, nameless, unremembered acts
Of kindness and of love.

WILLIAM WORDSWORTH

The only ones among you who will be really happy are those who will have sought and found how to serve.

ALBERT SCHWEITZER

IF I HAD KNOWN

If I had known what trouble you were bearing;
What griefs were in the silence of your face;
I would have been more gentle, and more
    caring,
And tried to give you gladness for a space.
I would have brought more warmth into the
    place,
    If I had known.

If I had known what thoughts despairing drew
    you;
(Why do we never try to understand?)
I would have lent a little friendship to you,
And slipped my hand within your hand,
And made your stay more pleasant in the land,
    If I had known.

MARY CAROLYN DAVIES

COURTESY

Of Courtesy, it is much less
Than Courage of Heart or Holiness,
Yet in my walks it seems to me
That the Grace of God is in Courtesy.

HILAIRE BELLOC

The best cure for worry, depression, melancholy, brooding, is to go deliberately forth and try to lift with one's sympathy the gloom of somebody else.

ARNOLD BENNETT

I sought to hear the
    voice of God
And climbed the
    topmost steeple,
But God declared:
    "Go down again—
I dwell among
    the people."

              JOHN HENRY NEWMAN

A house is built of logs and stone,
    Of tiles and posts and piers;
A home is built of loving deeds
    That stand a thousand years.

              VICTOR HUGO

A SALUTE TO A SCOUTMASTER

In almost every community in America you will find this man.

He is engaged in one of the most exciting tasks known, he works with boys—and in case you haven't worked with youngsters lately, they are still the most energetic, imaginative, enthusiastic animals ever to grace the earth.

He is an indoor worker who teaches how to get along in the outdoors.

He is a practicing expert in a multitudinous variety of minute-sized details.

He arms his charges with ideals, tents, cooking kits, and fervor and guides them into adventures to prepare them for life ahead.

He leads boys by arousing their enthusiasm until they run ahead of him to do the job.

He comforts them in perilous times with his presence and stability.

He teaches citizenship by letting them run a camp in the wilderness.

If he quits, moves away, or dies, his is one of the most difficult jobs to fill.

Yet, if he does his job well, his only pay will be the deep personal satisfaction of knowing that he has contributed immeasurably toward developing the kind of citizen that we consider ideal.

A strong man, who knows where he is going, and an extremely popular man in the eyes of the future generation—that is the Scoutmaster.

              THESE TIMES

Are you willing—

to stoop down and consider the needs and desires of little children;

to remember the weakness and loneliness of people who are growing old;

to stop asking how much your friends love you, and to ask yourself whether you love them enough;

to bear in mind the things that other people have to bear on their hearts;

to trim your lamp so that it will give more light and less smoke, and to carry it in front so that your shadow will fall behind you;

to make a grave for your ugly thoughts and a garden for your kindly feelings, with the gate open?

Are you willing to do these things for a day?

Then you are ready to keep Christmas!

              HENRY VAN DYKE

MARVEL

We marvel at the silence that divides
    the living and the dead
    Yet more apart
Are they who all life long live side by side
    Yet never heart by heart.

PRAYER

Lord of all pots and pans and tins, since I've
    no time to be
A saint by doing lovely things, or watching late
    with thee,
Or dreaming in the twilight, or storming
    heaven's gates,
Make me a saint by getting meals and washing
    up the plates.

Although I must have Martha's hands, I have
    a Mary mind;
And when I black the boots and shoes, thy
    sandals, Lord, I find;
I think of how they trod the earth, each time I
    scrub the floor;
Accept this meditation, Lord, I haven't time for
    more.

Warm all the kitchen with thy love and light
    it with thy peace;
Forgive me all my worrying and make all
    grumbling cease;
Thou who didst love to give men food—in
    room or by the sea—
Accept this service that I do, I do it unto thee.

LIGHT FOR DARKNESS

The hero is one who kindles a great light in
the world, who sets up blazing torches in the
dark streets of life for men to see by. The
saint is the man who walks through the dark
paths of the world, himself a light.

FELIX ADLER

No one is useless in this world who lightens
the burden of it to anyone else.

CHARLES DICKENS

OUR COMMON NATURE

No one is so rich that he does not need another's help; no one so poor as not to be useful
in some way to his fellow man; and the disposition to ask assistance from others with confidence, and to grant it with kindness, is part
of our very nature.

POPE LEO XIII

If any little thought of ours
Can make one life the stronger;
If any cheery smile of ours
Can make its brightness longer;
Then let us speak that thought today,
With tender eyes aglowing,
So God may grant some weary one
Shall reap from our glad sowing.

WORKING CAPITAL

Open your eyes and look for a human being,
or some work devoted to human welfare, which
needs from someone a little time or friendliness, a little sympathy, or sociability, or labor.
There may be a solitary or an embittered fellow-
man, an invalid, or an inefficient person to
whom you can be something. Perhaps it is an
old person or a child. Or some good work
needs volunteers who can offer a free evening,
or run errands. Who can enumerate the many
ways in which that costly piece of working
capital, a human being, can be employed? More
of him is wanted everywhere! Search, then,
for some investment for your humanity, and
do not be frightened away if you have to
wait, or to be taken on trial. And be prepared
for disappointments. But in any case, do not
be without some secondary work in which
you can give yourself as a man to men. It is
marked out for you, if you only truly will to
have it.

ALBERT SCHWEITZER

HOME

*There is no spectacle on earth more appealing
than that of a beautiful woman in the act of cooking dinner
for someone she loves.*

THOMAS WOLFE

WHAT IS A HOME?

A roof to keep out the rain. Four walls to keep out the wind. Floors to keep out the cold. Yes, but home is more than that. It is the laugh of a baby, the song of a mother, the strength of a father. Warmth of loving hearts, light from happy eyes, kindness, loyalty, comradeship. Home is first school and first church for young ones, where they learn what is right, what is good, and what is kind. Where they go for comfort when they are hurt or sick. Where joy is shared and sorrow eased. Where fathers and mothers are respected and loved. Where children are wanted. Where the simplest food is good enough for kings because it is earned. Where money is not so important as loving-kindness. Where even the teakettle sings from happiness. That is home. God bless it.

ERNESTINE SCHUMAN-HEINK

❧

Your house is your fortress in a warring world, where a woman's hand buckles on your armor in the morning and soothes your fatigue and wounds at night.

FRANK CRANE

❧

CONFIDENT LIVING

Home is the one place in all this world where hearts are sure of each other. It is the place of confidence. It is the place where we tear off that mask of guarded and suspicious coldness which the world forces us to wear in self-defense, and where we pour out the unreserved communications of full and confiding hearts. It is the spot where expressions of tenderness gush out without any sensation of awkwardness and without any dread of ridicule.

FREDERICK W. ROBERTSON

❧

SO LONG AS THERE ARE HOMES

So long as there are homes to which men turn
At close of day;
So long as there are homes where children are,
Where women stay—
If love and loyalty and faith be found
Across those sills—
A stricken nation can recover from
Its gravest ills.

So long as there are homes where fires burn
And there is bread;
So long as there are homes where lamps are lit
And prayers are said;
Although people falter through the dark—
And nations grope—
With God himself back of these little homes—
We have sure hope.

GRACE NOLL CROWELL

❧

HOME

Home is where
You hang
Your memories.

Home is the
Conscience of age,
The melody
At the end of
Eternity.
Home is truth
Guiding youth.
Home is the regret
In every madness.

Home is where
You begin again
To dream again.

CHARLES ANGOFF

❧

Let parents bequeath to their children not riches, but the spirit of reverence.

PLATO

LOVE AT HOME

There is beauty all around
When there's love at home;
There is joy in every sound
When there's love at home.

Peace and plenty here abide,
Smiling sweet on every side;
Time doth softly, sweetly glide
When there's love at home.

BLUEPRINT

Home—a world of strife shut out, a world of
love shut in.

Home—a place where the small are great, and
the great are small.

Home—the father's kingdom, the mother's
world, and the child's paradise.

Home—the place where we grumble the most,
and are treated the best.

Home—the center of our affection, round
which our heart's best wishes twine.

Home—the place where our stomachs get three
square meals a day and our hearts a thousand.

CHARLES M. CROWE

Anyone can build an altar; it requires a God to
provide the flame. Anybody can build a house;
we need the Lord for the creation of a home.

JOHN HENRY JOWETT

The Christian home is the Master's workshop
where the processes of character molding are
silently, lovingly, faithfully, and successfully
carried on.

LORD HOUGHTON

A FATHER'S PRAYER

Build me a son, O Lord, who will be strong
enough to know when he is weak, and brave
enough to face himself when he is afraid; one
who will be proud and unbending in honest
defeat, and humble and gentle in victory.

Build me a son whose wishbone will not be
where his backbone should be; a son who will
know thee and that to know himself is the
foundation stone of knowledge.

Lead him, I pray, not in the path of ease and
comfort, but under the stress and spur of difficulties and challenge. Here let him learn to
stand up in the storm; here let him learn compassion for those who fail.

Build me a son whose heart will be clear,
whose goal will be high; a son who will master
himself before he seeks to master other men;
one who will learn to laugh, yet never forget
how to weep; one who will reach into the
future, yet never forget the past.

And after all these things are his, add, I pray,
enough of a sense of humor, so that he may
always be serious, yet never take himself too
seriously. Give him humility, so that he may
always remember the simplicity of true greatness, the open mind of true wisdom, the meekness of true strength.

Then I, his father, will dare to whisper, "I
have not lived in vain."

DOUGLAS MAC ARTHUR

HOME VIRTUES

The beauty of a house is harmony.
The security of a house is loyalty.
The joy of a house is love.
The plenty of a house is in children.
The rule of a house is service.
The comfort of a house is in contented spirits.
The maker of a house, of a real human house,
    is God himself, the same who made the stars
    and built the world.

FRANK CRANE

130

FOUNDATIONS

It is, indeed, in the home that the foundations of the kind of world in which we live are laid, and in this sense it will always remain true that the hand that rocks the cradle is the hand that rules the world. And it is in this sense that women must assume the job of making men who will know how to make a world fit for human beings to live in.

ASHLEY MONTAGUE

INHERITANCE

I am most of all thankful for my birthplace and early nurture in the warm atmosphere of a spiritually-minded home, with a manifest touch of saintliness in it; thankful indeed that from the cradle I was saturated with the Bible and immersed in an environment of religion of experience and reality. It was a peculiar grace that I was born into that great inheritance of spiritual wisdom and faith, accumulated through generations of devotion and sacrificial love. I can never be grateful enough for what was done for me by my progenitors before I came on the scene. They produced the spiritual atmosphere of my youth. I became heir of a vast invisible inheritance. There is nothing I would exchange for that.

RUFUS M. JONES

Children can have no better inheritance than believing parents. Religion can become real in the midst of the family as in practically no other way. Many of us have inherited great riches from our parents—the bank account of their personal faith and family prayers.

NELS F. S. FERRÉ

PRAYER

Lord, this humble house we'd keep
Sweet with play and calm with sleep.
Help us so that we may give
Beauty to the lives we live.
Let Thy love and let Thy grace.
Shine upon our dwelling place.

EDGAR A. GUEST

HOUSE BLESSING

Bless the four corners of this house,
  And be the lintel blest;
And bless the hearth, and bless the board,
  And bless each place of rest;
And bless the door that opens wide
  To stranger, as to kin;
And bless each crystal windowpane
  That lets the starlight in;
And bless the rooftree overhead,
  And every sturdy wall,
The peace of man, the peace of God,
  The peace of love on all.

ARTHUR GUITERMAN

EXAMPLE

From the services in which I joined as a child I have taken with me into life a feeling for what is solemn, and a need for quiet self-recollection, without which I cannot realize the meaning of my life. I cannot, therefore, support the opinion of those who would not let children take part in grown-up people's services till they to some extent understand them. The important thing is not that they shall understand but that they shall feel something of what is serious and solemn. The fact that a child sees his elders full of devotion, and has to feel something of devotion himself, that is what gives the service its meaning for him.

ALBERT SCHWEITZER

MARRIAGE

Perhaps the greatest blessing in marriage is that it lasts so long. The years, like the varying interests of each year, combine to buttress and enrich each other. Out of many shared years, one life. In a series of temporary relationships, one misses the ripening, gathering, harvesting joys, the deep, hard-won truths of marriage.

RICHARD C. CABOT

TO BE HAPPY THOUGH MARRIED

1. Play the fifty-fifty game. Help the wife with the dishes, and she will help you with your charts and the signals.
2. Apply the rules of good sportsmanship to your married life. And that means follow the Golden Rule.
3. Be mutually unselfish.
4. Have mutual confidence. Keep no secrets from one another and let no jealousy creep in.
5. Never complain. Be cheerful.
6. Have children. A family without children is not normal, and the views of one or both of the couple are apt to become warped without children.
7. Work together. Find your happiness at home and in your play together. The couple that spend all their lives looking for pleasure won't find it.

AMOS ALONZO STAGG

Good family life is never an accident but always an achievement by those who share it.

JAMES H. S. BOSSARD

DEVOTION

There is an enduring tenderness in the love of a mother to a son that transcends all other affections of the heart. It is neither to be chilled by selfishness, nor daunted by danger, nor weakened by worthlessness, nor stifled by ingratitude. She will sacrifice every comfort to his convenience; she will surrender every pleasure to his enjoyment; she will glory in his fame and exult in his prosperity; and if adversity overtake him, he will be the dearer to her by misfortune; and if disgrace settle upon his name, she will still love and cherish him; and if all the world beside cast him off, she. will be all the world to him.

WASHINGTON IRVING

DOMESTIC STATESMAN

A woman who runs her house well is both its queen and its subject. She is the one who makes work possible for her husband and children; she protects them from worries, feeds them and cares for them. She is Minister of Finance, and, thanks to her, the household budget is balanced. She is Minister of Fine Arts, and it is to her doing if the house or apartment has charm. She is Minister of Family Education and responsible for the boys' entry into school and college and the girls' cleverness and cultivation. A woman should be as proud of her success in making her house into a perfect little world as the greatest statesman of his in organizing a nation's affairs.

ANDRÉ MAUROIS

Science has established two facts meaningful for human welfare: first, the foundation of the structure of human personality is laid down in early childhood; and second, the chief engineer in charge of this construction is the family.

MEYER FRANCIS NIMKOFF

When you educate a man you educate an individual; when you educate a woman you educate a whole family.

R. M. MAC IVER

THE HOUSEWIFE
Jesus, teach me how to be
Proud of my simplicity.

Sweep the floors, wash the clothes,
Gather for each vase a rose.

Iron and tend a tiny frock,
Keeping one eye on the clock.

Always having time kept free
For childish questions asked of me.

Grant me wisdom Mary had
When she taught her little Lad.

CATHERINE CATE COBLENTZ

A MOTHER'S CREED
I believe in the eternal importance of the home
    as the fundamental institution of society.
I believe in the immeasurable possibilities of
    every boy and girl.
I believe in the imagination, the trust, the hopes
    and the ideals which dwell in the hearts of
    all children.
I believe in the beauty of nature, of art, of
    books, and of friendship.
I believe in the satisfactions of duty.
I believe in the little homely joys of everyday
    life.
I believe in the goodness of the great design
    which lies behind our complex world.
I believe in the safety and peace which surround
    us all through the overbrooding love of God.

OZORA DAVIS

The mother's heart is the child's schoolroom.

HENRY WARD BEECHER

FOUR THINGS
Four things in any land must dwell,
If it endures and prospers well:
One is manhood true and good;
One is noble womanhood;
One is child life, clean and bright;
And one an altar kept alight.

MOTTO FOR A FRONT HALL
If you come cheerily,
Here shall be jest for you;
If you come wearily,
Here shall be rest for you.

If you come borrowing,
Gladly we'll loan to you;
If you come sorrowing,
Love shall be shown to you.

Under our thatch, friend,
Place shall abide for you,
Touch but the latch, friend,
The door will swing wide for you!

NANCY BYRD TURNE

CHRISTIAN COURTESY
He has callers every Sunday;
None are strangers, all are known.
Yet they quickly leave, and Monday
Finds Him in His house, alone.

Should we not on Sunday morning
After benediction's said,
Mend the manners we've been scorning,
Ask Him to our house instead?

RALPH W. SEAGER

SEVEN REASONS FOR FAMILY WORSHIP

1. It will enrich the life of the family and make the home fit for the presence of the Unseen Guest.
2. It will encourage tolerance and understanding, and put faith in the place of friction.
3. It will bring across the threshold an Infallible Guide for the youth of the home, to give their lives meaning and direction.
4. It will send us forth to the day's work in utter cheerfulness, dedicating the day to the glory of God.
5. It will so strengthen us against suffering, sorrow, and frustration that nothing the world can do to us can hurt us.
6. It will reinforce the work of church and church school, give us a Christ for *all* the week.
7. It will bring the consciousness of a family unity in God, a new dependence on his fatherhood, a new sense of the wider unity and brotherhood of man.

FAMILY WORSHIP

There is one practice which any family can maintain and that is the practice of a time of worship at each family meal. Nearly all families are together for at least one meal a day and, in any case, should sacrifice much else to make this possible. *The table is really the family altar!* Here those of all ages come together and help to sustain both their physical and their spiritual existence. If a sacrament is "an actual conveyance of spiritual meaning and power by a material process," then a family meal can be a sacrament. It entwines the material and the spiritual in a remarkable way. The food, in and of itself, is purely physical, but it represents human service in its use. Here, at one common table, is the father who has earned, the mother who has prepared or planned, and the children who share, according to need, whatever their antecedent participation may have been.

When we realize how deeply a meal together can be a spiritual and regenerating experience, we can understand something of why our Lord, when he broke bread with his little company toward the end of their earthly fellowship, told them, as often as they did it, to remember him. We, too, seek to be members of his sacred fellowship, and irrespective of what we do about the Eucharist, there is no reason why each family meal should not take on something of the character of a time of memory and hope.

ELTON TRUEBLOOD

ONLY ONE MOTHER

Most of all the other beautiful things in life come by twos and threes, by dozens and hundreds. Plenty of roses, stars, sunsets, rainbows, brothers and sisters, aunts and cousins, but only one mother in the whole world.

KATE DOUGLAS WIGGIN

TRIBUTE TO A MOTHER

Faith that withstood the shocks of toil and time;
   Hope that defied despair;
   Patience that conquered care;
And loyalty, whose courage was sublime;
The great deep heart that was a home for all—
   Just, eloquent, and strong
   In protest against wrong;
Wide charity, that knew no sin, no fall;
The Spartan spirit that made life so grand,
   Mating poor daily needs
   With high, heroic deeds,
That wrested happiness from Fate's hard hand.

LOUISA MAY ALCOTT

HOPE

If you have built castles in the air,
Your work need not be lost;
that is where they should be.
Now put foundations under them.

HENRY DAVID THOREAU

There are no rules of architecture for a castle in the clouds.

GILBERT KEITH CHESTERTON

❦

OUTREACHING DESIRE

Hope is outreaching desire with expectancy of good. It is a characteristic of all living beings. Birds, beasts, and men are always alert and striving for the fulfillment of their hungers. They are impelled forward in a ceaseless quest for satisfaction. The antennae of insects restlessly explore and feel their way ahead, and the imagination of man functions in the same manner, ranging through wide areas and far futures in search of the good which hope ever promises.

EDWARD S. AMES

❦

THE GATE OF THE YEAR

And I said to the man who stood at the gate of
　the year:
"Give me a light, that I may tread safely into
　the unknown."
And he replied:
"Go out into the darkness and put your hand
　into the Hand of God.
That shall be to you better than light and safer
　than a known way."
So, I went forth, and finding the Hand of God,
　trod gladly into the night.
And he led me towards the hills and the break-
　ing of the day in the lone East.
　So, heart, be still:
What need our little life,
Our human life, to know,
　If God hath comprehension?
In all the dizzy strife
Of things both high and low
　God hideth His intention.

M. LOUISE HASKINS

❦

Do not look forward to the changes and chances of this life in fear; rather look to them with full hope that, as they arise, God, whose you are, will deliver you out of them. He is your keeper. He has kept you hitherto. Do you but hold fast to his dear hand, and he will lead you safely through all things; and, when you cannot stand, he will bear you in his arms. Do not look forward to what may happen tomorrow. Our Father will either shield you from suffering, or he will give you strength to bear it.

ST. FRANCIS DE SALES

❦

Whoever falls from God's right hand
Is caught into his left.

EDWIN MARKHAM

❦

Even one's yesterdays could not continue to stir and move in a man's mind unless there were a future for those yesterdays to make.

MARY ELLEN CHASE

❦

Our humanity were a poor thing were it not for the divinity that stirs within us.

FRANCIS BACON

❦

TWO TRAILS

In the hills of life there are two trails. One lies along the higher, sunlit fields—where those who travel see afar, and the light lingers long after the sun is down. And one lies along the lower ground—where those who journey look over their shoulders with eyes of dread, and gloomy shadows gather long before the day is done.

HAROLD BELL WRIGHT

TEACHER OF HOPE

My experience of men has neither disposed me to think worse of them nor indisposed me to serve them; not, in spite of failures which I lament, of errors which I now see and acknowledge, or of the present aspect of affairs, do I despair of the future. The truth is this: The march of Providence is so slow and our desires so impatient; the work of progress is so immense and our means of aiding it so feeble; the life of humanity is so long, that of the individual so brief, that we often see only the ebb of the advancing wave and are thus discouraged. It is history that teaches us to hope.

ROBERT E. LEE

Why shouldst thou fill today with sorrow
About tomorrow,
　　My heart?
God watcheth all with care most true;
Doubt not that he will give thee too,
　　Thy part.

PAUL FLEMING

Yet all experience is an arch wherethro'
Gleams that untravell'd world whose margin
　　fades
For ever and for ever when I move.

ALFRED TENNYSON

We are haunted by an ideal life, and it is because we have within us the beginning and the possibility of it.

PHILLIPS BROOKS

JOURNEY TO THE STARS

If seeds in the black earth can turn into such beautiful roses, what might not the heart of man become in its long journey toward the stars?

GILBERT KEITH CHESTERTON

OVERHEARD IN AN ORCHARD

Said the Robin to the Sparrow:
　"I should really like to know
Why these anxious human beings
　Rush about and worry so."

Said the Sparrow to the Robin:
　"Friend, I think that it must be
That they have no heavenly Father
　Such as cares for you and me."

ELIZABETH CHENEY

HOPE—FAITH—LOVE

Nothing that is worth doing can be achieved in our lifetime; therefore we must be saved by hope. Nothing which is true or beautiful or good makes complete sense in any immediate context of history; therefore we must be saved by faith. Nothing we do, however virtuous, can be accomplished alone; therefore we are saved by love. No virtuous act is quite as virtuous from the standpoint of our friend or foe as it is from our standpoint. Therefore we must be saved by the final form of love which is forgiveness.

REINHOLD NIEBUHR

A NEW EARTH

God grant us wisdom in these coming days,
And eyes unsealed, that we clear visions see
Of that new world that he would have us build,
To Life's ennoblement and his high ministry.

JOHN OXENHAM

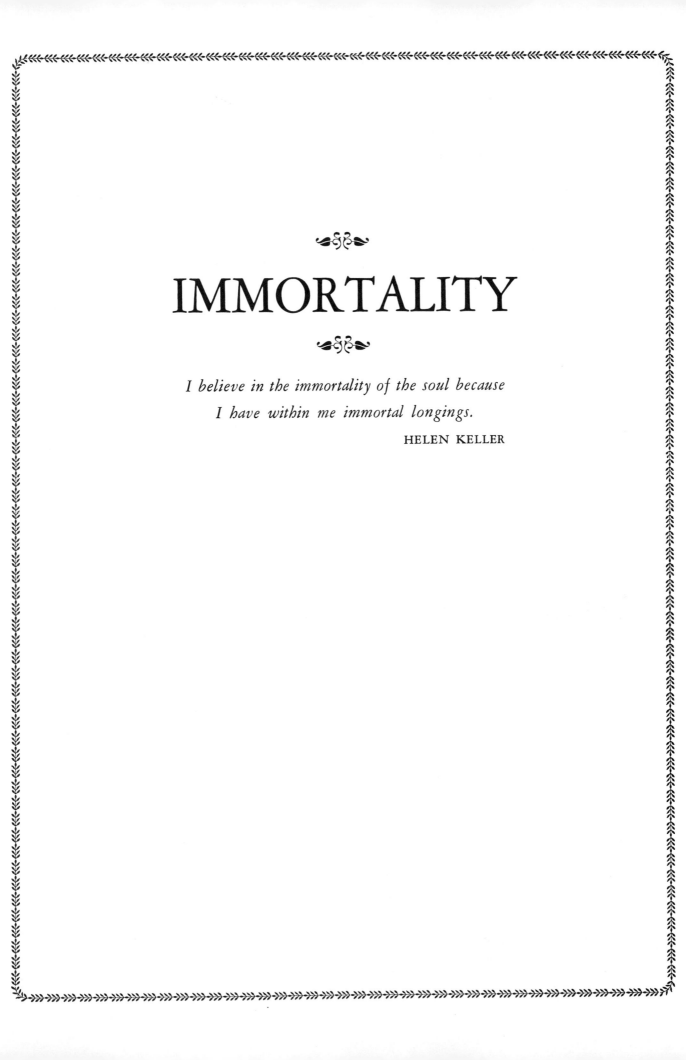

IMMORTALITY

*I believe in the immortality of the soul because
I have within me immortal longings.*

HELEN KELLER

The glory of the star, the glory of the sun—
we must not lose either in the other. We must
not be so full of the hope of heaven that we
cannot do our work on the earth; we must not
be so lost in the work of the earth that we
shall not be inspired by the hope of heaven.

PHILLIPS BROOKS

EVOLUTION

Out of the dusk a shadow,
  Then a spark;
Out of the cloud a silence,
  Then a lark;

Out of the heart a rapture,
  Then a pain;
Out of the dead, cold ashes,
  Life again.

JOHN BANISTER TABB

Heaven often seems distant and unknown, but
if he who made the road thither is our guide,
we need not fear to lose the way.

HENRY VAN DYKE

I NEVER SAW A MOOR

I never saw a moor,
I never saw the sea;
Yet know I how the heather looks,
And what a wave must be.

I never spoke with God,
Nor visited in heaven;
Yet certain am I of the spot
As if the chart were given.

EMILY DICKINSON

FRIEND

Death is not the enemy of life, but its friend,
for it is the knowledge that our years are
limited which makes them so precious. It is
the truth that time is but lent to us which
makes us, at our best, look upon our years as
a trust handed into our temporary keeping.

JOSHUA LOTH LIEBMAN

TRANSLATION

Our knowledge is but faith moving in the
dark, our joy is a gift of grace, our immortality
a subtle translation of time into eternity, where
all that we have missed is ours and where what
we call ours is the least part of ourselves. All
belongs to the necessary passion and death of
the spirit, that today rides upon an ass into its
kingdom, to be crucified tomorrow between
two thieves, and on the third day to rise again
from the dead.

GEORGE SANTAYANA

THERE'S MORE

We only see a little of the ocean,
A few miles distance from the rocky shore;
But oh! out there beyond—beyond the eyes'
    horizon
  There's more—there's more.

We only see a little of God's loving,
A few rich treasures from his mighty store;
But oh! out there beyond—beyond our life's
    horizon
  There's more—there's more.

LET ME DIE, WORKING

Let me die, working.
Still tackling plans unfinished, tasks undone!
Clean to its end, swift may my race be run.
No laggard steps, no faltering, no shirking;
　　Let me die, working!

Let me die, thinking.
Let me fare forth still with an open mind,
Fresh secrets to unfold, new truths to find,
My soul undimmed, alert, no question blink-
　　　　ing;
　　Let me die, thinking!

Let me die, laughing.
No sighing o'er past sins; they are forgiven.
Spilled on this earth are all the joys of Heaven;
The wine of life, the cup of mirth quaffing.
　　Let me die, laughing!

　　　　　　　　　　S. HALL YOUNG

Each departed friend is a magnet that attracts
us to the next world.

　　　　　　　　　　JEAN PAUL RICHTER

O HAPPY SOUL

O happy soul, be thankful now, and rest!
　　Heaven is a goodly land;
And God is love; and those he loves are blest;
　　Now thou dost understand
The least thou hast is better than the best
That thou didst hope for; now upon thine eyes
　　The new life opens fair;
Before thy feet the blessed journey lies
　　Through homelands everywhere;
And heaven to thee is all a sweet surprise.

　　　　　　　　　　WASHINGTON GLADDEN

All mankind is of one Author, and is one
volume; when one man dies, one chapter is not
torn out of the book, but translated into a better language; and every chapter must be so
translated; God employs several translators;
some pieces are translated by age, some by
sickness, some by war, some by justice; but
God's hand is in every translation; and his
hand shall bind up all our scattered leaves
again, for that library where every book shall
lie open to one another.

　　　　　　　　　　JOHN DONNE

The bustle in a house
The morning after death
Is solemnest of industries
Enacted upon earth—

The sweeping up the heart,
And putting love away
We shall not want to use again
Until eternity.

　　　　　　　　　　EMILY DICKINSON

HEAVEN

Heaven is like the life of Jesus with all the
conflict of human sin left out. Heaven is like
the feeding of the multitude in the wilderness,
with everybody sure to get ample to eat.
Heaven is like the woman sinner from the
streets who bathed the feet of Jesus in her tears
and wiped them with her hair. I do not want to
know more than that. It is peace, joy, victory,
triumph—it is life. It is love; it is tireless work
—faithful and unselfish service going on forever. The way to achieve all this is to try to
follow Christ today, tomorrow, and the day
after, through prayer and right living.

　　　　　　　　　　HENRY VAN DYKE

It was not until after the coming of Christ that time and man could breathe freely. It was not until after him that men began to live toward the future. Man does not die in a ditch like a dog—but at home in history, while the work toward the conquest of death is in full swing; he dies sharing in this work.

BORIS PASTERNAK

IMMORTAL SYMPHONIES

Winter is on my head but eternal spring is in my heart. The nearer I approach the end, the plainer I hear around me the immortal symphonies of the world to come. For half a century I have been writing my thoughts in prose and verse; but I feel that I have not said one-thousandth part of what is in me. When I have gone down to the grave I shall have ended my day's work; but another day will begin the next morning. Life closes in the twilight but opens with the dawn.

VICTOR HUGO

THERE IS NO DEATH

In one sense there is no death. The life of a soul on earth lasts beyond his departure. You will always feel that life touching yours, that voice speaking to you, that spirit looking out of other eyes, talking to you in the familiar things he touched, worked with, loved as familiar friends. He lives on in your life and in the lives of all others that knew him.

ANGELO PATRI

JOURNEY'S END

We go from God to God—then though
  The way be long,
We shall return to Heaven our home
  At evensong.

We go from God to God—so let
  The space between
Be filled with beauty, conquering
  Things base and mean.

We go from God to God—lo! what
  Transcendent bliss,
To know the journey's end will hold
  Such joy as this!

EVELYN H. HEALEY

THE CHARIOT

Because I could not stop for Death,
He kindly stopped for me;
The carriage held but just ourselves
And Immortality.

We slowly drove, he knew no haste,
And I had put away
My labor, and my leisure too,
For his civility.

We passed the school where children played,
Their lessons scarcely done;
We passed the fields of gazing grain,
We passed the setting sun.

We paused before a house that seemed
A swelling on the ground;
The roof was scarcely visible,
The cornice but a mound.

Since then 'tis centuries; but each
Feels shorter than the day
I first surmised the horses' heads
Were toward eternity.

EMILY DICKINSON

If God hath made this world so fair,
Where sin and death abound,
How beautiful, beyond compare,
Will paradise be found.

JAMES MONTGOMERY

THE JOURNEY

When Death, the angel of our higher dreams,
Shall come, far ranging from the hills of light
He will not catch me unaware; for I
Shall be as now communing with the dawn.
For I shall make all haste to follow him
Along the valley, up the misty slope
Where life lets go and Life at last is born.
There I shall find the dreams that I have lost
On toilsome earth, and they will guide me on,
Beyond the mists unto the farthest height.
I shall not grieve except to pity those
Who cannot hear the songs that I shall hear!

THOMAS CURTIS CLARK

INTIMATIONS OF IMMORTALITY

To every created thing God has given a tongue that proclaims a resurrection. If the Father designs to touch with divine power the cold and pulseless heart of the buried acorn, and make it burst forth from its prison wall, will he leave neglected the soul of man, who is made in the image of his Creator?

If he gives to the rosebush, whose withered blossoms float upon the breeze, the sweet assurance of another springtime, will he withhold the words of hope from the sons of men, when the frosts of winter come?

If matter, mute and inanimate, though changed by the force and nature into a multitude of forms, can never die, will the imperial spirit of man suffer annihilation after a brief sojourn, like a royal guest, in this tenement of clay?

Rather, let us believe that he—who in his apparent prodigality wastes not the raindrop, the blade of grass, or the evening's sighing zephyr, but makes them all to carry out his eternal plan—has given immortality to the mortal!

WILLIAM JENNINGS BRYAN

HIS HANDS

The hands of Christ
Seem very frail
For they were broken
By a nail.

But only they
Reach heaven at last
Whom these frail, broken
Hands hold fast.

JOHN RICHARD MORELAND

CONSOLATION

He is not dead, this friend; not dead,
But, in the path we mortals tread,
Gone some few, trifling steps ahead,
    And nearer to the end;
So that you, too, once past the bend,
Shall meet again, as face to face, this friend
    You fancy dead.

ROBERT LOUIS STEVENSON

What a man believes about immortality will color his thinking in every area of life.

JOHN SUTHERLAND BONNELL

144

AWAY

I cannot say, and I will not say
That he is dead. He is just away.

With a cheery smile, and a wave of the hand,
He has wandered into an unknown land.

And left us dreaming how very fair
It needs must be since he lingers there.

And you—O you, who the wildest yearn
For the old-time step and the glad return—

Think of him faring on, as dear
In the love of there as the love of here;

Think of him still as the same, I say;
He is not dead—he is just away!

JAMES WHITCOMB RILEY

WHEN LIFE'S DAY CLOSES

When on my day the evening shadows fall,
  I will go down to where a quiet river flows
Into a sea from whence no man returns;
  And there embark for lands where life
    immortal grows.

THOMAS TIPLADY

THE ABIDING LOVE

It singeth low in every heart,
  We hear it each and all,—
A song of those who answer not,
  However we may call;
They throng the silence of the breast,
  We see them as of yore,—
The kind, the brave, the true, the sweet,
  Who walk with us no more.

JOHN WHITE CHADWICK

HIGHER DESTINY

We are born for a higher destiny than that of earth; there is a realm where the rainbow never fades, where the stars will be spread before us like islands that slumber on the ocean, and where the beings that pass before us like shadows will stay in our presence forever.

EDWARD BULWER-LYTTON

Heaven is the soul finding its own perfect personality in God.

PHILLIPS BROOKS

NATURE

As a fond mother, when the day is o'er,
  Leads by the hand her little child to bed,
  Half willing, half reluctant to be led,
  And leave his broken playthings on the floor,
Still gazing at them through the open door,
  Nor wholly reassured and comforted
  By promises of others in their stead,
  Which, though more splendid, may not
    please him more;
So Nature deals with us, and takes away
  Our playthings one by one, and by the hand
  Leads us to rest so gently, that we go
Scarce knowing if we wish to go or stay,
  Being too full of sleep to understand
  How far the unknown transcends the what
    we know.

HENRY WADSWORTH LONGFELLOW

There is no dark despair that cannot be
Evicted from the heart's Gethsemane;
For faith is always more than unbelief,
And vibrant courage triumphs over grief.

MARY E. MC CULLOUGH

145

❦

Yet Love will dream, and Faith will trust,
(Since he who knows our need is just)
That somehow, somewhere, meet we must.
Alas for him who never sees
The stars shine through his cypress trees!
Who, hopeless, lays his dead away,
Nor looks to see the breaking day
Across the mournful marble play!
Who hath not learned, in hours of faith,
    The truth to flesh and sense unknown,
That Life is ever Lord of Death,
    And Love can never lose its own!

JOHN GREENLEAF WHITTIER

❦

Our Creator would never have made such lovely days and have given us the deep hearts to enjoy them, above and beyond all thought, unless we were meant to be immortal.

NATHANIEL HAWTHORNE

❦

From EAST OF EDEN
[Liza] looked forward to Heaven as a place where clothes did not get dirty and where food did not have to be cooked and dishes washed. Privately there were some things in Heaven of which she did not quite approve. There was too much singing, and she didn't see how even the Elect could survive for very long the celestial laziness which was promised. She could find something to do in Heaven. There must be something to take up one's time—some clouds to darn, some weary wings to rub with liniment. Maybe the collars of the robes needed turning now and then, and when you come right down to it, she couldn't believe that even in Heaven there would not be cobwebs in some corner to be knocked down with a cloth-covered broom.

JOHN STEINBECK

❦

Death stands above me, whispering low
    I know not what into my ear;
Of his strange language all I know
    Is, there is not a word of fear.

WALTER SAVAGE LANDOR

❦

If we are immortal, we are immortal now. If we are to survive, the future life will be a continuation of our life now. It will be different only in respect to its larger freedom, and the chief attribute of that freedom will be our escape from the dread of death and transition.

LLOYD C. DOUGLAS

❦

Music, when soft voices die,
Vibrates in the memory—
Odors, when sweet violets sicken,
Live within the sense they quicken.

Rose leaves, when the rose is dead,
Are heap'd for the beloved's bed;
And so thy thoughts, when thou art gone,
Love itself shall slumber on.

PERCY BYSSHE SHELLEY

❦

Faith may languish; creeds may be changed; churches may be dissolved. But one cannot imagine the time when Jesus will not be the fair image of perfection. He can never be superseded. He can never be exceeded. Religions may come and go, the passing shapes of an eternal instinct, but Jesus will remain the standard of the conscience and the satisfaction of men's final needs, whom all men seek and in whom all men will yet meet.

JOHN WATSON

INFLUENCE

*I could tell where the lamplighter was
by the trail he left behind him.*

HARRY LAUDER

A FABLE

A Persian fable says: One day
A wanderer found a piece of clay,
So redolent of perfume
Its odor scented all the room.
"What art thou?" was the quick demand;
"Art thou some gem of Samarcand?
Or spikenard rare in rich disguise,
Or other costly merchandise?"
"Nay, I am but a piece of clay."
"Then whence this wondrous sweetness, pray?"
"Friend, if the secret I disclose,
I have been dwelling with the rose."

❧

THERE ARE TWO SEAS

There are two seas in Palestine. One is fresh,
and fish are in it. Splashes of green adorn its
banks. Trees spread their branches over it,
and stretch out their thirsty roots to sip of its
healing waters.

Along its shores the children play, as children
played when He was there. He loved it. He
could look across its silver surface when He
spoke His parables. And on a rolling plain
not far away He fed five thousand people.

The river Jordan makes this sea with sparkling
water from the hills. Men build their houses
near to it, and birds build their nests; and
every kind of life is happier because it is
there.

The river Jordan flows on south into another
sea.

Here is no splash of fish, no fluttering leaf, no
song of birds, no children's laughter. Traveler's choose another route, unless on urgent
business. The air hangs heavy above its
water, and neither man nor beast nor fowl
will drink.

What makes this mighty difference in these
neighbor seas?

Not the river Jordan. It empties the same good
water into both. Not the soil in which they
lie, not the country round about.

This is the difference. The Sea of Galilee receives but does not keep the Jordan. For
every drop that flows into it another drop
flows out.

The other sea is shrewder, hoarding its income
jealously.

It will not be tempted into any generous impulse. Every drop it gets, it keeps.

The Sea of Galilee gives and lives. This other
sea gives nothing. It is named The Dead.

There are two seas in Palestine.

There are two kinds of people in the world.

BRUCE BARTON

❧

LIVING EXAMPLE

The greatness of Schweitzer—indeed the essence of Schweitzer—is the man as symbol. It
is not so much what he has done for others,
but what others have done because of him and
the power of his example. This is the measure
of the man. What has come out of his life and
thought is the kind of inspiration that can
animate a generation. He has supplied a working demonstration of reverence for life.

NORMAN COUSINS

❧

We are not driven from Behind, but lured from
Before! Not pushed, but pulled! Magnetized
from Beyond!

LLOYD C. DOUGLAS

❧

The most important part of the training of the
Twelve was one which was perhaps at the time
little noticed, though it was producing splendid
results—the silent and constant influence of His
character on them. It was this which made them
the men they became.

JAMES STALKER

❧

ONE SOLITARY LIFE

Here is a man who was born in an obscure village, the child of a peasant woman. He grew up in an obscure village. He worked in a carpenter shop until he was thirty, and then for three years he was an itinerant teacher. He never wrote a book. He never held an office. He never owned a home. He never had a family. He never went to college. He never traveled, except in his infancy, more than two hundred miles from the place where he was born. He never did one of the things that usually accompany greatness. He had no credentials but himself. While he was still a young man, the tide of popular opinion turned against him. His friends ran away. One of them denied him. He was turned over to his enemies. He went through the mockery of a trial. He was nailed upon a cross between two thieves. His executioners gambled for the only piece of property he had on earth, his seamless robe. When he was dead, he was taken down from the cross and laid in a borrowed grave through the courtesy of a friend. Nineteen wide centuries have come and gone, and today he is the centerpiece of the human race and the leader of all human progress. I am well within the mark when I say that all the armies that ever marched, all the navies that ever were built, all the parliaments that ever sat, and all the kings that ever reigned, put together, have not affected the life of man upon this earth as powerfully as has this one solitary personality.

JAMES A. FRANCIS

The world is a looking-glass, and gives back to every man the reflection of his own face. Frown at it, and it in turn will look sourly at you; laugh at it, and with it, and it is a jolly, kind companion.

WILLIAM MAKEPEACE THACKERAY

Do not think it wasted time to submit yourself to any influence which may bring upon you any noble feeling.

JOHN RUSKIN

LIFE'S MIRROR

There are loyal hearts, there are spirits brave,
    There are souls that are pure and true;
Then give to the world the best you have,
    And the best will come back to you.

Give love, and love to your life will flow,
    A strength in your utmost need;
Have faith, and a score of hearts will show
    Their faith in your word and deed.

Give truth, and your gift will be paid in kind,
    And honor will honor meet;
And a smile that is sweet will surely find
    A smile that is just as sweet.

Give sorrow and pity to those who mourn;
    You will gather in flowers again
The scattered seeds of your thought outborne,
    Though the sowing seemed but vain.

For life is the mirror of king and slave—
    'Tis just what we are and do;
Then give to the world the best you have,
    And the best will come back to you.

MADELINE BRIDGES

SHADOW-SELVES

This learned I from the shadow of a tree,
    That to and fro did sway against a wall:
    Our shadow-selves, our influence, may fall
Where we ourselves can never be.

ANNA E. HAMILTON

WHAT PEOPLE SAID

When people talked about Lincoln, it was nearly always about one or more of these five things: (1) how long, tall, quick, strong, or awkward in looks he was; (2) how he told stories and jokes, how he was comical or pleasant or kindly; (3) how he could be silent, melancholy, sad; (4) how he was ready to learn and looking for chances to learn; (5) how he was ready to help a friend, a stranger, or even a dumb animal in distress.

CARL SANDBURG

❦

AN INVISIBLE HOST

An American soldier wounded on a battlefield in the Far East owes his life to the Japanese scientist Kitasato, who isolated the bacillus of tetanus. A Russian soldier saved by a blood transfusion is indebted to Landsteiner, an Austrian. A German is shielded from typhoid fever with the help of a Russian, Metchnikoff. A Dutch marine in the East Indies is protected from malaria because of the experiments of an Italian, Grassi; while a British aviator in North Africa escapes death from surgical infection because a Frenchman, Pasteur, and a German, Koch, elaborated a new technique.

In peace, as in war, we are beneficiaries of knowledge contributed by every nation in the world. Our children are guarded from diphtheria by what a Japanese and a German did; they are protected from smallpox by the work of an Englishman; they are saved from rabies because of a Frenchman; they are cured of pellagra through the researches of an Austrian. From birth to death they are surrounded by an invisible host—the spirits of men who never thought in terms of flags or boundary lines and who never served a lesser loyalty than the welfare of mankind.

RAYMOND B. FOSDICK

❦

INFLUENCE

Drop a pebble in the water,
  And its ripples reach out far;
And the sunbeams dancing on them
  May reflect them to a star.

Give a smile to someone passing,
  Thereby making his morning glad;
It may greet you in the evening
  When your own heart may be sad.

Do a deed of simple kindness;
  Though its end you may not see,
It may reach, like widening ripples,
  Down a long eternity.

JOSEPH NORRIS

❦

There is no power on earth that can neutralize the influence of a high, pure, simple, and useful life.

BOOKER T. WASHINGTON

❦

THE MAN CHRIST

He built no temple, yet the farthest sea
Can yield no shore that's barren of his place
  For bended knee.

He wrote no book, and yet his words and prayer
Are intimate on many myriad tongues,
  Are counsel everywhere.

The life he lived has never been assailed,
Nor any precept, as he lived it, yet
  Has ever failed.

He built no kingdom, yet a King from youth
He reigned, is reigning yet; they call his realm
  The kingdom of the Truth.

THERESE LINDSEY

On the whole, ought I not to rejoice that God was pleased to give me such a father that from earliest years I had the example of a real man of God's own making continually before me? Let me learn of him. Let me write my books as he built his houses, and walk as blamelessly through this shadow world.

THOMAS CARLYLE

YOUR OWN VERSION

You are writing a Gospel,
    A chapter each day,
By deeds that you do,
    By words that you say.

Men read what you write,
    Whether faithless or true;
Say, what is the Gospel
    According to You?

PAUL GILBERT

MAKING LIFE WORTH WHILE

Every soul that touches yours—
Be it the slightest contact—
Gets therefrom some good;
Some little grace; one kindly thought;
One aspiration yet unfelt;
One bit of courage
For the darkening sky;
One gleam of faith
To brave the thickening ills of life;
One glimpse of brighter skies—
To make this life worthwhile
And heaven a surer heritage.

GEORGE ELIOT

TO POETS ALL

We shall not wholly die.
Perhaps some truth
That we have sung
Shall linger on,
And from some tongue
More eloquent
Shall hail the dawn
That we have glimpsed.
Though we be spent,
We shall be well content.

THOMAS CURTIS CLARK

IN HIS STEPS

He is a Christian who tries to be the kind of neighbor Christ would be, and the kind of citizen Christ would be, and who asks himself in all the alternatives of his business life, and his social life, and his personal life, What would the Master do in this case? The best Christian is he who most reminds the people with whom he lives of the Lord Jesus Christ. He who never reminds anybody of the Lord Jesus Christ is not a Christian at all.

GEORGE HODGES

TO LOVE THE HIGHEST

Plutarch's profoundest conviction was that we needs must love the highest when we see it— but who can see it if there are none to show it, first, of course, in their lives, but, second only to that, in their words? The one he raised to a pedestal was the man who made it easy for people to believe in goodness and greatness, in heroic courage and warm generosity and lofty magnanimity. In humble virtues, too, patience that never wearies; readiness to forgive; kindness to an erring servant, to an animal.

EDITH HAMILTON

JOY

*Real joy comes not from ease or riches or from the praise of men,
but from doing something worthwhile.*

WILFRED T. GRENFELL

ETERNAL JOY

Eternal joy is the end of the ways of God. The message of all religions is that the Kingdom of God is peace and joy. And it is the message of Christianity. But eternal joy is not to be reached by living on the surface. It is rather attained by breaking through the surface, by penetrating the deep things of ourselves, of our world, and of God. The moment in which we reach the last depth of our lives is the moment in which we can experience the joy that has eternity within it, the hope that cannot be destroyed, and the truth on which life and death are built. For in the depth is truth; and in the depth is hope; and in the depth is joy.

PAUL TILLICH

TRUE JOY

This is the true joy in life, the being used for a purpose recognized by yourself as a mighty one; the being thoroughly worn out before you are thrown on the scrap heap; the being a force of Nature instead of a feverish selfish little clod of ailments and grievances complaining that the world will not devote itself to making you happy.

GEORGE BERNARD SHAW

UNEXPECTED SURPRISES

Into all our lives, in many simple, familiar, homely ways, God infuses this element of joy from the surprises of life, which unexpectedly brighten our days, and fill our eyes with light. He drops this added sweetness into his children's cup, and makes it to run over. The success we are not counting on, the blessing we were not trying after, the strain of music in the midst of drudgery, the beautiful morning picture or sunset glory thrown in as we pass to

or from our daily business, the unsought word of encouragement or expression of sympathy, the sentence that meant for us more than a writer or speaker thought—these and a hundred others that everyone's experience can supply are instances of what I mean.

SAMUEL LONGFELLOW

PRAYER

God, give me sympathy and sense
    And help me keep my courage high.
God, give me calm and confidence—
    And, please—a twinkle in my eye.

MARGARET BAILEY

The south wind is driving
His splendid cloud-horses
Through vast fields of blue.
The bare woods are singing,
The brooks in their courses
Are bubbling and springing,
And dancing and leaping,
The violets peeping,
I'm glad to be living:
    Aren't you?

GAMALIEL BRADFORD

ALCHEMY

I lift my heart as spring lifts up
    A yellow daisy to the rain;
My heart will be a lovely cup
    Altho' it holds but pain.

For I shall learn from flower and leaf
    That color every drop they hold,
To change the lifeless wine of grief
    To living gold.

SARA TEASDALE

155

CHRISTIANITY

Christianity is not the religion of sorrow and gloom; it is the religion of the morning, and it carries in its heart the happiness of heaven.

Christianity is not a restraint but an inspiration—not a weight but wings; not subtraction but addition.

Christianity brings bloom for faded hearts, rejuvenation for the prematurely old, imagination for the dry, literal mind.

Christianity is not a kill-joy at the feast of life, nor a kind of incarnate "don't"; it bristles with great affirmatives, fires the soul with permanent enthusiasms and durable loyalties.

Christianity leaves a trail of light wherever it goes; it can keep you cool under any confusion, bring you up smiling from any deeps, and utterly banish your fret and worry.

Christianity brings zest and sparkle to life; it is sunshine on the flowers rather than moonshine on the snow; it is life more abundant; it is leaving the little narrow life behind and leaving it forever.

HUGH ELMER BROWN

❧

Alas for the worn and heavy soul if it has outlived its privilege of springtime and sprightliness.

NATHANIEL HAWTHORNE

❧

HOW TO BE CHEERFUL

The voluntary path to cheerfulness, if our spontaneous cheerfulness be lost, is to sit up cheerfully, and act and speak as if cheerfulness were already there. To feel brave, *act* as if we were brave, use all our will to that end, and courage will very likely replace fear. If we act as if from some better feeling, the bad feeling soon folds its tent like an Arab and silently steals away.

WILLIAM JAMES

❧

I would be always in the thick of life,
Threading its mazes, sharing its strife,
    Yet—somehow singing!
ROSELLE MERCIER MONTGOMERY

❧

NO REGRETS

There is only one thing about which I shall have no regrets when my life ends. I have savored to the full all the small, daily joys. The bright sunshine on the breakfast table; the smell of the air at dusk; the sound of the clock ticking; the light rains that start gently after midnight; the hour when the family come home; Sunday-evening tea before the fire! I have never missed one moment of beauty, not ever taken it for granted. Spring, summer, autumn, or winter. I wish I had failed as little in other ways.

AGNES SLIGH TURNBULL

❧

A characteristic of the great saints is their power of levity. Angels can fly because they can take themselves lightly. One "settles down" into a sort of selfish seriousness; but one has to rise to a gay self-forgetfulness. A man falls into a "brown study"; he reaches up at a blue sky.

GILBERT KEITH CHESTERTON

❧

As a countenance is made beautiful by the soul's shining through it, so the world is beautiful by the shining through it of God.

FRIEDRICH HEINRICH JACOBI

❧

Because the way was steep and long,
And through a strange and lonely land,
God placed upon my lips a song,
And put a lantern in my hand.

JOYCE KILMER

❧❧❧

HIGHEST JOY

A new day rose upon me. It was as if another sun had risen into the sky; the heavens were indescribably brighter, and the earth fairer; and that day has gone on brightening to the present hour. I have known the other joys of life, I suppose, as much as most men; I have known art and beauty, music and gladness; I have known friendship and love and family ties; but it is certain that till we see God in the world—God in the bright and boundless universe—we never know the highest joy. It is far more than if one were translated to a world a thousand times fairer than this; for that supreme and central Light of Infinite Love and Wisdom, shining over this world and all worlds, alone can show us how noble and beautiful, how fair and glorious they are.

ORVILLE DEWEY

❧❧❧

PHILOSOPHY OF FOCUS

One morning in the throes of a dismal headache I took my pen and sketched a philosophy of focus:

The truth which cannot alter,
The hope that cannot fail,
The faith that cannot falter,
The peace which shall prevail,
The strength which God has promised,
The life his love made real,
I leave unto his keeping
Come woe or come weal.

I exchanged the headache for a joyful heart.

NELS F. S. FERRÉ

❧❧❧

ELOQUENCE

The hands of those I meet are dumbly eloquent to me. I have met people so empty of joy that when I clasped their frosty fingertips it seemed as if I were shaking hands with a northeast storm. Others there are whose hands have sunbeams in them, so that their grasp warms my heart. It may be only the clinging touch of a child's hand, but there is as much potential sunshine in it for me as there is in a loving glance for others.

HELEN KELLER

❧❧❧

The men whom I have seen succeed have always been cheerful and hopeful, who went about their business with a smile on their faces, and took the changes and chances of this mortal life like men.

CHARLES KINGSLEY

❧❧❧

PRAYER

Give me a sense of humor, Lord;
Give me the grace to see a joke,
To get some happiness from life,
And pass it on to other folk.

CHESTER CATHEDRAL

❧❧❧

Let us be of good cheer, remembering that the misfortunes hardest to bear are those which never come.

AMY LOWELL

❧❧❧

TESTIMONY

This is a cheerful world as I see it from my garden under the shadows of my vines. But *if* I were to ascend some high mountain and look out over the wide lands, you know very well what I should see: brigands on the highways, pirates on the sea, armies fighting, cities burning; in the amphitheaters men murdered to please applauding crowds; selfishness and cruelty and misery and despair under all roofs. It is a bad world, Donatus, an incredibly bad world. But I have discovered in the midst of it a quiet and holy people who have learned a great secret. They have found a joy which is a thousand times better than any pleasure of our sinful life. They are despised and persecuted, but they care not. They are masters of their souls. They have overcome the world. These people, Donatus, are the Christians—and I am one of them.

ST. CYPRIAN (*Third-century martyr*)

CHOICE

Our lives are songs; God writes the words
And we set them to music at pleasure;
And the song grows glad, or sweet or sad,
As we choose to fashion the measure.

ELLA WHEELER WILCOX

A form of gratitude seems to come as a product of sound growth. This is gratitude for the amazing common decencies of most people; for the simple fact that most people, most of the time, take the brunt of circumstances without falling apart; that most of them, given half a chance, are friendly rather than hostile; that most of them would rather help than hurt.

HARRY *and* BONARO OVERSTREET

I asked God for strength, that I might achieve,
I was made weak, that I might learn humbly to obey . . .
I asked for health, that I might do greater things,
I was given infirmity, that I might do better things . . .
I asked for riches, that I might be happy,
I was given poverty, that I might be wise . . .
I asked for power, that I might have the praise of men,
I was given weakness, that I might feel the need of God . . .
I asked for all things, that I might enjoy life,
I was given life, that I might enjoy all things . . .
I got nothing that I asked for—but everything I had hoped for,
Almost despite myself, my unspoken prayers were answered.
I am among all men, most richly blessed.

HIS COMING

He comes to us as one unknown, without a name, as of old by the lakeside he came to those men who knew him not. He speaks to us the same word, "Follow thou me," and sets us to the tasks which he has to fulfill for our time. He commands. And to those who obey, whether they be wise or simple, he will reveal himself in the toils, the conflicts, the suffering which they shall pass through in his fellowship, and as an ineffable mystery, they shall learn in their own experience who he is.

ALBERT SCHWEITZER

RESURGENCE

Out of the earth, the rose,
Out of the night, the dawn,
Out of my heart, with all its woes,
High courage to press on.

LAURA LEE RANDALL

LIFE

God asks no man whether he will accept life.
That is not the choice.
You must take it.
The only choice is how.

HENRY WARD BEECHER

VOYAGE

Think of life as a voyage. The truest liver of the truest life is like a voyager who, as he sails, is not indifferent to all the beauty of the sea around him. The morning and the evening sun, the moonlight and the starlight, the endless change of the vast water that he floats on, the passing back and forth of other ships between him and the sky, the incidents and company on his own vessel—all these are pleasant to him; but their pleasure is borne up by and woven in with his interest in the purpose for which he undertook the voyage. That lies beyond and that lies under the voyage all the while. He is not sailing just for the sake of sailing. He would never have undertaken the voyage for his own sake. Another man, who has no purpose beyond the voyage, is vexed and uneasy. He is so afraid of not getting the best out of it that he loses its best. The spots and imperfections in its pleasure worry him. Those are the differences of the ways in which men live. One man forgets his own life in the purposes for which his life is lived, and he is the man whose life grows richest and brightest. Another man is always thinking about himself, and so never gets beyond himself into those purposes of living out of which all the fullness of personal life may flow back to him.

PHILLIPS BROOKS

MAN'S LIFE

The life of man seems to me like the flight of a sparrow through the hall wherein you are sitting at supper in the winter time, a warm fire lighted on the hearth while storms rage without. The sparrow flies in at one door, tarries for a moment in the light and heat, and then flying forth through another door vanishes into the wintry darkness whence it had come. So tarries man for a brief space, but of what went before or what is to follow, we know not.

THE VENERABLE BEDE

Life is a pure flame, and we live by an invisible sun within us.

THOMAS BROWNE

Life is like a library owned by an author. In it are a few books which he wrote himself, but most of them were written for him.

HARRY EMERSON FOSDICK

Life is a series of surprises, and would not be worth taking or keeping if it were not.

RALPH WALDO EMERSON

The great use of life is to spend it for something that outlasts it.

WILLIAM JAMES

If we made God a little more real than otherwise he would be to any single human being, we have not wasted our little lives in a large world or lived in vain.

WILLARD L. SPERRY

METAPHORS

Life is currently described in one of four ways: a journey, a battle, a pilgrimage, or a race. Select your own metaphors, but the necessity of finishing is all the same. For if life is a journey, it must be completed. If life is a battle, it must be finished. If life is a pilgrimage, it must be concluded. And if life is a race, it must be won.

THE WAR CRY

WHAT LIFE IS

Life is a race. Don't whimper if the track is rough and the goal is distant. One day you shall reach it.

Life is a voyage. Don't complain if the storms batter the hull or the winds tatter to shreds the sails. One day you shall come to your haven.

Life is growth. Don't find fault if the seed lies smothered and submerged in the dark earth before it blooms and blossoms. One day you shall have your harvest.

Life is a pilgrimage. Don't falter on the road through self-pity because stones cut your feet and leave your blood on the trail. One day you will come to Immanuel's land.

The God who through the boundless sky guides the flight of the sparrow, who builds the blind bird's nest, will see to it that in his good time you shall arrive.

JOSEPH R. SIZOO

FOR A CONTENTED LIFE

Health enough to make work a pleasure.

Wealth enough to support your needs.

Strength to battle with difficulties and overcome them.

Grace enough to confess your sins and forsake them.

Patience enough to toil until some good is accomplished.

Charity enough to see some good in your neighbor.

Love enough to move you to be useful and helpful to others.

Faith enough to make real the things of God.

Hope enough to remove all anxious fears concerning the future.

JOHANN WOLFGANG VON GOETHE

Be not afraid of life. Believe that life is worth living, and your belief will help create the fact.

WILLIAM JAMES

HOW—WHEN—WHERE

It is not so much WHERE you live,
As HOW, and WHY, and WHEN you live,
That answers in the affirmative,
Or maybe in the negative,
The question—Are you fit to live?

It is not so much WHERE you live,
As HOW you live, and whether good
Flows from you through your neighborhood.

And WHY you live, and whether you
Aim high and noblest ends pursue,
And keep Life brimming full and true.

And WHEN you live, and whether Time
Is at its nadir or its prime,
And whether you descend or climb.

It is not so much WHERE you live,
As whether while you live you *live*
And to the world your highest give,
And so make answer positive
That you are truly fit to live.

JOHN OXENHAM

Be a life long or short, its completeness depends on what it was lived for.

DAVID STARR JORDAN

The real art of life consists in finding out what is the question to be solved, and the person who can find out what problem is to be solved is the man who really makes contributions to life.

ABBOTT LAWRENCE LOWELL

THE DIFFERENCE

Granted that man is only a more highly developed animal; that the ring-tailed monkey is a distant relative who had gradually developed acrobatic tendencies, and the humpbacked whale a far-off connection who in early life took to the sea—granted that back of these he is kin to the vegetable, and is still subject to the same laws as plants, fishes, birds, and beasts. Yet there is still this difference between man and other animals—he is the only animal whose desires increase as they are fed; the only animal that is never satisfied. The wants of every other living thing are uniform and fixed. The ox of today aspires to no more than did the ox when man first yoked him. The sea gull of the English Channel, who poises himself above the swift steamer, wants no better food or lodging than the gulls who circled round as the keels of Caesar's galleys first grated on a British beach. Of all that nature offers them, be it ever so abundant, all living things save man can take, and care for, only enough to supply wants which are definite and fixed.

HENRY GEORGE

May you live all the days of your life.

JONATHAN SWIFT

Life is no brief candle to me. It is a sort of splendid torch which I have got hold of for the moment, and I want to make it burn as brightly as possible before handing it on to future generations.

GEORGE BERNARD SHAW

Life truly lived is a risky business, and if one puts up too many fences against risk one ends by shutting out life itself.

KENNETH S. DAVIS

Every man's life is a plan of God.

HORACE BUSHNELL

LIFE'S COMPLETENESS

A love that lasts forever:
A friendship naught can sever;
A courage never failing,
Though evil seems prevailing;
And joyous, radiant living,
Made glorious by its giving;
A faith strong and enduring,
Unworthy thoughts obscuring;
And eyes for seeing beauty
In work, in play, in duty;
Life ever onward flowing
And more abundant growing;
Love, courage, faith, and sweetness
To make up life's completeness.

S. G. FISHER

GRAMMAR

Live in the active voice, rather than in the passive. Think more about what you make happen than what is happening to you.

Live in the indicative mood, rather than in the subjunctive. Be concerned with things as they are, rather than as they might be.

Live in the present tense, facing the duty at hand without regret for the past or worry over the future.

Live in the singular number, caring more for the approval of your own conscience than for the applause of the crowd.

WILLIAM DE WITT HYDE

❧❦❧

THE WINDS OF FATE
One ship drives east and another drives west
 With the selfsame winds that blow.
 'Tis the set of the sails
 And not the gales
Which tells us the way to go.

Like the winds of the sea are the ways of fate,
 As we voyage along through life:
 'Tis the set of a soul
 That decides its goal,
And not the calm or the strife.

ELLA WHEELER WILCOX

❧❦❧

Every man has a train of thought on which he rides when he is alone. The dignity and nobility of his life, as well as his happiness, depend upon the direction in which that train is going, the baggage it carries, and the scenery through which it travels.

JOSEPH FORT NEWTON

❧❦❧

I believe that man will not merely endure: he will prevail. He is immortal, not because he alone among creatures has an inexhaustible voice, but because he has a soul, a spirit capable of compassion and sacrifice and endurance.

WILLIAM FAULKNER

❧❦❧

WHAT WE KNOW
Life is too complex to be described in simple terms, yet we know much about it.
First, life comes from life. When we trace back to the beginning, we come face to face with God, who is Life, original and underived.

"In him was life; and the life was the light of men."

Second, we know God is anxious to impart his life to us, for God is Love and love seeks to share and enrich others.

Third, life is creative. Animals leave this world as they found it; man affects great changes, because so much of God is in him. Together with God, it is our privilege to make a new world.

Fourth, life grows. All activities of man revolve around making life fuller and more meaningful. When we receive God, we become with him co-creators. Perhaps heaven is our opportunity to go on forever growing more and more like God.

Fifth, at birth we are candidates for the full life. We possess within ourselves the possibilities, and we have a God, able and willing to work with us. By co-operating with him who is Life, we have life, and can use and enjoy and bestow life.

J. J. RIVES

❧❦❧

YOUR PLACE
Is your place a small place?
 Tend it with care;—
 He set you there.

Is your place a large place?
 Guard it with care!—
 He set you there.

Whate'er your place, it is
 Not yours alone, but his
 Who set you there.

JOHN OXENHAM

Our business in life is not to get ahead of other people, but to get ahead of ourselves.

MALTBIE D. BABCOCK

164

LOVE

Love cannot be forced, love cannot be coaxed and teased.
It comes out of Heaven, unasked and unsought.

PEARL BUCK

ALL-EMBRACING LOVE

Love all God's creation, both the whole and every grain of sand. Love every leaf, every ray of light. Love the animals, love the plants, love each separate thing. If thou love each thing thou will perceive the mystery of God in all; and when once thou perceive this, thou wilt thenceforward grow every day to a fuller understanding of it: until thou come at last to love the whole world with a love that will then be all-embracing and universal.

FYODOR DOSTOEVSKI

A CHILD LEARNS ABOUT LOVE

In her autobiography, *The Story of My Life,* Helen Keller tells how as a deaf and blind child she learned from Anne Sullivan the meaning of love.

"I remember the morning that I first asked the meaning of the word, 'love.' This was before I knew many words. I had found a few early violets in the garden and brought them to my teacher. She tried to kiss me; but at that time I did not like to have anyone kiss me except my mother. Miss Sullivan put her arm gently round me and spelled into my hand, 'I love Helen.'

" 'What is love?' I asked.

"She drew me closer to her and said, 'It is here,' pointing to my heart. . . . Her words puzzled me very much because I did not then understand anything unless I touched it.

"I smelled the violets in her hand and asked, half in words, half in signs, a question which meant, 'Is love the sweetness of flowers?'

" 'No,' said my teacher.

"Again I thought. The warm sun was shining on us.

" 'Is this not love?' I asked, pointing in the direction from which the heat came. . . .

"A day or two afterward . . . the sun had been under a cloud all day, and there had been brief showers, but suddenly the sun broke forth in all its southern splendor. Again I asked my teacher, 'Is this not love?'

" 'Love is something like the clouds that were in the sky before the sun came out,' she replied. Then in simpler words than these, which at that time I could not have understood, she explained: 'You cannot touch the clouds, you know; but you feel the rain and know how glad the flowers and the thirsty earth are to have it after a hot day. You cannot touch love either; but you feel the sweetness that it pours into everything. Without love you would not be happy or want to play.'

"The beautiful truth burst upon my mind— I felt that these were invisible lines stretched between my spirit and the spirits of others."

HALLMARKS OF TRUE LOVE

1. A genuine interest in the other person and all that he or she says and does.
2. A community of tastes, ideals, and standards with no serious clashes.
3. A greater happiness in being with the one person than with any other.
4. A real unhappiness when the other person is absent.
5. A great feeling of comradeship.
6. A willingness to give and take.
7. A pride in the other person when comparisons are made.

NEWELL W. EDSON

I never knew a night so black
Light failed to follow on its track.
I never knew a storm so gray
It failed to have its clearing day.
I never knew such bleak despair
That there was not a rift, somewhere.
I never knew an hour so drear
Love could not fill it full of cheer!

JOHN KENDRICK BANGS

167

He who would have beautiful roses in his garden must have beautiful roses in his heart. He must love them well and always. He must have not only the glowing admiration, the enthusiasm, and the passion, but the tenderness, the thoughtfulness, the reverence, the watchfulness of love.

S. R. HOLE

LIGHT AND LOVE
The night has a thousand eyes,
  And the day but one;
Yet the light of the bright world dies
  With the dying sun.

The mind has a thousand eyes,
  And the heart but one;
Yet the light of a whole life dies
  When love is done.

FRANCIS W. BOURDILLON

Love does not consist in gazing at each other, but in looking outward together in the same direction.

ANTOINE DE SAINT-EXUPÉRY

No cord or cable can draw so forcibly, or bind so fast, as love can do with a single thread.

ROBERT BURTON

'Tis better to have loved and lost
Than never to have loved at all.

ALFRED TENNYSON

Two persons who love each other are in a place more holy than the interior of a church.

WILLIAM LYON PHELPS

Love is not blind—it sees more, not less. But because it sees more, it is willing to see less.

JULIUS GORDON

THE LOVE OF GOD
There is an ocean—cold water without motion. In this ocean, however, is the Gulf Stream, hot water flowing from the equator toward the Pole. Inquire of all scientists how it is physically imaginable that a stream of hot water flows between the waters of the ocean, which, so to speak, form its banks, the moving within the motionless, the hot within the cold. No scientist can explain it. Similarly, there is the God of love within the God of the forces of the universe—one with him, and yet so totally different. We let ourselves be seized and carried away by that vital stream.

ALBERT SCHWEITZER

He loves each one of us, as if there were only one of us.

ST. AUGUSTINE

We like someone *because*. We love someone *although*.

HENRI DE MONTHERLANT

I like not only to be loved, but to be told that I am loved; the realm of silence is large enough beyond the grave.

GEORGE ELIOT

LIGHTED LAMP

Love is something eternal—the aspect may change, but not the essence. There is the same difference in a person before and after he is in love as there is in an unlighted lamp and one that is burning. The lamp was there and it was a good lamp, but now it is shedding light, too, and that is its real function.

VINCENT VAN GOGH

FOR A WEDDING ANNIVERSARY

Companioned years have made them comprehend
The comradeship that lies beyond a kiss.
The young ask much of life—they ask but this,
To fare the road together to its end.

ROSELLE MERCIER MONTGOMERY

SEASON OF LOVE

We miss the spirit of Christmas if we consider the incarnation as an indistinct and doubtful, far-off event unrelated to our present problems. We miss the purport of Christ's birth if we do not accept it as a living link which joins us together in spirit as children of the ever-living and true God. In love alone—the love of God and the love of man—will be found the solution of all the ills which afflict the world today. Slowly, sometimes painfully, but always with increasing purpose, emerges the great message of Christianity: Only with wisdom comes joy, and with greatness comes love.

HARRY S. TRUMAN

'Tis sweet to feel by what fine-spun threads our affections are drawn together.

LAURENCE STERNE

How do I love thee? Let me count the ways.
I love thee to the depth and breadth and height
My soul can reach, when feeling out of sight
For the ends of Being and ideal Grace.
I love thee to the level of everyday's
Most quiet need, by sun and candlelight.
I love thee freely, as men strive for Right;
I love thee purely, as they turn from Praise.
I love thee with the passion put to use
In my old griefs, and with my childhood's faith.
I love thee with a love I seemed to lose
With my lost saints,—I love thee with the breath,
Smiles, tears, of all my life!—and, if God choose,
I shall but love thee better after death.

ELIZABETH BARRETT BROWNING

Of all the music that reached farthest into heaven, it is the beating of a loving heart.

HENRY WARD BEECHER

LOVE OR PERISH

To say that one will perish without love does not mean that everyone without adequate love dies. Many do, for without love the will to live is often impaired to such an extent that a person's resistance is critically lowered and death follows. But most of the time, lack of love makes people depressed, anxious, and without zest for life. They remain lonely and unhappy, without friends or work they care for, their life a barren treadmill, stripped of all creative action and joy.

SMILEY BLANTON

The race will never know salvation unless it is love-lifted and star-led.

JOSEPH FORT NEWTON

LEARNING TO LOVE

There are many who want me to tell them of secret ways of becoming perfect and I can only tell them that the sole secret is a hearty love of God, and the only way of attaining that love is by loving. You learn to speak by speaking, to study by studying, to run by running, to work by working; and just so you learn to love God and man by loving. Begin as a mere apprentice and the very power of love will lead you on to become a master of the art.

ST. FRANCIS DE SALES

We never live so intensely as when we love strongly. We never realize ourselves so vividly as when we are in the full glow of love for others.

WALTER RAUSCHENBUSCH

REFRESHMENT

Talk not of wasted affection, affection never was wasted;
If it enrich not the heart of another, its waters, returning
Back to their springs, like the rain, shall fill them full of refreshment.

HENRY WADSWORTH LONGFELLOW

Love is never lost. If not reciprocated, it will flow back and soften and purify the heart.

WASHINGTON IRVING

PRAYER AT EVENTIDE

This day is almost done. When the night and morning meet it will be only an unalterable memory. So let no unkind word, no careless doubting thought, no guilty secret, no neglected duty, no wisp of jealous fog becloud its pass-ing. Now, in token of our deep and abiding love, we would lay aside all disturbing thoughts, all misunderstandings, all unworthiness. If things have gone awry, let neither of us lift an accusing finger. Who is to blame is not important; only how shall we set the situation right. And so, serving and being served, loving and being loved, we shall make a peaceful home, where we and our children shall learn to face life joyfully, triumphantly, so near as God shall give us grace.

F. ALEXANDER MAGOUN

Go often to the house of thy friend, for weeds choke the unused path.

RALPH WALDO EMERSON

THE PRAYER PERFECT

Dear Lord! Kind Lord!
 Gracious Lord! I pray
Thou wilt look on all I love,
 Tenderly today!
Weed their hearts of weariness;
 Scatter every care
Down a wake of angel-wings
 Winnowing the air.

Bring unto the sorrowing
 All release from pain;
Let the lips of laughter
 Overflow again;
And with all the needy
 O divide, I pray,
This vast measure of content
 That is mine today!

JAMES WHITCOMB RILEY

The kindest and the happiest pair
Will find occasion to forbear;
And something, every day they live,
To pity, and perhaps forgive.

WILLIAM COWPER

NATION

We must have many Lincoln-hearted men.

VACHEL LINDSAY

THE GIFT OUTRIGHT

The land was ours before we were the land's.
She was our land more than a hundred years
Before we were her people. She was ours
In Massachusetts, in Virginia,
But we were England's, still colonials,
Possessing what we still were unpossessed by,
Possessed by what we now no more possessed.
Something we were withholding made us weak
Until we found out that it was ourselves
We were withholding from our land of living,
And forthwith found salvation in surrender.
Such as we were we gave ourselves outright
(The deed of gift was many deeds of war)
To the land vaguely realizing westward,
But still unstoried, artless, unenhanced,
Such as she was, such as she would become.

ROBERT FROST

❧

AMERICA'S GREATNESS

I sought for the greatness and genius of America in her commodious harbors and her ample rivers, and it was not there.

I sought for the greatness and genius of America in her fertile fields and boundless forests, and it was not there.

I sought for the greatness and genius of America in her rich mines and her vast world commerce, and it was not there.

I sought for the greatness and genius of America in her public school system and her institutions of learning, and it was not there.

I sought for the greatness and genius of America in her democratic congress and her matchless constitution, and it was not there.

Not until I went into the churches of America and heard her pulpits flame with righteousness did I understand the secret of her genius and power.

America is great because America is good, and if America ever ceases to be good, America will cease to be great.

ALEXIS DE TOCQUEVILLE

❧

BORN OUT OF FAITH

The men who laid the foundations and reared the soaring arches of our great republic had a vigorous, indomitable, and all-encompassing belief in God. Faith permeated their thoughts, their words and deeds. We see Thomas Jefferson's hand guiding the quill which wrote, "I have sworn upon the altar of God, eternal hostility against every form of tyranny over the mind of man." We see George Washington, when the fires of hope had flickered to embers, kneeling in the snow at Valley Forge. And we see wise old Ben Franklin suggesting to a Constitutional Convention, deadlocked time after time, that "we have prayers every morning."

This nation was born out of faith in God. It can continue to exist in freedom only as that faith remains forthright and strong. A statesman of a past age said, "Despotism may govern without faith, but Liberty cannot."

Faith in God remains the solid rock that stands unmoved amid the sliding sands. The antithesis of cynicism, it is the dynamo which sparks the minds and actions of men who think beyond the pettiness of self. It is the tie which binds mankind in mystic unity, exalting the human creature until, indeed, he is "little lower than the angels." And it is the balm which salves the sting of time and death.

Faith in God has meant to me the enjoyment of those manifold "blessings of liberty" which the Founding Fathers sought to secure for all posterity. It is a fathomless source from which to draw strength in times of adversity. And it has helped me to catch a glimpse of the wisdom implicit in those immutable laws by which He rules His universe.

J. EDGAR HOOVER

❧

The true discovery of America is before us.

THOMAS WOLFE

AMERICA

God built him a continent of glory and filled
  it with treasures untold;
He carpeted it with soft-rolling prairies and
  columned it with thundering mountains;
He studded it with sweet-flowing fountains and
  traced it with long-winding streams;
He planted it with deep-shadowed forests, and
  filled them with song.
Then he called unto a thousand peoples and
  summoned the bravest among them.
They came from the ends of the earth, each
  bearing a gift and a hope.
The glow of adventure was in their eyes, and
  in their hearts the glory of hope.
And out of the bounty of earth and the labor
  of men,
Out of the longing of hearts and the prayer of
  souls,
Out of the memory of ages and hopes of the
  world,
God fashioned a nation in love, blessed it with
Purpose sublime—and called it America!

ABBA HILLEL SILVER

Give me your tired, your poor,
Your huddled masses yearning to breathe free,
The wretched refuse of your teeming shore.
Send these, the homeless, tempest-tost to me,
I lift my lamp beside the golden door.

WRITTEN BY EMMA LAZARUS
AND INSCRIBED ON
THE STATUE OF LIBERTY

Democracy is a small hard core of common
agreement, surrounded by a rich variety of
individual differences.

JAMES CONANT

What were you carrying, Pilgrims, Pilgrims?
What did you carry beyond the sea?
  We carried the Book, we carried the Sword,
  A steadfast heart in the fear of the Lord,
  And a living faith in His plighted word
  That all men should be free.

What were your memories, Pilgrims, Pilgrims?
What of the dreams you bore away?
  We carried the songs our fathers sung
  By the hearths of home when they were
    young,
  And the comely words of the mother-tongue
  In which they learnt to pray.

What did you find there, Pilgrims, Pilgrims?
What did you find beyond the waves?
  A stubborn land and a barren shore,
  Hunger and want and sickness sore:
  All these we found and gladly bore
  Rather than be slaves.

How did you fare there, Pilgrims, Pilgrims?
What did you build in that stubborn land?
  We felled the forest and tilled the sod
  Of a continent no man had trod
  And we established there, in the Grace of
    God,
  The rights whereby we stand.

What are you bringing us, Pilgrims, Pilgrims?
Bringing us back in this bitter day?
  The selfsame things we carried away:
  The Book, the Sword,
  The fear of the Lord,
  And the boons our fathers dearly bought:
  Freedom of Worship, Speech and Thought,
  Freedom from Want, Freedom from Fear,
  The liberties we hold most dear,
  And who shall say us Nay?

FRANCIS BRETT YOUNG

America is a tune; it must be sung together.

GERALD STANLEY LEE

PLYMOUTH ROCK INSCRIPTION

This spot marks the final resting-place of the Pilgrims of the *Mayflower*. In weariness and hunger and in cold, fighting the wilderness and burying their dead in common graves that the Indians should not know how many had perished, they here laid the foundations of a state in which all men for countless ages should have liberty to worship God in their own way. All ye who pass by and see this stone remember, and dedicate yourselves anew to the resolution that you will not rest until this lofty ideal shall have been realized throughout the earth.

SPIRIT OF LIBERTY

What is the spirit of liberty? I cannot define it; I can only tell you my own faith. The spirit of liberty is the spirit which is not too sure that it is right. The spirit of liberty is the spirit which seeks to understand the minds of other men and women. The spirit of liberty is the spirit which weighs their interests alongside its own without bias. The spirit of liberty remembers that not even a sparrow falls to the earth unheeded. The spirit of liberty is the spirit of Him who, nearly two thousand years ago, taught mankind that lesson it has never learned, but has never quite forgotten: that there may be a kingdom where the least shall be heard and considered side by side with the greatest.

LEARNED HAND

This generation of Americans has a rendezvous with destiny.

FRANKLIN D. ROOSEVELT

FREEDOM

Freedom is a breath of air,
Pine-scented, or salty like the sea;
Freedom is a field new-plowed . . .
Furrows of democracy!

Freedom is a forest,
Trees tall and straight as men!
Freedom is a printing press . . .
The power of the pen!

Freedom is a country church,
A cathedral's stately spire;
Freedom is a spirit
That can set the soul on fire!

Freedom is man's birthright,
A sacred, living rampart;
A pulsebeat of humanity . . .
The throb of a nation's heart!

CLARA SMITH REBER

THE FOUR FREEDOMS

In the future days, which we seek to make secure, we look forward to a world founded upon four essential human freedoms.

The first is freedom of speech and expression—everywhere in the world.

The second is freedom of every person to worship God in his own way—everywhere in the world.

The third is freedom from want—which, translated into world terms, means economic understanding which will secure to every nation a healthy peacetime life for its inhabitants—everywhere in the world.

The fourth is freedom from fear—which, translated into world terms, means a worldwide reduction of armaments to such a point and in such a fashion that no nation will be in a position to commit an act of physical aggression against any neighbor—anywhere in the world.

FRANKLIN D. ROOSEVELT

❦

When an American says that he loves his country, he means not only that he loves the New England hills, the prairies glistening in the sun, the wide and rising plains, the great mountains, and the sea. He means that he loves an inner air, an inner light in which freedom lives and in which a man can draw the breath of self-respect.

ADLAI STEVENSON

❦

TEN MARKS OF A GOOD CITIZEN

1. He is well informed on local and world affairs. "Knowledge is the food of the soul" (Plato).
2. He is courteous, unselfish, friendly—gets along well with others—is a good neighbor. "All is well with him who is beloved by his neighbors" (George Herbert).
3. He is sincere, dependable, and takes an active part in the church or religious community of his choice. "Religion is the basis of civil society" (Edmund Burke).
4. He appreciates what others have done for him and accepts responsibility for the future betterment of his community. "A community is like a ship; everyone ought to be prepared to take the helm" (Henrik Ibsen).
5. He is fair and just in his relations with others. "Hear the other side" (Augustine).
6. He obeys the laws of his community and nation. "No man is above the law" (Theodore Roosevelt).
7. He votes regularly and intelligently at election time. "The greatest menace to freedom is an inert people" (Louis D. Brandeis).
8. He is interested in the freedom and welfare of all the world's peoples and does his part to secure them. "Slav, Teuton, Celt, I count them all my friends and brother souls" (Tennyson).
9. He is productive—renders a worthwhile service to his fellow man. "The highest of distinctions is service to others" (King George VI).
10. He sets a good example to the youth of his community. "A good example is the best sermon" (Thomas Fuller).

HERBERT J. TAYLOR

❦

WHAT THE FLAG MEANS

The Flag is many things. It is a mark of identification of ships at sea and of armies in the field. It is a means of communication. When you see our Flag in front of a home, it says for all the world to read, "Here lives a family that is American in spirit as well as in name." The Flag is a mirror, reflecting to each person his own ideals and dreams. It is a history. Its thirteen stripes and fifty stars embrace a record written greatly during these years since 1776. It is a mark of pride in a great word—the word "American." It is an aspiration of what small children want their lives to be. It is a memory at the end of life of all that life has been. It is a ribbon of honor for those who have served it well—in peace and war. It is a warning not to detour from the long road that has brought our country and its people to a degree of prosperity and happiness never even approached under any other banner.

EDWARD F. HUTTON

❦

ONE PURE SOURCE

The meaning of our word America flows from one pure source. Within the soul of America is the freedom of mind and spirit in man. Here alone are the open windows through which pours the sunlight of all the human spirit. Here alone human dignity is not a dream but a major accomplishment.

HERBERT HOOVER

OUR COMMON LABOR

Before all else we seek, upon our common labor as a nation, the blessings of Almighty God. And the hopes in our hearts fashion the deepest prayers of our whole people.

May we pursue the right—without self-righteousness.

May we know unity—without conformity.

May we grow in strength—without pride in self.

May we, in our dealings with all peoples of the earth, ever speak truth and serve justice.

May the light of freedom, coming to all darkened lands, flame brightly—until at last the darkness is no more.

May the turbulence of our age yield to a true time of peace, when men and nations share a life that honors the dignity of each, the brotherhood of all.

DWIGHT D. EISENHOWER

DEDICATION

I was born an American; I live an American; I shall die an American; and I intend to perform the duties incumbent upon me in that character to the end of my career. I mean to do this with absolute disregard of personal consequences. What are the personal consequences? What is the individual man, with all the good or evil that may betide him, in comparison with the good or evil which may befall a great country, and in the midst of great transactions which concern that country's fate? Let the consequences be what they will, I am careless. No man can suffer too much, and no man can fall too soon, if he suffer, or if he fall, in the defense of the liberties and constitution of his country.

DANIEL WEBSTER

HERITAGE

Let us not forget the religious character of our origin. Our fathers were brought here by their high veneration for the Christian religion. They journeyed by its light, and labored in its hope. They sought to incorporate its principles with the elements of their society, and to diffuse its influence through all their institutions—civil, political and literary. Let us cherish these sentiments, and extend this influence still more widely, in the full conviction that this is the happiest society, which partakes in the highest degree of the mild and peaceable spirit of Christianity.

DANIEL WEBSTER

THE ATHENIAN OATH

We will never bring disgrace to this, our nation, by any act of dishonesty or cowardice, nor ever desert our suffering comrades in the ranks.

We will fight for the ideals of the nation both alone and with others.

We will revere and respect our nation's laws, and do our best to incite a like respect and reverence in those above us who are prone to annul and set them at naught.

We will strive unceasingly to quicken the public's sense of civic duty.

Thus in all these ways we will transmit this nation not only not less but greater, better, and more beautiful than it was transmitted to us.

AMERICA'S GOSPEL

Our country hath a gospel of her own
To preach and practice before all the world—
The freedom and divinity of man,
The glorious claims of human brotherhood,
And the soul's fealty to none but God.

JAMES RUSSELL LOWELL

MOUNT VERNON INSCRIPTION

Washington, the brave, the wise, the good,
Supreme in war, in council, and in peace.
Valiant without ambition, discreet without fear,
Confident without presumption.
In disaster, calm; in success, moderate; in all,
    himself.
The hero, the patriot, the Christian.
The father of nations, the friend of mankind,
Who, when he had won all, renounced all,
And sought in the bosom of his family and
    of nature, retirement,
And in the hope of religion, immortality.

In the long view of history, these years are the
early summer of America. Our land is young.
Our strength is great. Our course is far from
run.

LYNDON B. JOHNSON

THE AMERICAN'S CREED

I believe in the United States of America
    as a government of the people, by the people,
    for the people;
Whose just powers are derived from the con-
    sent of the governed;
A democracy in a republic, a sovereign nation
    of many sovereign states;
A perfect union one and inseparable;
Established upon those principles of freedom,
    equality, justice, and humanity for which
    American patriots sacrificed their lives and
    fortunes.
I therefore believe it is my duty to my country
    to love it, to support its Constitution, to
    obey its laws, to respect its flag, and to de-
    fend it against all enemies.

WILLIAM TYLER PAGE

CREDO

I believe in America because in it we are free—
    free to choose our government, to speak our
    minds, to observe our different religions;
Because we are generous with our freedom—
    we share our rights with those who disagree
    with us;
Because we hate no people and covet no people's
    land;
Because we are blessed with a natural and
    varied abundance;
Because we set no limit to a man's achievement:
    in mine, factory, field, or service in business
    or the arts, an able man, regardless of class
    or creed, can realize his ambition;
Because we have great dreams—and because
    we have the opportunity to make those
    dreams come true.

WENDELL L. WILLKIE

American life is a powerful solvent. It seems
to neutralize every intellectual element, however tough and alien it may be, and to fuse it
in the native good-will, complacency, thought-
lessness, and optimism.

GEORGE SANTAYANA

MY COUNTRY

God grant that not only
    the love of liberty
But a thorough knowledge
    of the rights of man
May pervade all nations
    of the earth, so that
A philosopher may set
    his foot anywhere
On its surface, and say,
    "This is my country."

BENJAMIN FRANKLIN

NATURE

Earth's crammed with heaven,
And every common bush afire with God.
ELIZABETH BARRETT BROWNING

I SAW GOD WASH THE WORLD

I saw God wash the world last night
   With his sweet showers on high,
And then, when morning came, I saw
   Him hang it out to dry.

He washed each tiny blade of grass
   And every trembling tree;
He flung his showers against the hill,
   And swept the billowing sea.

The white rose is a cleaner white,
   The red rose is more red,
Since God washed every fragrant face
   And put them all to bed.

There's not a bird, there's not a bee
   That wings along the way
But is a cleaner bird and bee
   Than it was yesterday.

I saw God wash the world last night.
   Ah, would he had washed me
As clean of all my dust and dirt
   As that old white birch tree.

WILLIAM L. STIDGER

SIGNATURE

Everywhere I find the signature, the autograph of God, and he will never deny his own handwriting. God hath set his tabernacle in the dewdrop as surely as in the sun. No man can any more create the smallest flower than he could create the greatest world.

JOSEPH PARKER

Familiarity with nature never breeds contempt. The more one learns, the more he expects surprises, and the more he becomes aware of the inscrutable.

ARCHIBALD RUTLEDGE

A BALLAD OF TREES AND THE MASTER

Into the woods my Master went,
Clean forspent, forspent.
Into the woods my Master came,
Forspent with love and shame.
But the olives they were not blind to him;
The little gray leaves were kind to him;
The thorn-tree had a mind to him
When into the woods he came.

Out of the woods my Master went,
And he was well content.
Out of the woods my Master came,
Content with death and shame.
When Death and Shame would woo him last,
From under the trees they drew him last:
'Twas on a tree they slew him—last
When out of the woods he came.

SIDNEY LANIER

A happy life is not built up of tours abroad and pleasant holidays, but of little clumps of violets noticed by the roadside, hidden away almost so that only those can see them who have God's peace and love in their hearts; in one long continuous chain of little joys, little whispers from the spiritual world, and little gleams of sunshine on our daily work.

EDWARD WILSON

LESSONS OF NATURE

As never before it is the duty of parents to train their children to behold the creatures of Nature which can never lose their identities because they can only be what they already are: the flowers "fresh and laughing as on the days of great battles," the beasts who "walk the earth, ignorant, while their splendor lasts, of any weakness," and, most of all, perhaps, the stars of the night sky, in all their unchanging majesty and stateliness of movement.

W. H. AUDEN

❧❦❧

OUT OF THE VAST

There's a part of the sun in the apple,
　There's a part of the moon in a rose;
There's a part of the flaming Pleiades
　In every leaf that grows.

Out of the vast comes nearness;
　For the God whose love we sing
Lends a little of his heaven
　To every living thing.

AUGUSTUS WRIGHT BAMBERGER

❧❦❧

Nature is man's religious book, with lessons
for every day.

THEODORE PARKER

❧❦❧

I love to think of nature as an unlimited broad-
casting station, through which God speaks to
us every hour, if we will only tune in.

GEORGE WASHINGTON CARVER

❧❦❧

Nature is the living, visible garment of God.

JOHANN WOLFGANG VON GOETHE

❧❦❧

Rightly considered, modern scientific development gives us a profound conception of God
because it gives us a better idea than heretofore
of the inexhaustible activity of God. In enlarging indefinitely the limits of the universe created by God, we have enlarged our understanding of the Creator's power.

J. ELLIOTT ROSS

❧❦❧

PRAYER

Like summer seas that lave with silent tides a
lonely shore, like whispering winds that stir
the tops of forest trees, like a still small voice
that calls us in the watches of the night, like a
child's hand that feels about a fast-closed door;
gentle, unnoticed, and oft in vain; so is thy
coming unto us, O God.

Like ships storm-driven into port, like starv-
ing souls that seek the bread they once despised,
like wanderers begging refuge from the whelm-
ing night, like prodigals that seek the father's
home when all is spent; yet welcomed at the
open door, arms outstretched and kisses for
our shame; so is our coming unto thee, O God.

Like flowers uplifted to the sun, like trees
that bend before the storm, like sleeping seas
that mirror cloudless skies, like a harp to the
hand, like an echo to a cry, like a song to the
heart; for all our stubbornness, our failure and
our sin; so would we have been to thee, O God.

WILLIAM E. ORCHARD

❧❦❧

STOPPING BY WOODS ON
A SNOWY EVENING

Whose woods these are I think I know.
His house is in the village though;
He will not see me stopping here
To watch his woods fill up with snow.

My little horse must think it queer
To stop without a farmhouse near
Between the woods and frozen lake
The darkest evening of the year.

He gives his harness bells a shake
To ask if there is some mistake.
The only other sound's the sweep
Of easy wind and downy flake.

The woods are lovely, dark and deep,
But I have promises to keep,
And miles to go before I sleep,
And miles to go before I sleep.

ROBERT FROST

Flower in the crannied wall,
I pluck you out of the crannies,
I hold you, root and all, in my hand,
Little flower—but *if* I could understand
What you are, root and all, and all in all,
I should know what God and man is.

ALFRED TENNYSON

THE CANTICLE OF THE SUN

O most high, almighty, good Lord God, to thee belong praise, glory, honor, and all blessing!

Praised by my Lord God with all his creatures; and specially our brother the sun, who brings us the day, and who brings us the light; fair is he, and shining with a very great splendor: O Lord, to us he signifies thee!

Praised be my Lord for our sister the moon, and for the stars, the which he has set clear and lovely in heaven.

Praised be my Lord for our brother the wind, and for air and cloud, calms and all weather, by the which thou upholdest in life all creatures.

Praised be my Lord for our sister water, who is very serviceable unto us, and humble, and precious, and clean.

Praised by my Lord for our brother fire, through whom thou givest us light in the darkness; and he is bright, and pleasant, and very mighty, and strong.

Praised be my Lord for our mother the earth, the which doth sustain us and keep us, and bringeth forth divers fruits, and flowers of many colors, and grass.

Praised be my Lord for all those who pardon one another for his love's sake and who endure weakness and tribulation; blessed are they who peaceably shall endure, for thou, O most Highest, shalt give them a crown!

Praised be my Lord for our sister, the death of the body, from whom no man escapeth. Woe to him who dieth in mortal sin! Blessed are they who are found walking by thy most holy will, for the second death shall have no power to do them harm.

Praise ye, and bless ye the Lord, and give thanks unto him, and serve him with great humility.

ST. FRANCIS OF ASSISI

CELESTIAL MATHEMATICS

The naturalist William Beebe tells of visits he made to Theodore Roosevelt, another naturalist. After an evening's talk in Roosevelt's home at Sagamore Hill, the two men would go out on the lawn and gaze up at the sky and see who first could detect the faint spot of light-mist beyond the lower left-hand corner of the Great Square of Pegasus, and then one or the other would recite:

That is the Spiral Galaxy of Andromeda.
It is as large as our Milky Way.
It is one of a hundred million galaxies.
It is 750,000 light-years away.
It consists of one hundred billion suns,
    each larger than our sun.

After an interval Beebe reports Mr. Roosevelt would grin at him and say, "Now, I think we are small enough. Let's go to bed."

HENRY SLOANE COFFIN

Kepler stood before his telescope, viewing the star clusters of a night sky, and cried out, "O God, I think thy thoughts after thee."

To him who in the love of Nature holds
Communion with her visible forms, she speaks
A various language.

WILLIAM CULLEN BRYANT

Some keep the Sabbath going to church;
I keep it staying at home,
With a bobolink for a chorister,
And an orchard for a dome.

Some keep the Sabbath in surplice;
I just wear my wings,
And instead of tolling the bell for church,
Our little sexton sings.

God preaches,—a noted clergyman,—
And the sermon is never long;
So instead of getting to heaven at last,
I'm going all along!

EMILY DICKINSON

❦

SILENCE

I need not shout my faith. Thrice eloquent
    Are quiet trees and the green listening sod;
Hushed are the stars, whose power is never spent;
    The hills are mute: yet how they speak of God!

CHARLES HANSON TOWNE

❦

AUTUMN

When Autumn flings her banners wide upon
    October air,
All nature seems to thank its God for making
    life so fair.
The hills go robed in amethyst, the trees are
    dressed in fire,
The very air seems thrilling with a passionless
    desire.
One somehow feels that God on high must love
    this season best,
He holds it as a mother holds her babe close to
    her breast.
The pressure of his hand is on all nature like
    a prayer—
When Autumn flings her banners wide upon
    October air.

MARGARET E. SANGSTER

❦

MY GALILEES

Although my eyes may never see
That hallowed Lake of Galilee,

Still I have found each little lake
More fraught with meaning for His sake.

Upon a floor of amethyst
He walks in early morning mist,

While on a grassy slope is spread
Once more the Feast of Living Bread.

BELLE CHAPMAN MORRILL

❦

OUR DAILY BREAD

Back of the loaf is the snowy flour,
    And back of the flour the mill;
And back of the mill is the wheat and the
        shower,
    And the sun and the Father's will.

MALTBIE D. BABCOCK

❦

If spring came but once in a century instead of
once a year, or burst forth with the sound of an
earthquake and not in silence, what wonder
and expectation there would be in all hearts
to behold the miraculous change.

HENRY WADSWORTH LONGFELLOW

❦

MY GARDEN

A garden is a lovesome thing, God wot!
    Rose plot,
    Fringed pool,
Fern'd grot—
    The veriest school
    Of peace; and yet the fool
Contends that God is not—
Not God! in gardens! when the eve is cool?
    Nay, but I have a sign;
    'Tis very sure God walks in mine.

THOMAS EDWARD BROWN

OPORTUNITY

*The pessimist sees the difficulty in every opportunity;
the optimist, the opportunity in every difficulty.*

L. P. JACKS

ENLARGEMENT

The night sky does something to the star-gazer. There is silent, uplifting inspiration from the Absolute. It does us creative good to look up and "see Orion driving his hunting dogs across the Zenith or Andromeda shaking out her tresses over limitless space." It enlarges the self to know great art, to have studied great architecture, to have felt the spell of epic heroisms, to have swung to the rhythmic pulse of Homer's strophes, to have shaken to the passion of Roland, or Romeo, or Francis of Assisi, to have wrestled with Kant's categorical imperatives, to have seen the twin-flower in Linnaeus' companionship, to have heard the roll of Drake's drum, to have been borne on the music stream of Beethoven's symphonies, to engrave the prologue to John's Gospel on the heart, to have said the sonorous, searching affirmations of the Nicene Creed.

PHILLIPS ENDICOTT OSGOOD

❧

THE LITTLE TASK

Always keep your eyes open for the little task, because it is the little task that is important to Jesus Christ. The future of the Kingdom of God does not depend on the enthusiasm of this or that powerful person; those great ones are necessary too, but it is equally necessary to have a great number of little people who will do a little thing in the service of Christ.

The great flowing rivers represent only a small part of all the water that is necessary to nourish and sustain the earth. Beside the flowing river there is the water in the earth—the subterranean water—and there are the little streams which continually enter the river and feed it and prevent it from sinking into the earth. Without these other waters—the silent hidden subterranean waters and the trickling streams—the great river could no longer flow. Thus it is with the little tasks to be fulfilled by us all.

ALBERT SCHWEITZER

❧

The lure of the distant and the difficult is deceptive. The great opportunity is where you are.

JOHN BURROUGHS

❧

ONE VISIT

The fairy Opportunity
   Knocks at so many doors
She can but linger fleetingly
   At mine or yours.

And if we wait to draw the blind
   Or challenge, "Who goes there?"
Her wings beat skyward, and we find
   But empty air.

❧

SPIRITUAL EXERCISE

Every trouble is an opportunity to win the grace of strength. Whatever else trouble is in the world for, it is here for this good purpose—to develop strength. For a trouble is a moral and spiritual task. It is something which is hard to do. And it is in the spiritual world as in the physical, strength is increased by encounter with the difficult. A world without any trouble in it would be, to people of our kind, a place of spiritual enervation and moral laziness. Fortunately, every day is crowded with care. Every day to every one of us brings its questions, its worries, and its tasks, brings its sufficiency of trouble. Thus we get our daily spiritual exercise. Every day we are blessed with new opportunities for the development of strength of soul.

GEORGE HODGES

❧

We should all be concerned about the future because we will have to spend the rest of our lives there.

CHARLES F. KETTERING

NO RETURN

Three things return not, even for prayers and
    tears—
The arrow which the archer shoots at will;
The spoken word, keen-edged and sharp to
    sting;
The opportunity left unimproved.
If thou would'st speak a word of loving cheer,
Oh, speak it now. This moment is thine own.

WHAT MIGHT HAVE BEEN

I held a moment in my hand,
    Brilliant as a star,
    Fragile as a flower,
    A shiny sliver out of one hour.
I dropped it carelessly.
    O God! I knew not
    I held opportunity.

HAZEL LEE

From THE ROAD NOT TAKEN

I shall be telling this with a sigh
Somewhere ages and ages hence;
Two roads diverged in a wood, and I,
I took the one less traveled by—
And that has made all the difference.

ROBERT FROST

SCULPTURING

It is something to be able to paint a particular
picture, or to carve a statue, and so to make a
few objects beautiful; but it is far more glorious
to carve and paint the very atmosphere and
medium through which we look. To affect the
quality of the day—that is the highest of arts.

HENRY DAVID THOREAU

Lost yesterday, somewhere between sunrise and
sunset, two golden hours, each set with sixty
diamond minutes. No reward is offered, for
they are gone forever.

HORACE MANN

Hell begins on the day when God grants us a
clear vision of all that we might have achieved,
of all the gifts which we have wasted, of all
that we might have done which we did not do.

GIAN-CARLO MENOTTI

DAYS

Daughters of Time, the hypocritic Days,
Muffled and dumb like barefoot dervishes,
And marching single in an endless file,
Bring diadems and fagots in their hands.
To each they offer gifts after his will,
Bread, kingdom, stars, and sky that holds them
    all.
I, in my pleached garden, watched the pomp,
Forgot my morning wishes, hastily
Took a few herbs and apples, and the Day
Turned and departed silent. I, too late,
Under her solemn filet saw the scorn.

RALPH WALDO EMERSON

When a man's pursuit gradually makes his
face shine and grow handsome, be sure it is a
worthy one.

WILLIAM JAMES

THE TIDE

There is a tide in the affairs of men
Which taken at the flood, leads on to fortune;
Omitted, all the voyage of their life,
Is bound in shallows and in miseries.

WILLIAM SHAKESPEARE

PEACE

*Lord, thou madest us for thyself, and we can find no rest
till we find rest in thee.*

ST. AUGUSTINE

Matthew Arnold counted as the greatest single line in all poetry that saying of Dante's poetic insight: "In Thy will is our peace."

PHILEMON F. STURGES

❧

GUIDEPATHS TO PEACE

Be glad of life because it gives you the chance to love and to work and to play and to look up at the stars; to be satisfied with your possessions but not content with yourself until you have made the best of them; to despise nothing in the world except falsehood and meanness, and to fear nothing except cowardice; to be governed by your admirations rather than by your disgusts; to covet nothing that is your neighbor's except his kindness of heart and gentleness of manners; to think seldom of your enemies, often of your friends, and every day of Christ; and to spend as much time as you can with body and spirit in God's out-of-doors—these are little guidepaths to peace.

HENRY VAN DYKE

❧

THE PEACE OF CHRIST

The peace of Christ is the peace of trust in the cause we serve, when service seems to fail of its end. It is the peace of confidence in God when all the forces of the universe seem working for ends that are undivine. It is the peace which can accept unexplained mysteries, which can bear heartbreaking sorrows, which can see natural instincts thwarted, holy aspirations unrealized, Christlike purposes broken off, and yet be unperturbed. It is the peace of a Paul rejected by his countrymen. It is the peace of all those who have given their lives for causes too high and sacred for immediate success and who yet have been able to believe that even their failures were being overruled by God for good.

WILLIAM ADAMS BROWN

❧

WHAT GOD HATH PROMISED

God hath not promised
Skies always blue,
Flower-strewn pathways
All our lives through;
God hath not promised
Sun without rain,
Joy without sorrow,
Peace without pain.

But God hath promised
Strength for the day,
Rest for the labor,
Light for the way,
Grace for the trials,
Help from above,
Unfailing sympathy,
Undying love.

ANNIE JOHNSON FLINT

❧

WAIT ON

To talk with God,
No breath is lost—
  Talk on!

To walk with God,
No strength is lost—
  Walk on!

To wait on God,
No time is lost—
  Wait on!

DNYANODAYA

❧

Some people have just enough religion to make them uncomfortable.

JOHN WESLEY

❧

SLOW ME DOWN, LORD!

Slow me down, Lord!
Ease the pounding of my heart by the quieting
    of my mind.
Steady my hurried pace,
With a vision of the eternal reach of time.
Give me, amidst the confusion of my day,
The calmness of the everlasting hills.
Break the tension of my nerves
With the soothing music of the singing streams
That live in my memory.
Help me to know the magical restoring power
    of sleep.
Teach me the art of taking minute vacations of
    slowing down.
To look at a flower;
To chat with an old friend or make a new one;
To pat a stray dog; to watch a spider build a
    web;
To smile at a child; or to read from a good
    book.
Remind me each day
That the race is not always to the swift;
That there is more to life than increasing its
    speed.
Let me look upward into the towering oak
And know that it grew great and strong
Because it grew slowly and well.

ORIN L. CRAIN

❧

But sometimes, through the Soul of Man,
    Slow moving o'er his pain,
The moonlight of a perfect peace
    Floods heart and brain.

FIONA MACLEOD

❧

All men's miseries derive from not being able
to sit quiet in a room alone.

BLAISE PASCAL

❧

THE MYSTIC'S PRAYER

Lay me to sleep in sheltering flame,
    O Master of the Hidden Fire!
Wash pure my heart, and cleanse for me
    My soul's desire.

In flame of sunrise bathe my mind,
    O Master of the Hidden Fire,
That, when I wake, clear-eyed may be
    My soul's desire.

FIONA MACLEOD

❧

SECRET OF PEACE

The saints reveal to other men what a man can be; they smash the body to atoms and come forth a living flame with a body newly refreshed; they unearth the hidden beauty in human beings who have been passed over as the waste product of humanity and they thread together on one golden cord of the love of God virtues whose existence was scarcely known, whose combination seemed incredible, ardor and patience, meekness and power, detachment and affection, lowly hope and high humility. But above all, the saints possess some secret of peace, as if, like the successful lover, they were in possession of their heart's desire, and in this fulfillment some joy sang within them to which all their faculties made response. They are not lonely nor stoical; they are well acquainted with sorrow and they embrace pain, but everywhere they go they are accompanied by the sunshine of spring.

M. C. D'ARCY

❧

Let us not go faster than God. It is our emptiness and our thirst that he needs, not our plenitude.

JACQUES MARITAIN

TO GAIN EMOTIONAL POISE

1. Get the right mental picture of your own life.
2. Scale down the demands you are making on other people.
3. At any cost in effort, keep your world from growing small.

JAMES GORDON GILKEY

FROM A COUNTRY HILL

If you have watched with inarticulate delight,
From the free vantage of a country hill,
The change from sunset into twilight, dusk, and night,
Then you have felt how deep peace is, how still.

You see the benediction of the afterglow
Accent each detail of the widespread scene,
Before the twilight sky, rimmed with pink, rose and mauve,
Securely cups your world, safe and serene.

Then dark, pricked there—and there—and there by neighbor's light;
Bright stars, and silence stabbed by cricket song.
You feel cares slip away. Here on this hill to-night
The tang is clean, the pulse is strong.

EMMA GLASER

SUNSET

The day is done,
    The sun has set,
Yet light still tints the sky;

My heart stands still
    In reverence,
For God is passing by.

RUTH ALLA WAGER

GOD'S WILL

Thy will, O God, is joy to me,
    A gladsome thing;
For in it naught but love I see
    Whate'er it bring.

Within the circle of thy will
    All things abide;
So I, exulting, find no ill
    When thou dost guide.

In that resplendent will of thine
    I calmly rest;
Triumphantly I make it mine,
    And count it best.

JAMES MUDGE

FISHING

To go fishing is the chance to wash one's soul with pure air, with the rush of the brook, or with the shimmer of the sun on blue water. It brings meekness and inspiration from the decency of nature, charity toward tackle-makers, patience toward fish, a mockery of profits and cgos, a quieting of hate, a rejoicing that you do not have to decide a darned thing until next week. And it is discipline in the equality of men—for all men are equal before fish.

HERBERT HOOVER

PRAYER

Calm soul of all things! make it mine
To feel, amid the city's jar,
That there abides a peace of thine,
Man did not make, and cannot mar!

The will to neither strive nor cry,
The power to feel with others give!
Calm, calm me more! nor let me die
Before I have begun to live.

MATTHEW ARNOLD

PAUSES

In our whole life melody the music is broken off here and there by rests, and we foolishly think we have come to the end of time. God sends a time of forced leisure, a time of sickness and disappointed plans, and makes a sudden pause in the hymns of our lives, and we lament that our voice must be silent and our part missing in the music which ever goes up to the ear of our Creator. Not without design does God write the music of our lives. Be it ours to learn the time and not be dismayed at the rests. If we look up, God will beat the time for us.

JOHN RUSKIN

ALL'S WELL

My heart,
   The sun hath set.
Night's paths
   With dews are wet.

Sleep comes
   Without regret;
Stars rise
   When sun is set.

All's well.
   God loves thee yet,
Heart, smile,
   Sleep sweet, nor fret.

WILLIAM A. QUAYLE

Have courage for the great sorrows of life and patience for the small ones; and when you have laboriously accomplished your daily task, go to sleep in peace. God is awake.

VICTOR HUGO

TRUE REST

Rest is not quitting
The busy career;
Rest is the fitting
Of self to one's sphere.

'Tis the brook's motion
Clear without strife,
Fleeting to ocean,
After this life.

'Tis loving and serving,
The highest and best;
'Tis onward, unswerving,
And this is true rest.

JOHANN WOLFGANG VON GOETHE

HIS ENTRANCE

"Where is the dwelling of God?"
This was the question with which the Rabbi of
   Kotzk surprised a number of learned men
   who happened to be visiting him.
They laughed at him. "What a thing to ask! Is
   not the whole world full of his glory?"
Then he answered his own question. "God
   dwells wherever man lets him in."

MARTIN BUBER

A room of quiet . . . a temple of peace;
The home of faith . . . where doubtings cease;
A house of comfort . . . where hope is given;
A source of strength . . . to make earth heaven;
A shrine of worship . . . a place to pray—
I found all this . . . in my church today.

CYRUS E. ALBERTSON

194

PRAYER

God warms his hands at man's heart when he prays.

JOHN MASEFIELD

Prayer is need finding a voice. Prayer is embarrassment seeking relief. Prayer is friend in search of friend. Prayer is a quest in the darkness of midnight. Prayer is knocking on a barred door. Prayer is communion through both darkness and closed doors. Prayer is shameless insistence in the name of another. Prayer is expecting and receiving all things whatsoever we need to meet the demands when Jesus our Friend calls on us.

RALPH A. HERRING

A prayer in its simplest definition is merely a wish turned Godward.

PHILLIPS BROOKS

Prayer is the contemplation of the facts of life from the highest point of view.

RALPH WALDO EMERSON

PROOF

If radio's slim fingers can pluck a melody
From night—and toss it over a continent or
    sea;
If the petalled white notes of a violin
Are blown across the mountains or the city's
    din;
If songs, like crimson roses, are culled from
    thin blue air—
Why should mortals wonder if God hears
    prayer?

ETHEL ROMIG FULLER

Pray till prayer makes you forget your own wish, and leave it or merge it in God's will.

FREDERICK W. ROBERTSON

HOW TO PRAY

I. Pray where you are. God is present everywhere and ready to listen.

II. Pray when possible in a quiet spot where you can be alone. It is well to fix your mind deliberately on God, apart from confusing distractions.

III. Pray to God simply and naturally, as to a friend. Tell him what is on your mind. Get help from the prayers of others.

IV. Pray remembering the good things God has done for you. Reckon up your blessings from time to time and give thanks for them.

V. Pray for God's forgiveness for the unworthy things that you may have done. He is near to a humble and contrite heart.

VI. Pray for the things that you need, especially for those that will make your life finer and more Christlike.

VII. Pray for others, remembering the situations they confront and the help they need.

VIII. Pray for the world in its need, asking God to bring better things and offering your plan to help him.

IX. Pray above everything else that God's will may be done in you and in the world. His purposes are deeper and wiser than anything we can imagine.

X. Pray, and then start answering your prayer.

DEANE EDWARDS

THE SECRET PLACE

Each soul has its secret place,
Where none may enter in
Save it and God—to them alone
What goeth on therein is known—
To it and God alone.

JOHN OXENHAM

EIGHT SENATE PRAYERS

These prayers by Peter Marshall were given in his capacity of Chaplain of the United States Senate.

I. Our Father, when we long for life without trials and work, without difficulties, remind us that oaks grow strong in contrary winds and diamonds are made under pressure. With stout hearts may we see in every calamity an opportunity and not give way to the pessimist that sees in every opportunity a calamity.

II. Lord, when we are wrong, make us willing to change. And when we are right, make us easy to live with.

III. Let us not be frightened by the problems that confront us, but rather give thee thanks that thou hast matched us with this hour. May we resolve, God helping us, to be part of the answer, and not part of the problem.

IV. Save us from hotheads that would lead us to act foolishly, and from cold feet that would keep us from acting at all.

V. Help us, our Father, to show other nations an America to imitate—not the America of loud jazz music, self-seeking indulgence, and love of money, but the America that loves fair play, honest dealing, straight talk, real freedom, and faith in God. Make us to see that it cannot be done as long as we are content to be coupon clippers on the original investment made by our forefathers. Give us faith in God and love for our fellow men, that we may have something to deposit on which the young people of today can draw interest tomorrow.

VI. Help us, O Lord, when we want to do the right thing, but know not what it is. But help us most when we know perfectly well what we ought to do, and do not want to do it.

VII. Lord Jesus, thou who art the way, the truth, and the life, hear us as we pray for the truth that shall make men free. Teach us that liberty is not only to be loved but also to be lived. Liberty is too precious a thing to be buried in books. It costs too much to be hoarded. Make us to see that our liberty is not the right to do as we please, but the opportunity to please to do what is right.

VIII. Deliver us, we pray thee, from the tyranny of trifles. Teach us how to listen to the prompting of thy Spirit, and thus save us from floundering in indecision that wastes time, subtracts from our peace, divides our efficiency, and multiplies our troubles.

RENEWAL

To keep God at the center of one's life requires frequent renewal of power through prayer. But such renewal is not measured by the amount of time it takes, rather by the degree to which one is able even for a short time to have relaxed and unhurried communion with God. One can pray inwardly at any time and anywhere—in a subway or on an athletic field. But one prays best either alone or with understanding friends. To avoid neglecting to pray, it is best to have a time-habit and a place-habit. This is so important that it is worth great effort, in spite of the hurry of life and our lack of privacy.

GEORGIA HARKNESS

Prayer introduces us to the Great Companion who meets our human need with his divine response. The man who has learned to pray is no longer alone in the universe. He is living in his Father's house.

WILLIAM ADAMS BROWN

Who riseth from prayer a better man, his prayer is answered.

GEORGE MEREDITH

Prayer is self-discipline which comes as a result of discovering God's will and then making the necessary adjustments within one's thoughts, feelings, and acts.

CHARLES L. ALLEN

KNEELING

It matters not how oft you kneel
In attitude of prayer so true,
Unless inside, where no man sees,
Your very soul is kneeling too.

MARY L. O'HARA

A METHOD OF PRAYING

1. Be simple and direct in your secret prayer. The grace of simplicity is not to be despised in public prayer; but when we call on God in secret, any formality or elaborateness in our petitions is an offense.

2. Pray audibly. You need not lift your voice to be heard in the street, but it is vastly better to pray not merely in your thoughts but also with words. The utterance of our wants helps to define them.

3. Be honest in your secret prayer. Do not express any want that you do not feel. Do not confess any fault that you do not mean to forsake. Do not keep anything back. Remember that it is He that searcheth the heart to whom you are speaking.

4. Pray earnestly. The words need not be loud, but the desire should be intense. "The fervent, energetic prayer of a righteous man availeth much." "The kingdom of heaven suffereth violence, and the violent take it by force." No listless, drowsy petitioning will serve.

5. Do not mock God in your prayers. Do not beg him to come to you. You know that he is never far from any soul that seeks him. That prayer is answered before you utter it. Do not ask God to do for you that which he has expressly bidden you to do.

6. Pray always with special reference to the needs of the day and the hour;—the warfare to be waged, the temptations to be resisted, the work to be done, the sorrow to be borne; put your life into your prayer; and let it be the most real and the most immediate business of your life.

WALTER RAUSCHENBUSCH

TWO-WAY STREET

Prayer is neither black magic nor is it a form of demand note. Prayer is a relationship. The act of praying is more analogous to clearing away the underbrush which shuts out a view than it is to begging in the street. There are many different kinds of prayer. Yet all prayer has one basic purpose. We pray not to get something, but to open up a two-way street between us and God, so that we and others may inwardly become something.

JOHN HEUSS

TESTIMONY

Personal prayer, it seems to me, is one of the simplest necessities of life, as basic to the individual as sunshine, food and water—and at times, of course, more so. By prayer I believe we mean an effort to get in touch with the Infinite. We know that our prayers are imperfect. Of course they are. We are imperfect human beings. A thousand experiences have convinced me beyond room of doubt that prayer multiplies the strength of the individual and brings within the scope of his capabilities almost any conceivable objective.

DWIGHT D. EISENHOWER

THE MEANING OF PRAYER

A breath of prayer in the morning
  Means a day of blessing sure;
A breath of prayer in the evening
  Means a night of rest secure;

A breath of prayer in our weakness
  Means a clasp of a mighty hand;
A breath of prayer when we're lonely
  Means Someone to understand;

A breath of prayer in our sorrows
  Means comfort and peace and rest;
A breath of prayer in our doubtings
  Assures us the Lord knows best;

A breath of prayer in rejoicing
  Gives joy and added delight,
For they that remember God's goodness
  Go singing far into the night.

There's never a year nor a season
  That prayer may not bless every hour,
And never a soul need be helpless
  When linked with God's infinite power.

FRANCES MC KINNON MORTON

THE LITTLE GATE TO GOD

In the castle of my soul
Is a little postern gate,
Whereat, when I enter,
I am in the presense of God.
In a moment, in the turning of a thought,
I am where God is.

WALTER RAUSCHENBUSCH

There are times in a man's life when, regardless of the attitude of the body, the soul is on its knees in prayer.

VICTOR HUGO

THE MASTER'S TOUCH

In the still air the music lies unheard;
  In the rough marble beauty hides unseen:
To make the music and the beauty, needs
  The master's touch, the sculptor's chisel keen.

Great Master, touch us with thy skillful hand;
  Let not the music that is in us die!
Great Sculptor, hew and polish us; nor let,
  Hidden and lost, thy form within us lie!

Spare not the stroke! do with us as thou wilt!
  Let there be naught unfinished, broken marred;
Complete thy purpose, that we may become
  Thy perfect image, thou our God and Lord!

HORATIUS BONAR

TIME EXPOSURE

Prayer is the time exposure of the soul to the highest that we know and he who practices it will learn its central, primary, and transforming importance. Prayer is the fulfillment of man's highest capacity to look not down alone nor out, but up, and to adore. Prayer is the road to the crowning experience of human life, being carried out of ourselves by something greater than ourselves to which we give ourselves. Prayer is taking in earnest the central affirmation of religion that there is a responsive Spirit at the heart of reality in communion with whom is our power and peace. True prayer is never an endeavor to change the divine purpose but is always an endeavor to release it through the one who prays into the world.

HARRY EMERSON FOSDICK

If you would never cease to pray, never cease to long for it. The continuance of your longing is the continuance of your prayer.

ST. AUGUSTINE

⊷⧉⊷

NINE MEMORABLE PRAYERS

I.

O God, grant us the serenity to accept
What cannot be changed;
The courage to change what can be changed;
And wisdom to know one from the other.

REINHOLD NIEBUHR

II.

Beloved Pan, and all ye other gods who haunt
this place, give me beauty in the inward soul;
and may the outward and inward man be at one.

SOCRATES

III.

Grant us grace, Almighty Father, so to pray as
to deserve to be heard.

JANE AUSTEN

IV.

Great Spirit, help me never to judge another
until I have walked in his moccasins.

SIOUX INDIAN PRAYER

V.

O Lord, thou knowest that which is best for us.
Let this or that be done, as thou shalt please.
Give what thou wilt, how much thou wilt, and
when thou wilt.

THOMAS A KEMPIS

VI.

May the wisdom of God instruct me, the eye of
God watch over me, the ear of God hear me,
the word of God give me sweet talk, the hand
of God defend me, the way of God guide me.
  Christ be with me.
  Christ before me.
  Christ in me.
  Christ under me.
  Christ over me.
  Christ on my right hand.
  Christ on my left hand.
  Christ on this side.
  Christ on that side.

Christ in the head of everyone to whom I
  speak.
Christ in the mouth of every person who
  speaks to me.
Christ in the eye of every person who looks
  upon me.
Christ in the ear of everyone who hears me
  today. Amen.

ST. PATRICK

VII.

O Lord, thou knowest how busy I must be this
day. If I forget thee, do not thou forget me.

LORD ASHLEY BEFORE
THE BATTLE OF EDGE HILL

VIII.

Father in Heaven, when the thought of thee
wakes in our hearts, let it not awaken like a
frightened bird that flies about in dismay, but
like a child waking from its sleep with a
heavenly smile.

SØREN KIERKEGAARD

IX.

Teach us, good Lord, to serve thee as thou
  deservest:
  to give and not to count the cost;
  to fight and not to heed the wounds;
  to toil and not to seek for rest;
  to labor and not to ask for any reward
  save that of knowing that we do thy will.

ST. IGNATIUS OF LOYOLA

⊷⧉⊷

THE UNSEEN BRIDGE

There is a bridge whereof the span
Is hidden in the heart of man,
And reaches, without pile or rod,
Into the plenitude of God.

It carries all that honestly
Is faith or hope or charity.
No other traffic will it bear:
This broad yet narrow Bridge of Prayer.

GILBERT THOMAS

⊷⧉⊷

THE EXAMPLE OF CHRIST

His prayer before temptation (Luke 3:21; 4:1-13).

His prayer before appointing the twelve (Luke 6:12-16).

His prayer before the Sermon on the Mount (Luke 6:12, 17-49).

His practice of common prayer (Luke 4:16-32; Mark 1:21-22).

His teaching as to the manner of prayer (Matthew 6:5-8).

His teaching as to the matter of prayer (Matthew 6:9-15).

His teaching as to earnestness in prayer (Matthew 7:7-11; Luke 11:5-10; 18:1-8).

His teaching as to the objective of prayer (Luke 11:11-13).

His prayer after serving the people (Matthew 14:22-23).

His prayer before his glory was manifested (Luke 9:28-36).

His story about vain prayer (Luke 18:9-14).

His prayer in joy (Luke 10:17-24; Matthew 11:25-30).

His teaching as to the condition and power of prayer (Matthew 18:19-20; Mark 11:22-25).

His warning concerning too much formal prayer (Luke 20:45-47; Matthew 6:7-8).

His exhortation to vigilant prayer (Luke 21:34-36; Matthew 24:32; 25:13).

His promises to the prayerful (John 14:12-17; 15:7-10; 16:23-24).

His prayer for all Christians (John 17).

His prayer for himself (Matthew 26:36-44).

His prayers from the cross (Luke 23:34, 46).

WORSHIP RESOURCES FOR
THE CHRISTIAN YEAR

Step softly, under snow or rain,
To find the place where men can pray;
The way is all so very plain
That we may lose the way.

GILBERT KEITH CHESTERTON

LEAVING ALL TO GOD

"Surely," one sometimes hears it said, "it is absurd to try to change the will of God. Who are we that we should tell God what to do? If we believe in God at all, we must believe that he is already ordering all things for the best." Well, let me say that Christian prayer is not telling God what to do; it is rather telling him what we think we need. It is "making our requests known unto him." In the last resort Christian prayer has always left it to God's own wisdom to decide what precisely he is to do about our need. With all his importunity the Christian never ventures to *dictate* to the Most High; he always adds, "If it be thy will."

JOHN BAILLIE

PRIVATE PRAYER

Prayer, the basic exercise of the spirit, must be actively practiced in our private lives. The neglected soul of man must be made strong enough to assert itself once more. For if the power of prayer is again released and used in the lives of common men and women; if the spirit declares its aims clearly and boldly, there is yet hope that our prayers for a better world will be answered.

ALEXIS CARREL

The privilege of prayer to me is one of the most cherished possessions, because faith and experience alike convince me that God himself sees and answers, and his answers I never venture to criticize. It is only my part to ask. If it were otherwise, I would not dare to pray at all.

WILFRED T. GRENFELL

A MEDITATION ON THE LORD'S PRAYER

Our Father, who art in heaven.

Help me to believe this day that there is a power to lift me up which is stronger than all the things that hold me down.

Hallowed be Thy Name.

Help me to be sensitive to what is beautiful, and responsive to what is good, so that day by day I may grow more sure of the holiness of life in which I want to trust.

Thy Kingdom come.

Help me to be quick to see, and ready to encourage, whatever brings the better meaning of God into that which otherwise might be the common round of the uninspired day.

Thy will be done, on earth as it is in heaven.

Help me to believe that the ideals of the spirit are not a far-off dream, but a power to command loyalty and direct my life here on our real earth.

Give us this day our daily bread.

Open the way for me to earn an honest living without anxiety; but let me never forget the needs of others, and make me want only that benefit for myself which will also be their gain.

And forgive us our trespasses, as we forgive those who trespass against us.

Make me patient and sympathetic with the shortcomings of others, especially of those I love; and keep me sternly watchful only of my own. Let me never grow hard with the unconscious cruelty of those who measure themselves by mean standards, and so think they have excelled. Keep my eyes lifted to the highest, so that I may be forgiving, because I know how much there is of which I need to be forgiven.

And lead us not into temptation, but deliver us from evil.

Let me not go carelessly this day within the reach of any evil I cannot resist, but if in the path of duty I must go where temptation is, give me strength of spirit to meet it without fear.

For thine is the kingdom, and the power, and the glory for ever and ever. Amen.

WALTER RUSSELL BOWIE

ANSWERS

Answers to prayer often come in unexpected ways. We pray, for instance, for a certain virtue; but God seldom delivers Christian virtues all wrapped in a package and ready for use. Rather he puts us in situations where by his help we can develop those virtues. Henry Ward Beecher told of a woman who prayed for patience, and God sent her a poor cook. The best answers to prayer may be the vision and strength to meet a circumstance or to assume a responsibility.

C. R. FINDLEY

NO LIMIT

Let there be no limit to what we take to God in prayer, so that there may be no limit to God's reign and rule in all of life. It is far better to ask God for whatever we desire than to play God by deciding on our own what we ought to pray for. That would simply be pious magic all over again, wanting to control God by praying for the right things in a way that is sure to get results. God himself will be the judge; ours is the task of putting everything up to him.

ROGER HAZELTON

PRAYER

Lord, what a change within us one short hour
Spent in thy presence will prevail to make!
What heavy burdens from our bosoms take,
What parched grounds refresh as with a
    shower!
We kneel, and all around us seems to lower;
We rise, and all, the distant and the near,
Stands forth in sunny outline brave and clear;
We kneel, how weak! we rise, how full of
    power!
Why, therefore, should we do ourselves this
    wrong,
Or others, that we are not always strong,
That we are ever overborne with care,
That we should ever weak or heartless be,
Anxious or troubled, when with us is prayer,
And joy and strength and courage are with thee!

RICHARD CHENEVIX TRENCH

❦

He that enjoys aught without thanksgiving is
as though he robbed God.

ST. CHRYSOSTOM

❦

GOD'S COMMUNICATIONS

It is a mistake to assume that God's communications to us are limited to technical speech,
whether of the written or the spoken word.
Even our friends who walk by our side have
many languages other than words. They speak
to us in gestures, in the glow or gloom of their
faces, in a touch of the hand, in a token secretly
left where we shall find it. Often their most
meaningful communication is by the way of
silence. So also God speaks to us in the multitudinous voices of nature, the blessings of his
providence, the turning of an event. All our environment is vocal with his goodness, and those
voiceless promptings from out the silence of
our soul are the fleet messengers of his will.

THE DAILY ALTAR

❦

AMEN

This little word has entered more languages
(perhaps over 1000) than any other single
word in a human speech. How that came to be
is a fascinating story. It is said that in Alexandria, Egypt, around 250 B.C.E., King Ptolemy
desired a translation of the Hebrew Bible. He
set 70 or 72 scholars, chosen from the Jewish
community, to work on the translation. They
reached the word "Amen," first cousin of *Emet*
(truth). "Amen" meant "So be it" or "May
this prayer come true." There was no single
Greek word expressing this thought, so they
turned it into a Greek word—"Amen." When
the Bible was translated into Latin, "Amen"
became a Latin word. And so it went.

❦

A PRAYER

Teach me, Father, how to go
Softly as the grasses grow;
Hush my soul to meet the shock
Of the wild world as a rock;
But my spirit, propt with power,
Make as simple as a flower.
Let the dry heart fill its cup,
Like a poppy looking up;
Let life lightly wear her crown,
Like a poppy looking down,
When its heart is filled with dew,
And its life begins anew.

Teach me, Father, how to be
Kind and patient as a tree.
Joyfully the crickets croon
Under shady oak at noon;
Beetle, on his mission bent,
Tarries in that cooling tent.
Let me, also, cheer a spot,
Hidden field or garden grot—
Place where passing souls can rest
On the way and be their best.

EDWIN MARKHAM

RELIGION

The universe is centered on neither the earth nor the sun.
It is centered on God.

ALFRED NOYES

Religion does not occupy any one part of man's life. It is the reaction of a man's whole being to his object of highest loyalty. Religion must be felt and thought. It must be lived out; it must translate itself into action. Religion is not a segment of life, nor is it connected with any one time or place. It is not just ritual, ceremony, doctrines, or the church, even though these may all be aids in stimulating it. The great religious leaders of the race have spoken of religion as a vital, personal experience. This experience grows out of real needs—the need for courage and companionship in life. Micah speaks of man's chief duty "To love mercy, to do justly, and to walk humbly with thy God." For Jesus the great commandments were love of God and love of one's neighbor. Whether religion has been interpreted as man's co-operative quest for the values of life or as "the Spirit of God in the soul of man," it has been stressed as involving the whole of life.

HAROLD H. TITUS

❧❀☙

Religion's place in the world is to help, to speak to men and women, certainly in the whole range of their lives, but especially at their deepest levels of need. In sickness and sorrow, in failure and despair, in the face of the baffling complexities, inconsistencies, seeming injustices, the sheer idiotism of much of our world— it is here especially, and not on happy, sunny Sunday mornings, that Christ seeks to come, and it is in such situations that men's real need for him is born.

NATHAN M. PUSEY

❧❀☙

Jesus is God spelling himself out in language that man can understand.

S. D. GORDON

❧❀☙

To fall in love with God is the greatest of all romances;
To seek him, the greatest adventure;
To find him, the greatest human achievement.

RAPHAEL SIMON

❧❀☙

TRUE SOURCE

Your religion is good if it is vital and active; if it nourishes in you confidence, hope, love, and a sentiment of the infinite value of existence; if it is allied with what is best in you against what is worst, and holds forever before you the necessity of becoming a new man; if it makes you understand that pain is a deliverer; if it increases your respect for the conscience of others; if it renders forgiveness more easy, fortune less arrogant, duty dear, the beyond less visionary. If it does these things, it is good, little matter its name; however rudimentary it may be when it fills this office, it comes from the true source, it binds you to man and to God.

CHARLES WAGNER

❧❀☙

THE GOAL

All roads that lead to God are good;
What matters it, your faith or mine;
Both center at the goal divine
Of love's eternal brotherhood.

A thousand creeds have come and gone;
But what is that to you or me?
Creeds are but branches of a tree,
The root of love lives on and on.

Though branch by branch proves withered wood,
The root is warm with precious wine;
Then keep your faith, and leave me mine;
All roads that lead to God are good.

ELLA WHEELER WILCOX

WHAT IS RELIGION?

Religion in the life of man is a momentary glance from time into eternity.

It is Augustine visioning his *Civitas Dei* when the City of Man is about to crumble.

It is Pythagoras discerning eternal truths in the framework of a right triangle.

It is Plato grasping Beauty, Truth, and Goodness as eternal verities through human reason.

It is Edna St. Vincent Millay writing "Renascence" and crying out,

> The soul can split the sky in two,
> And let the fact of God shine through

It is Socrates saying, "Knowledge is virtue."

It is Newton at twenty-four discovering the binomial theorem and the law of gravitation.

It is Händel with a paralyzed limb, destitute of money, facing imprisonment, gathering new courage and writing his greatest oratorio, *The Messiah.*

It is Paul hearing the voice of his Lord on the Damascus Road.

It is Jesus in terrible agony crying, "Father, into thy hands I commit my spirit."

It is an ordinary man dedicating every fiber of himself to the betterment of the world.

It is Albrecht Dürer painting his "Praying Hands."

It is Washington praying alone at Valley Forge.

It is Isaiah changing his purple garments of a prince for the tattered cloth of a prophet to save a nation from chaos.

It is Augustine forsaking a lustful heart and fleeing into the arms of God, and later becoming the Bishop of Hippo.

It is a priest jotting down the last words of a dying marine at Guadalcanal and composing a letter of comfort to a widowed mother in St. Louis.

It is Jesus saying to his disciples, "Take up your cross and follow me."

It is a teacher refusing a gainful salary elsewhere that he may instruct youth in the wisdom of the ages.

It is Mary weeping at the foot of the cross.

It is Clement of Alexandria interpreting the divine Logos as the inspiration for all truth.

It is a father sacrificing a suit of clothes that his son may stay in college.

It is a widow in a tenement taking in washing to support three orphaned children of a former neighbor across the hall.

It is Luther standing firm at Worms saying, "I cannot and will not recant anything, since it is unsafe and dangerous to do anything against the conscience."

It is Francis of Assisi preaching to the birds and the flowers.

It is a man centering his focus on God and not himself, and finding his life changed from a state of worry to a state of wonder.

It is Edith Cavell before a firing squad in Brussels saying, "Patriotism is not enough."

It is a man saying, "My soul is so absorbed in the bigger issues of life that I cannot afford to be jealous and suspicious of any person."

It is the sacrifice of a meal by an American family in order that starvation in China may be averted.

It is Bernard at a monastery in Clairvaux in love with Christ and married to the church.

It is Servetus burning at the stake in Geneva for the sake of truth.

It is Amos forsaking his flock at Tekoa to preach against hypocrisy at Bethel.

It is Schleiermacher discerning religion as man's feeling of absolute dependence upon God.

It is Katherine Mansfield saying about her literary creations shortly before her death, "Not one of these writings dare I show to God."

It is Thomas Aquinas wedding reason and faith.

It is my feeling of humility when I contemplate God as the Life of a universe extending a million light years into space.

It is Deutero-Isaiah discerning the nations as

specks of sand when compared to God's majesty and infinity.

It is my little self on a second-rate planet eradicating fear, self-centeredness, resentment, and guilt in order that it may become an instrument of God's energetic redemptive love.

It is the writer of the Gospel of John reporting, "Let not your hearts be troubled; believe in God."

Yes, these are all religion. For religion is as big as life and as normal an experience as breathing, eating, and sleeping.

THOMAS S. KEPLER

UNBELIEF

There is no unbelief;
Whoever plants a seed beneath the sod
And waits to see it push away the clod,
 He trusts in God.

Whoever says when clouds are in the sky,
"Be patient, heart; light breaketh by and by,"
 Trusts the Most High.

Whoever sees 'neath winter's field of snow,
The silent harvest of the future grow,
 God's power must know.

Whoever lies down on his couch to sleep,
Content to lock each sense in slumber deep,
 Knows God will keep.

Whoever says "To-morrow," "The unknown,"
"The future," trusts that Power alone
 He dares disown.

The heart that looks on when the eye-lids close,
And dares to live when life has only woes,
 God's comfort knows.

There is no unbelief;
For thus by day and night unconsciously
The heart lives by the faith the lips deny.
 God knoweth why!

ELIZABETH YORK CASE

The nature of God is a circle whose center is everywhere and whose circumference is nowhere.

ST. AUGUSTINE

PATHWAY

Religion is the first beautiful companion that man encountered in his wilderness. It is the pathway between life and death that is worn deepest by the feet of perpetually seeking generations. It is never far away when man knows exaltation and rapture. It is always present when he transcends himself in unearthly consecrations. It opens the door of vision when his genius hungers and thirsts for the substance behind all symbols, and other hands that can open it there is none. It is by his side when he walks the high and lonely places where he makes the discovery of himself. In life it is with him, illuminating him at his noblest, scourging him at his basest—the latter presence even more wistfully loved than the former. Neither in death does it leave him; but when al other voices mourn of irreparable defeat, it alone lifts the cry of defiance and stands on the ruins of mortality announcing mysterious and splendid victory for the fallen.

WILLIAM L. SULLIVAN

GOD'S ALTAR

There is in all the sons of men
A love that in the spirit dwells,
That panteth after things unseen,
And tidings of the future tells.

And God hath built his altar here
To keep this fire of faith alive,
And sent his priests in holy fear
To speak the truth—for truth to strive.

RALPH WALDO EMERSON

SANCTUARY

Let us put by some hour of every day
For holy things—whether it be when dawn
Peers through the window pane, or when noon
Flames, like a burnished topaz, in the vault,
Or when the thrush pours in the ear of eve
Its plaintive melody; some little hour
Wherein to hold rapt converse with the soul,
From sordidness and self a sanctuary,
Swept by the winnowings of unseen things,
And touched by the White Light ineffable!

CLINTON SCOLLARD

CERTAINTY

Religion exists not to answer all questions, or to clear up all mysteries; if that were its purpose, it could never be accomplished, for life grows, not less, but more mysterious as the intellect enters more fully into its truth.

The stars were wonderful enough in all conscience, when we thought of them as lamps of light set in a solid sky to guide the sailors on their journey over the trackless sea; but they are a million times more wonderful, now that we know them to be blazing worlds, that move through the vast infinities of space in accordance with exact mathematical laws.

Our own bodies were wonderful enough, when we thought of them as created in a moment by the fiat of the Almighty from the dust of the earth; but how much more wonderful they have become since the sciences of physiology and embryology have taught us to trace their growth through countless stages, from the humblest kind of beginning to their present complex end.

Knowledge does not take from, it adds to, the wonder of the world. It is an infallible rule that the more a man knows the less he knows. He knows that he knows nothing compared with what there is to know—that he is but a child playing on the shore of an infinite sea of truth and picking up tiny pearls of wisdom that, by the grace of God, are cast up at his feet.

Religion leaves a million questions unanswered and apparently unanswerable. Its purpose and object is not to make a man certain and cock-sure about everything, but to make him certain about those things of which he must be certain if he is to live a human life at all. Religion does not relieve us from the duty of thought; it makes possible for a man to begin thinking.

G. A. STUDDERT-KENNEDY

WHAT IS GOD?

Creator of minds to receive his own fullness,
imparting to them life to be conscious of him,
prompting them to desire him,
enlarging them to receive him,
fitting them to be worthy of him,
enkindling them with zeal,
aiding them to yield fruit,
directing them to equity,
fashioning them to benevolence,
tempering them for wisdom,
strengthening them for virtue,
visiting them for consolation,
illuminating them for knowledge,
preserving them for immortality,
enriching them for felicity,
surrounding them with protection.

ST. BERNARD OF CLAIRVAUX

It is hard enough to make one Christian, harder still to make a Christian church. To make a Christian nation is a task to stagger the imagination; to make a Christian world may well seem all but impossible. Yet this, no less, is the goal to which our religion sets us.

WILLIAM ADAMS BROWN

HIS NAME

Does he keep you from sin? Call him Savior.

Does he free you from the slavery of your passions? Call him Redeemer.

Does he teach you as no one else has taught you? Call him Teacher.

Does he mold and master your life? Call him Master.

Does he shine upon the pathway that is dark to you? Call him Guide.

Does he reveal God to you? Call him the Son of God.

Does he reveal man? Call him the Son of Man.

Or in following him are your lips silent in your incapacity to depict him and his influence upon you? Call him by no name, but follow him.

CARL HOPKINS ELMORE

There's a divinity that shapes our ends,
Rough hew them how we will.

WILLIAM SHAKESPEARE

WHAT DOES CHRISTIANITY MEAN?

In the home—kindness.
In business—honesty.
In society—courtesy.
In work—thoroughness.
In play—fairness.
To the unfortunate—pity.
To sin—resistance.
To the strong—trust and good will.
To the weak—help.
To the penitent—forgiveness.
To all men—reverence and love.
To God—worship and service.

CHARLES F. BANNING

Religion means faith that man's ideals are achievable and will be achieved.

JEROME FRANK

Religion should be our steering wheel, not our spare tire.

CHARLES L. WHEELER

SERMON ON THE MOUNT

If you were to take the sum total of all the authoritative articles ever written by the most qualified of psychologists and psychiatrists on the subject of mental hygiene, if you were to combine them and refine them and cleave out the excess verbiage, if you were to take the whole of the meat and none of the parsley, and if you were to have these unadulterated bits of pure scientific knowledge concisely expressed by the most capable of living poets, you would have an awkward and incomplete summation of the Sermon on the Mount.

JAMES T. FISHER

GOD'S MEDICINE

During the past thirty years, people from all civilized countries on the earth have consulted me. Among all my patients in the second half of life—that is to say, over thirty-five—there has not been one whose problem in the last resort was not that of finding a religious outlook on life. It is safe to say that every one of them fell ill because he had lost that which the living religions of every age have given to their followers, and none of them has been really healed who did not regain his religious outlook.

C. G. JUNG

EXPERIMENT

In its essence the Gospel is a call to make the experiment of comradeship, the experiment of fellowship, the experiment of trusting the heart of things, throwing self-care to the winds, in the sure and certain faith that you will not be deserted, forsaken nor betrayed, and that your ultimate interests are perfectly secure in the hands of the Great Companion. This insight is the center, the kernel, the growing point of the Christian religion, which, when we have it, all else is secure, and when we have it not, all else is precarious.

L. P. JACKS

This is what I found out about religion: it gives you courage to make the decisions you must make in a crisis and the confidence to leave the results to a higher Power. Only by trust in God can a man carrying responsibility find repose.

DWIGHT D. EISENHOWER

No man has a right to lead such a life of contemplation as to forget in his own ease the service due to his neighbor; nor has any man a right to be so immersed in active life as to neglect the contemplation of God.

ST. AUGUSTINE

God has a purpose for each one of us, a work for each one to do, a place for each one to fill, an influence for each one to exert, a likeness to his dear Son for each one to manifest, and then, a place for each one to fill in his holy temple.

ARTHUR C. A. HALL

SO MANY!

So many stars in the infinite space—
So many worlds in the light of God's face.

So many storms ere the thunders shall cease—
So many paths to the portals of Peace.

So many years, so many tears—
Sighs and sorrows and pangs and prayers.

So many ships in the desolate night—
So many harbors, and only one Light.

So many creeds like the weeds in the sod—
So many temples, and only one God.

FRANK L. STANTON

GOD BE IN MY HEAD

God be in my head,
   And in my understanding;

God be in my eyes,
   And in my looking;

God be in my mouth,
   And in my speaking;

God be in my heart,
   And in my thinking;

God be at my end,
   And at my departing.

SARUM PRIMER

Even a little Christianity personally possessed is worth an infinite amount of Christianity externally copied.

HARRY EMERSON FOSDICK

Christainity even when watered down is hot enough to boil all modern society to rags.

GILBERT KEITH CHESTERTON

THANKFULNESS

*A single grateful thought
toward heaven
is the most complete prayer.*

GOTTHOLD LESSING

PRAYER

Oh, Lord, I thank you for the privilege and gift of living in a world filled with beauty and excitement and variety.

I thank you for the gift of loving and being loved, for the friendliness and understanding and beauty of the animals on the farm and in the forest and marshes, for the green of the trees, the sound of a waterfall, the darting beauty of the trout in the brook.

I thank you for the delights of music and children, of other men's thoughts and conversation and their books to read by the fireside or in bed with the rain falling on the roof or the snow blowing past outside the window.

LOUIS BROMFIELD

❧❦❧

Gratitude consists in a watchful, minute attention to the particulars of our state, and to the multitude of God's gifts, taken one by one. It fills us with a consciousness that God loves and cares for us, even to the least event and smallest need of life. It is a blessed thought that from our childhood God has been laying his fatherly hands upon us, and always in benediction, and that even the strokes of his hands are blessings, and among the chiefest we have ever received.

HENRY EDWARD MANNING

❧❦❧

THE HEART'S GRATITUDE

As flowers carry dewdrops, trembling on the edges of the petals, and ready to fall at the first waft of the wind or brush of bird, so the heart should carry its beaded words of thanksgiving. At the first breath of heavenly flavor, let down the shower, perfumed with the heart's gratitude.

HENRY WARD BEECHER

❧❦❧

THANKSGIVING

We thank thee, Father, for the care
That did not come to try us;
The burden that we did not bear,
The trouble that passed by us;
The task we did not fail to do,
The hurt we did not cherish;
The friend who did not prove untrue,
The joy that did not perish.
We thank thee for the blinding storm
That did not lose its swelling;
And for the sudden blight of harm
That came not nigh our dwelling.
We thank thee for the dart unsped,
The bitter word unspoken,
The grave unmade, the tear unshed,
The heart-tie still unbroken.

❧❦❧

God is glorified, not by our groans, but by our thanksgivings.

EDWIN PERCY WHIPPLE

❧❦❧

THANK YOU

It was inevitable, I suppose, that in the garden I should begin, at long last, to ask myself what lay behind all this beauty. When guests were gone and I had the flowers to myself, I was so happy that I wondered why at the same time I was haunted by a sense of emptiness. It was as though I wanted to thank somebody, but had nobody to thank; which is another way of saying that I felt the need for worship. That is, perhaps, the kindliest way in which a man may come to his God. There is an interminable literature on the origins of the religious impulse, but to me it is simpler than that. It is summed up in the image of a man at sundown, watching the crimson flowering of the sky and saying—to somebody—"Thank you."

BEVERLY NICHOLS

FATHER, WE THANK THEE

Father, we thank thee:
For peace within our favored land,
For plenty from thy bounteous hand,
For means to give to those in need,
For grace to help in thought and deed,
For faith to walk, our hands in thine,
For truth to know thy law divine,
For strength to work with voice and pen,
For love to serve our fellow men,
For light the goal ahead to see,
For life to use alone for thee,
Father, we thank thee.

GRENVILLE KLEISER

THE ART OF THANKSGIVING

The art of thanksgiving is thanksliving. It is gratitude in action. It is applying Albert Schweitzer's philosophy: "In gratitude for your own good fortune you must render in return some sacrifice of your life for other life."

It is thanking God for the gift of life by living it triumphantly.

It is thanking God for your talents and abilities by accepting them as obligations to be invested for the common good.

It is thanking God for all that men and women have done for you by doing things for others.

It is thanking God for opportunities by accepting them as a challenge to achievement.

It is thanking God for happiness by striving to make others happy.

It is thanking God for beauty by helping to make the world more beautiful.

It is thanking God for inspiration by trying to be an inspiration to others.

It is thanking God for health and strength by the care and reverence you show your body.

It is thanking God for the creative ideas that enrich life by adding your own creative contributions to human progress.

It is thanking God for each new day by living it to the fullest.

It is thanking God by giving hands, arms, legs, and voice to your thankful spirit.

It is adding to your prayers of thanksgiving, acts of thanksliving.

WILFERD A. PETERSON

THANKS BE TO GOD

I do not thank thee, Lord,
That I have bread to eat while others starve;
Nor yet for work to do
While empty hands solicit heaven;
Nor for a body strong
While other bodies flatten beds of pain.
No, not for these do I give thanks!

But I am grateful, Lord,
Because my meager loaf I may divide;
For that my busy hands
May move to meet another's need;
Because my doubled strength
I may expend to steady one who faints.
Yes, for all these do I give thanks!

For heart to share, desire to bear
And will to lift,
Flamed into one by deathless Love—
Thanks be to God for this!
Unspeakable! His Gift!

JANIE ALFORD

SUREST WAY

If anyone would tell you the shortest, surest way to happiness and all perfection, he must tell you to make it a rule to yourself to thank and praise God for everything that happens to you. For it is certain that whatever seeming calamity happens to you, if you thank and praise God for it, you turn it into a blessing.

WILLIAM LAW

216

TODeAY

I have no Yesterdays,
Time took them away;
Tomorrow may not be—
But I have Today.
PEARL YEADON McGINNIS

THE DAY

The day will bring some lovely thing,
I say it over each new dawn;
"Some gay, adventurous thing to hold
Against my heart, when it is gone."
And so I rise and go to meet
The day with wings upon my feet.

I come upon it unaware—
Some sudden beauty without name;
A snatch of song, a breath of pine;
A poem lit with golden flame;
High tangled bird notes, keenly thinned,
Like flying color on the wing.

No day has ever failed me quite—
Before the grayest day is done,
I come upon some misty bloom
Or a late line of crimson sun.
Each night I pause, remembering
Some gay, adventurous, lovely thing.

GRACE NOLL CROWELL

❧

JUST FOR TODAY

Just for today, I will try to live through this
day only, and not tackle my whole life problem at once. I can do something for twelve
hours that would appall me if I felt that I
had to keep it up for a lifetime.

Just for today, I will be happy. This assumes to
be true what Abraham Lincoln said, that
"most folks are as happy as they make up
their minds to be."

Just for today, I will try to strengthen my mind.
I will study. I will learn something useful.
I will not be a mental loafer. I will read
something that requires effort, thought and
concentration.

Just for today, I will adjust myself to what is,
and not try to adjust everything to my own
desires. I will take my "luck" as it comes,
and fit myself to it.

Just for today, I will exercise my soul in three
ways: I will do somebody a good turn, and
not get found out. I will do at least two

things I don't want to do—just for exercise.
I will not show anyone that my feelings are
hurt; they may be hurt, but today I will not
show it.

Just for today, I will be agreeable. I will look
as well as I can, dress becomingly, talk low,
act courteously, criticize not one bit, not
find fault with anything and not try to im-
prove or regulate anybody except myself.

Just for today, I will have a program. I may not
follow it exactly, but I will have it. I will
save myself from two pests: hurry and indecision.

Just for today, I will have a quiet half hour all
by myself, and relax. During this half hour,
sometime, I will try to get a better perspective
of my life.

Just for today, I will be unafraid. Especially I
will not be afraid to enjoy what is beautiful,
and to believe that as I give to the world, so
the world will give to me.

KENNETH L. HOLMES

❧

Let us then think only of the present, and not
even permit our minds to wander with curiosity
into the future. This future is not yet ours;
perhaps it never will be. It is exposing ourselves to temptation to wish to anticipate God,
and to prepare ourselves for things which he
may not destine for us. If such things should
come to pass, he will give us light and strength
according to the need. Why should we desire
to meet difficulties prematurely, when we have
neither strength nor light as yet provided for
them? Let us give heed to the present, whose
duties are pressing; it is fidelity to the present
which prepares us for fidelity in the future.

FRANÇOIS FÉNELON

❧

We live on a moving line between past and
future. That line is our lifeline.

GEORGE A. BUTTRICK

219

THREE DAYS

Yesterday . . .
Like mintage spent, is past recall;
Its echo dimmed beyond time's wall.

Tomorrow . . .
It never promised earthly man,
Nor does it often fit a plan.

Today . . .
Is gold that covers hills and dell,
And rich are they who use it well.

PEARL PHILLIPS

THE SALUTATION OF THE DAWN

Listen to the Exhortation of the Dawn!
Look to this Day!
For it is Life, the very Life of Life.
In its brief course lie all the
Verities and Realities of your Existence:
 The Bliss of Growth,
 The Glory of Action,
 The Splendor of Beauty,
For Yesterday is but a Dream,
And Tomorrow is only a Vision:
But Today well-lived makes
Every Yesterday a Dream of Happiness,
And every Tomorrow a Vision of Hope.
Look well therefore to this Day!
Such is the Salutation of the Dawn!

BASED ON THE SANSKRIT

There is a kind of release that comes directly to those who have undergone an ordeal and who know, having survived it, that they are equal to all of life's occasions.

LEWIS MUMFORD

A FENCE OF TRUST

Build a little fence of trust around today,
Fill the space with loving deeds and therein
 stay;
Look not through the sheltering bars upon
 tomorrow,
God will help thee bear what comes of joy or
 sorrow.

MARY FRANCES BUTTS

TIME

Take time to pray . . . it helps to bring God near and washes the dust of earth from your eyes.
Take time for friends . . . it is the source of happiness.
Take time for work . . . it is the price of success.
Take time to think . . . it is the source of power.
Take time to read . . . it is the foundation of knowledge.
Take time to laugh . . . it is the singing that helps with life's loads.
Take time to love . . . it is the one sacrament of life.
Take time to dream . . . it hitches the soul to the stars.
Take time to play . . . it is the secret of youth.
Take time to worship . . . it is the highway to reverence.

ONE DAY AT A TIME

Finish every day and be done with it. You have done what you could. Some blunders and absurdities no doubt crept in; forget them as soon as you can. Tomorrow is a new day; begin it well and serenely and with too high a spirit to be cumbered with your old nonsense. This day is all that is good and fair. It is too dear, with its hopes and invitations, to waste a moment on yesterdays.

RALPH WALDO EMERSON

PRAYER AT EVENTIDE

I bring thee now, O God, the parcel of a completed day. For I have wrapped it in my thoughts, tied it with my acts, and stored it in the purposes for which I live.

As the evening falls and while I seek thy face in prayer, grant unto me the joy of good friends, the curative power of new interests, the peace of the quiet heart.

Bestow upon me, Eternal Spirit, light as darkness comes—

Light not of the sun but of the soul, not for the eye but for the mind.

Light by which to judge the errors and the wisdom of the day's work.

Light for the path that the soul must find in the tangled ways of coming days.

And grant thou again the healing touch of sleep.

PERCY ROY HAYWARD

EARLY RISERS

Abraham rose early to stand before the Lord (Genesis 19:27).

Jacob rose early to worship the Lord (Genesis 28:18).

Moses rose early to give God's message to Pharaoh (Exodus 8:20).

Moses rose early to build an altar to God (Exodus 24:4).

Moses rose early to meet God at Sinai (Exodus 34:4).

Joshua rose early to lead Israel over Jordan (Joshua 3:1).

Joshua rose early to capture Jericho (Joshua 6:12).

Joshua rose early to take Ai (Joshua 8:10).

Gideon rose early to examine the fleece (Judges 6:38).

Hannah and Elkanah rose early to worship God (I Samuel 1:9).

Samuel rose early to meet Saul (I Samuel 15:12).

David rose early to do as his father bade him (I Samuel 17:20).

Job rose early to offer sacrifices for his children (Job 1:5).

The Son of God rose early to go to a solitary place to pray (Mark 1:35).

Jesus rose early to go to the temple to pray (John 8:2).

The people rose early to go hear him (Luke 21:38).

The women rose early to go to the sepulcher (Mark 16:2).

ROBERT G. LEE

Most of us wait until we're in trouble, and then we pray like the dickens. Wonder what would happen if, some morning, we'd wake up and say, "Anything I can do for *You* today, Lord?"

BURTON HILLIS

TODAY

So here hath been dawning
   Another blue day:
Think, wilt thou let it
   Slip useless away?

Out of Eternity
   This new day is born;
Into Eternity,
   At night, will return.

Behold it aforetime
   No eye ever did;
So soon it forever
   From all eyes is hid.

Here hath been dawning
   Another blue day:
Think, wilt thou let it
   Slip useless away?

THOMAS CARLYLE

≈§§≈

God broke the years to hours and days,
That hour by hour   1.5
And day by day,
Just going on a little way,
We might be able all along
To keep quite strong.

GEORGE KLINGLE

≈§§≈

He who every morning plans the transactions of the day and follows out that plan carries a thread that will guide him through the labyrinth of the most busy life. The orderly arrangement of his time is like a ray of light which darts itself through all his occupations. But where no plan is laid, where the disposal of time is surrendered merely to the chance of incidents, chaos will soon reign.

VICTOR HUGO

≈§§≈

LIVE TODAY

Forget the past and live the present hour;
Now is the time to work, the time to fill
The soul with noblest thoughts, the time to will
Heroic deeds, to use whatever dower
Heaven has bestowed, to test our utmost power.

Now is the time to love, and better still,
To serve our loved ones, over passing ill
To rise triumphant; thus the perfect flower
Of life shall come to fruitage; wealth amass
For grandest giving ere the time be gone.

Be glad today, tomorrow may bring tears;
Be brave today, the darkest night will pass,
And golden rays will usher in the dawn;
Who conquers now shall rule the coming years.

SARAH KNOWLES BOLTON

≈§§≈

Human nature craves a certain amount of variety. We plant several kinds of flowers in our gardens. We enjoy our meals most when the selection of food is varied from day to day. The same principle applies to our daily activities.

HAROLD SHRYOCK

≈§§≈

APPOINTED MOMENT

Things come to pass as they do and when they do because the time is ripe. Events come into being because the world is ready for them. Nothing comes unannounced or unexpected. If we could interpret accurately the forces and the tumults that play in the world we should never be caught off guard. Nothing ever happens until the hour has struck. Life in this universe runs on a divine schedule. The celestial calendar marks with an unerring precision the exact arrival of events. In the belfry of heaven the clock always strikes on time; it is never early, and it is never late. The ships of destiny arrive at their ports of call at the moment they should arrive. If we could untangle the mysteries of life and unravel the energies which run through the world; if we could evaluate correctly the significance of passing events; if we could measure the struggles, dilemmas, and aspirations of mankind, we would find that nothing is born out of time. Everything comes at its appointed moment.

JOSEPH R. SIZOO

≈§§≈

PROCRASTINATION

One of the most tragic things I know about human nature is that all of us tend to put off living. We are all dreaming of some magical rose garden over the horizon—instead of enjoying the roses that are blooming outside our windows today.

DALE CARNEGIE

TROUBLE

We shall steer safely through every storm,
so long as our heart is right,
our intention fervent, our courage steadfast,
and our trust fixed on God.

ST. FRANCIS DE SALES

All problems become smaller if you don't dodge them but confront them. Touch a thistle timidly, and it pricks you; grasp it boldly, and its spines crumble.

WILLIAM S. HALSEY

❧

OUT IN THE FIELDS WITH GOD

The little cares that fretted me,
  I lost them yesterday,
Among the fields above the sea,
  Among the winds at play,
Among the lowing of the herds,
  The rustling of the trees,
Among the singing of the birds,
  The humming of the bees.

The foolish fears of what might pass
  I cast them all away
Among the clover-scented grass
  Among the new-mown hay,
Among the rustling of the corn
  Where drowsy poppies nod,
Where ill thoughts die and good are born—
  Out in the fields with God!

❧

Man is born broken. He lives by mending. The grace of God is glue!

EUGENE O'NEILL

❧

PRAYER

White Captain of my soul, lead on;
I follow thee, come dark or dawn.
Only vouchsafe three things I crave:
Where terror stalks, help me be brave!
Where righteous ones can scarce endure
The siren call, help me be pure!
Where vows grow dim, and men dare do
What once they scorned, help me be true!

ROBERT FREEMAN

❧

I am an old man and have known a great many troubles, but most of them have never happened.

MARK TWAIN

❧

Trouble and perplexity drive us to prayer, and prayer driveth away trouble and perplexity.

PHILIP MELANCHTHON

❧

GIVING BACK

Some people have a belief that every tree, when it burns, gives back the colors that went into its making—they see in the flaming logs the red of many sunsets, the purple of early dawn, the silver of moonrise and the sparkle of stars. So it is with us: what we have accepted into our hearts and made a permanent part of ourselves is given back in times of trials.

FULTON J. SHEEN

❧

MAKE A PEARL

Most of us can afford to take a lesson from the oyster. The most extraordinary thing about the oyster is this. Irritations get into his shell. He does not like them; he tries to get rid of them. But when he cannot get rid of them he settles down to make of them one of the most beautiful things in the world. He uses the irritation to do the loveliest thing that an oyster ever has a chance to do. If there are irritations in our lives today, there is only one prescription: make a pearl. It may have to be a pearl of patience, but, anyhow, make a pearl. And it takes faith and love to do it.

HARRY EMERSON FOSDICK

❧

REMEMBRANCE

Undaunted by Decembers,
  The sap is faithful yet.
The giving earth remembers
  And only men forget.

JOHN G. NEIHARDT

What life means to us is determined not so much by what life brings to us as by the attitude we bring to life; not so much by what happens to us as by our reaction to what happens.

LEWIS L. DUNNINGTON

PLEASURE AND SORROW

I walked a mile with Pleasure,
  She chattered all the way,
But left me none the wiser
  For all she had to say.

I walked a mile with Sorrow,
  And ne'er a word said she;
But, oh, the things I learned from her
  When Sorrow walked with me!

ROBERT BROWNING HAMILTON

GETHSEMANE

All those who journey, soon or late,
Must pass within the garden's gate;
Must kneel alone in darkness there,
And battle with some fierce despair.
God pity those who cannot say:
"Not mine but thine"; who only pray:
"Let this cup pass," and cannot see
The purpose in Gethsemane.

ELLA WHEELER WILCOX

Only in winter can you tell which trees are truly green. Only when the winds of adversity blow can you tell whether an individual or a country has courage and steadfastness.

JOHN F. KENNEDY

CHANGE

We do not succeed in changing things according to our desire, but gradually our desire changes. The situation that we hoped to change because it was intolerable becomes unimportant. We have not managed to surmount the obstacle, as we were absolutely determined to do, but life has taken us round it, led us past it, and then if we turn round to gaze at the remote past, we can barely catch sight of it, so imperceptible has it become.

MARCEL PROUST

There is in every true woman's heart a spark of heavenly fire, which lies dormant in the broad daylight of prosperity; but which kindles up, and beams and blazes in the dark hour of adversity.

WASHINGTON IRVING

Worry is a thin stream of fear trickling through the mind. If encouraged, it cuts a channel into which all other thoughts are drained.

ARTHUR SOMERS ROCHE

Never a tear bedims the eye
That time and patience will not dry.

BRET HARTE

226

Our God is at home with the rolling spheres,
And at home with broken hearts.

M. P. FERGUSON

❧❦❧

ONE BY ONE

In the old *McGuffey's Reader* is a story about
the clock that had been running for a long,
long time on the mantelpiece. One day the
clock began to think about how many times
during the year ahead it would have to tick. It
counted up the seconds—31,536,000 in the
year—and the old clock just got too tired and
said, "I can't do it," and stopped right there.
When somebody reminded the clock that it did
not have to tick the 31,536,000 seconds all at
one time, but rather one by one, it began to run
again and everything was all right.

NENIEN C. MC PHERSON, JR.

❧❦❧

APRIL RAIN

It is not raining rain to me,
   It's raining daffodils;
In every dimpled drop I see
   Wild flowers on the hills.

The clouds of gray engulf the day
   And overwhelm the town;
It is not raining rain to me,
   It's raining roses down.

It is not raining rain to me,
   But fields of clover bloom,
Where any buccaneering bee
   May find a bed and room.

A health unto the happy!
   A fig for him who frets!—
It is not raining rain to me,
   It's raining violets.

ROBERT LOVEMAN

❧❦❧

THINK OR WORRY?

You can think about your problems or you can
worry about them, and there is a vast difference
between the two. Worry is thinking that has
turned toxic. It is jarring music that goes round
and round and never comes to either climax or
conclusion. Thinking works its way through
problems to conclusions and decisions; worry
leaves you in a state of tensely suspended ani-
mation. When you worry, you go over the same
ground endlessly and come out the same place
you started. Thinking makes progress from one
place to another; worry remains static. The
problem of life is to change worry into thinking
and anxiety into creative action.

HAROLD B. WALKER

❧❦❧

TO ONE IN SORROW

Let me come in where you are weeping, friend,
And let me take your hand.
I, who have known a sorrow such as yours,
Can understand.
Let me come in—I would be very still
Beside you in your grief;
I would not bid you cease your weeping, friend,
Tears bring relief.
Let me come in—I would only breathe a prayer,
And hold your hand,
For I have known a sorrow such as yours,
And understand.

GRACE NOLL CROWELL

❧❦❧

All sunny skies would be too bright,
All morning hours mean too much light,
All laughing days too gay a strain;
There must be clouds, and night, and rain,
And shut-in days, to make us see
The beauty of life's tapestry.

❧❦❧

HOW TO COUNT YOUR BLESSINGS

Welcome all the passing showers,
Count your garden by its flowers,
Count your days by joys, not fears;
Count the rainbows through your tears.

Count your world by friends, not strangers.
Count your town by hearts made strong;
Gratitude admits no dangers . . .
Count your blessings with a song.

Count your night by stars, not blackness,
Count your time by good deeds done;
God's sweet promise knows no slackness . . .
Count yourself His precious son!

ETHEL COLWELL SMITH

THE OLD AND THE NEW

Let this New Year be the beginning of a new life in each of us wherein "old things are passed away." Not the old thoughts, of course, which are still true: but those that remain to nurse and encourage our prejudices. Not the old emotions that are filled with kindness: but all anger and bitter feeling and railing. Not the old reverence for the authority of God: but all fears born of our unworthy service apart from him.

Not the old gracious ministries that blessed mankind: but the harsh words, the suspicious looks, the clenched hands, and unwilling feet. Not the old habits that keep us in the straight way: but the new fashions that make us unmindful of those things which hold life together in the unity of good manners. Not the old friends who grow more beloved each year because their worth is better appreciated: but the new associations made from mercenary motives.

Let all blessed old things stay, but let the clutter of our heads and hearts be removed, that new inspirations and new affections may come in to gladden our lives.

CHESTER BURGE EMERSON

Nothing happens to anybody which he is not fitted by nature to bear.

MARCUS AURELIUS

If God really rules the world, why does he allow things like earthquakes and floods and epidemics to happen? This old question has often been put in the form: "If God cannot stop such things, he is not Almighty; if he could stop them and does not, he is not good." But the fact is that the question has been put in quite the wrong way. The right question is: "Why did God choose to make a dangerous world?" If God made the world and human beings for a purpose, that purpose must be one which can be achieved only in a world in which life for all of us will always be short and dangerous; there seem to be lessons that we can learn only through danger and suffering.

STEPHEN C. NEILL

In the hour of adversity be not without hope
For crystal rain falls from black clouds.

NIZAMI (*Persian poet*)

WHY WORRY?

40% will never happen, for anxiety is the result of a tired mind,
30% concerns old decisions which cannot be altered,
12% centers in criticisms, mostly untrue, made by people who feel inferior,
10% is related to my health which worsens while I worry, and only
8% is "legitimate," showing that life does have real problems which may be met head-on when I have eliminated senseless worries.

WISDOM

*The best cosmetic in the world is an active mind
that is always finding something new.*

MARY MEEK ATKESON

HEART-THROBS

Knowledge is happiness, because to have knowledge—broad deep knowledge—is to know true ends from false, and lofty things from low. To know the thoughts and deeds that have marked man's progress is to feel the great heart-throbs of humanity through the centuries; and if one does not feel in these pulsations a heavenward striving, one must indeed be deaf to the harmonies of life.

HELEN KELLER

The journey of a thousand miles begins with one step.

LAO-TSE

To be a philosopher is not merely to have subtle thoughts, nor even to found a school, but so to love wisdom as to live, according to its dictates, a life of simplicity, independence, magnanimity, and trust.

HENRY DAVID THOREAU

WISDOM ABOUT LIFE

The differences in human life depend, for the most part, not on what men do, but upon the meaning and purpose of their acts. All are born, all die, all lose their loved ones, nearly all marry and nearly all work, but the significance of these acts may vary enormously. The same physical act may be in one situation vulgar and in another holy. The same work may be elevating or degrading. The major question is not "What act do I perform?" but "In what frame do I put it?" Wisdom about life consists in taking the inevitable ventures which are the very stuff of common existence, and glorifying them.

ELTON TRUEBLOOD

Knowledge is proud that it knows so much; wisdom is humble that it knows no more.

WILLIAM COWPER

Besides the noble art of getting things done, there is the noble art of leaving things undone. The wisdom of life consists in the elimination of nonessentials.

LIN YUTANG

Education consists in being afraid at the right time.

ANGELO PATRI

LESSONS HISTORY TEACHES

1. When it gets dark enough, you can see the stars.
2. The bee fertilizes the flower that it robs.
3. Whom the gods would destroy, they first make mad.
4. The mills of the gods grind slowly, but they grind exceeding fine.

CHARLES A. BEARD

Courage is the power of being mastered by and possessed with an idea.

PHILLIPS BROOKS

I find the great thing in this world is not so much where we stand as in what direction we are moving.

OLIVER WENDELL HOLMES

The farther backward you can look, the farther forward you are likely to see.

WINSTON CHURCHILL

❦

ADVENTURE OF FAITH

My message has been very simple. To live well we must have a faith fit to live by, a self fit to live with, and a work fit to live for—something to which we can give ourselves and thus get ourselves off our hands. We cannot tell what may happen to us in the strange medley of life. But we can decide what happens in us—how we can take it, what we do with it—and that is what really counts in the end. How to take the raw stuff of life and make it a thing of worth and beauty—that is the test of living. Life is an adventure of faith, if we are to be victors over it, not victims of it. Faith in the God above us, faith in the little infinite soul within us, faith in life and in our fellow souls—without faith, the plus quality, we cannot really live.

JOSEPH FORT NEWTON

❦

No man really becomes a fool until he stops asking questions.

CHARLES P. STEINMETZ

❦

The larger the island of knowledge, the longer the shore line of wonder.

RALPH W. SOCKMAN

❦

Whoever it was who searched the heavens with a telescope and found no God would not have found the human mind if he had searched the brain with a microscope.

GEORGE SANTAYANA

❦

It wasn't until quite late in life that I discovered how easy it is to say, "I don't know."

SOMERSET MAUGHAM

❦

My grandfather always said that living is like licking honey off a thorn.

LOUIS ADAMIC

❦

Most of the shadows of this life are caused by standing in one's own sunshine.

RALPH WALDO EMERSON

❦

Worry never robs tomorrow of its sorrow; it only saps today of its strength.

A. J. CRONIN

❦

POINTS OF VIEW

We men are from one point of view mere trivial microbes, but from another the crown of creation: both views are true, and we must hold them together, interpenetrating, in our thought. From the point of view of the stellar universe, whose size and meaningless spaces baffle comprehension and belief, man may appear a mere nothing, and all his efforts destined to disappear like the web of a spider brushed down from the corner of a little room in the basement of a palace; but meanwhile he is engaged upon a task which by him can be imagined, the task of imposing mind and spirit upon matter and outer force. This he does by confronting the chaos of outer happenings with his intellect, and generating ordered knowledge; with his aesthetic sense, and generating beauty; with his purpose, and generating control of nature; with his ethical sense and his sense of humor, and generating character; with his reverence, and generating religion.

JULIAN HUXLEY

Life's greatest tragedy is to lose God and not to miss him.

F. W. NORWOOD

If God shuts one door, he opens another.

IRISH PROVERB

CONTENTMENT

Let us learn to be content with what we have. Let us get rid of our false estimates, set up all the higher ideals—

a quiet home,

vines of our own planting,

a few books full of the inspiration of genius,

a few friends worthy of being loved and able to love in return,

a hundred innocent pleasures that bring no pain or remorse,

a devotion to the right that will never swerve,

a simple religion empty of all bigotry, full of trust and hope and love—

and to such a philosophy this world will give up all the joy it has.

DAVID SWING

The worst sin toward our fellow creatures is not to hate them, but to be indifferent to them: that's the essence of inhumanity.

GEORGE BERNARD SHAW

I deem nothing alien to my feelings that concerns a human being.

TERENCE

THE FREE MIND

I call that mind free which is not passively framed by outward circumstances, which is not swept away by the torrent of events, which is not the creature of accidental impulse, but which bends events to its own improvement, and acts from an inward spring, from immutable principles which it has deliberately espoused.

WILLIAM ELLERY CHANNING

The marksman hitteth the target partly by pulling, partly by letting go. The boatsman reacheth the landing partly by pulling, partly by letting go.

EGYPTIAN PROVERB

We cannot swing up a rope that is attached only to our own belt.

WILLIAM ERNEST HOCKING

To put yourself in the second place is the whole significance of life.

RICHARD ROBERTS

INSCRIPTION

Man's ultimate destiny depends not on whether he can learn new lessons or make new discoveries and conquests, but on his acceptance of the lesson taught him close upon two thousand years ago.

ROCKEFELLER CENTER

We should take from the past its fires and not its ashes.

JEAN JUARES

DESERT PLACES

Snow falling and night falling fast, oh, fast
In a field I looked into going past,
And the ground almost covered smooth in
    snow,
But a few weeds and stubble showing last.

The woods around it have it—it is theirs.
All animals are smothered in their lairs.
I am too absent-spirited to count;
The loneliness includes me unawares.

And lonely as it is that loneliness
Will be more lonely ere it will be less—
A blanker whiteness of benighted snow
With no expression, nothing to express.

They cannot scare me with their empty spaces
Between stars—on stars where no human race
    is.
I have it in me so much nearer home
To scare myself with my own desert places.

ROBERT FROST

The lowest ebb is the turn of the tide.

HENRY WADSWORTH LONGFELLOW

THE HEART'S REASONS

The heart has its reasons, which reason does not
know. We feel it in a thousand things. I say that
the heart naturally loves the Universal Being,
and also itself naturally, according as it gives
itself to them; and it hardens itself against one
or the other at its will.

BLAISE PASCAL

NEVER FORSAKEN

God is the hardest taskmaster I have known
on this earth, and he tries you through and
through. And when you find that your faith is
failing or your body is failing you, and you
are sinking, he comes to your assistance somehow or other and proves to you that you must
not lose your faith and that he is always at
your beck and call, but on his terms, not on
your terms. So I have found. I cannot really
recall a single instance when, at the eleventh
hour, he has forsaken me.

MAHATMA GANDHI

Storms make oaks take deeper root.

GEORGE HERBERT

DREAMS LEAD THE HEART

There is no dream so small you cannot make it
A lovely thing of vivid blue and white;
There is no hope so tiny but its glowing
May touch the dark of centuries with light.

There is no flower so faded that its petals
May hold a hint of fragrance that will last;
There is no memory so lost and so broken
That it can fail to glorify the past.

There is no vision in this world of striving
That does not help the tired soul to peace;
There is no suffering, however bitter,
That does not end at last in glad release.

There is no dream so small but its slim fingers
May point the path to all that life holds best;
There is no road, no matter how it falters,
That does not lead the heart, at last, to rest.

MARGARET E. SANGSTER

Men are wise in proportion not to their experience but to their capacity for experience.

GEORGE BERNARD SHAW

WORK

I can more easily see our Lord sweeping the streets of London than issuing edicts from its cathedral.

DICK SHEPPARD

Work is doing what you now enjoy for the sake of a future which you clearly see and desire. Drudgery is doing under strain what you don't now enjoy and for no end that you can now appreciate.

RICHARD C. CABOT

❧

Thank God every morning when you get up that you have something to do that day which must be done, whether you like it or not.

CHARLES KINGSLEY

❧

The highest reward for man's toil is not what he gets for it but what he becomes by it.

JOHN RUSKIN

❧

A BAG OF TOOLS

Isn't it strange
That princes and kings,
And clowns that caper
In sawdust rings,
And common people
Like you and me
Are builders for eternity?

Each is given a bag of tools,
A shapeless mass,
A book of rules;
And each must make,
Ere life is flown,
A stumbling-block
Or a stepping-stone.

R. L. SHARPE

❧

Have thy tools ready. God will find thee work.

CHARLES KINGSLEY

❧

The beauty of work depends upon the way we meet it, whether we arm ourselves each morning to attack it as an enemy that must be vanquished before night comes—or whether we open our eyes with the sunrise to welcome it as an approaching friend who will keep us delightful company and who will make us feel at evening that the day was well worth its fatigue.

LUCY LARCOM

❧

THREE THINGS ARE NEEDED

In order that people may be happy in their work, these three things are needed: they must be fit for it; they must not do too much of it; and they must have a sense of success in it—not a doubtful sense, such as needs some testimony of other people for its confirmation, but a sure sense, or rather knowledge, that so much work has been done well, and fruitfully done, whatever the world may say or think about it.

JOHN RUSKIN

❧

THE COMMON TASKS

The common tasks are beautiful if we
Have eyes to see their shining ministry.
The plowman with his share deep in the loam,
The carpenter whose skilled hands build a
  home,
The gardener working with reluctant sod,
Faithful to his partnership with God—
These are the artisans of life, and oh,
A woman with her eyes and cheeks aglow,
Watching a kettle, tending a scarlet flame,
Guarding a little child—there is no name
For these great ministries, and eyes are dull
That do not see that they are beautiful,
That do not see within the common tasks
The simple answer to the thing God asks
Of any child, a pride within his breast:
That at our given work we do our best.

GRACE NOLL CROWELL

No man is born into the world whose work
Is not born with him; there is always work,
And tools to work withal, for those who will;
And blessed are the horny hands of toil!

JAMES RUSSELL LOWELL

I AM WORK

I am the foundation of all business.

I am the source of all prosperity.

I am the parent of genius.

I am the salt that gives life its savour.

I laid the foundation of every fortune.

I can do more to advance youth than his own parents, be they ever so wealthy.

I must be loved before I can bestow my greatest blessings and achieve my greatest ends.

Loved, I make life sweet, purposeful, and fruitful.

I am represented in the humblest savings, in the largest block of investments.

All progress springs from me.

Anyone can carry his burden, however hard, until nightfall. Anyone can do his work, however hard, for one day.

ROBERT LOUIS STEVENSON

THE PROPER TASK

Would'st shape a noble life? Then cast
No backward glances toward the past,
And though somewhat be lost and gone,
Yet do thou act as one new-born;
What each day needs, that shalt thou ask,
Each day will set its proper task.

JOHANN WOLFGANG VON GOETHE

A WORKER'S RESOLUTION

One thing I am resolved upon: I will not be a sponge or a parasite. I will give an honest equivalent for what I get. I want no man's money for which I have not rendered a full return. I want no wages that I have not earned. If I work for any man or any company or any institution, I will render a full, ample, generous service. If I work for the city or the state or the nation, I will give my best thought, my best effort, my most conscientious and efficient endeavor. No man, no body of men, shall ever be made poor by their dealings with me. If I can give a little more than I get every time, in that shall be my happiness. The great commonwealth of human society shall not be the loser through me. I will take good care to put into the common fund more than I take out.

WASHINGTON GLADDEN

St. Francis of Assisi was hoeing his garden when someone asked what he would do if he were suddenly to learn that he would die before sunset that very day. "I would finish hoeing my garden," he replied.

LOUIS FISCHER

DIVINE TRADITION

The handling of tools need not put a gulf between man and God; it does not demean their user, does not cheat life of dignity, does not of itself desert men to the impersonal world of things. To use hammer, plane, chisel, and saw belongs to a tradition which the Son of God himself reverenced. When he used the plumbline, the God-man lost none of his glory. The workshop is a legitimate area for week-long service of God and man. Indeed, the profound hope of the labor world in the twentieth century is the hammer and sickle in the hand of Christ and his servants.

CARL F. H. HENRY

YOUR CHRIST AND MINE

To the artist he is the One Altogether Lovely.
To the architect he is the Chief Cornerstone.
To the baker he is the Living Bread.
To the banker he is the Hidden Treasure.
To the builder he is the Sure Foundation.
To the doctor he is the Great Physician.
To the educator he is the Great Teacher.
To the farmer he is the Sower and the Lord of Harvest.
To the florist he is the Lily of the Valley and the Rose of Sharon.
To the geologist he is the Rock of Ages.
To the judge he is the Righteous Judge.
To the lawyer he is the Counsellor, the Lawgiver, the Advocate.
To the newspaperman he is the Good Tidings of Great Joy.
To the philanthropist he is the Unspeakable Gift.
To the philosopher he is the Wisdom of God.
To the preacher he is the Word of God.
To the lonely he is the Friend that sticketh closer than a brother.
To the servant he is the Good Master.
To the toiler he is the Giver of Rest.

CYCLOPEDIA OF BIBLE ILLUSTRATIONS

SOURCE OF HAPPINESS

So much unhappiness, it seems to me, is due to nerves; and bad nerves are the result of having nothing to do, or doing a thing badly, unsuccessfully or incompetently. Of all the unhappy people in the world, the unhappiest are those who have not found something they want to do. True happiness comes to him who does his work well, followed by a relaxing and refreshing period of rest. True happiness comes from the right amount of work for the day.

LIN YUTANG

The time of business does not with me differ from the time of prayer. In the noise and clatter of my kitchen, while several persons are at the same time calling different things, I possess God in as great tranquillity as if I were upon my knees. We should establish ourselves in a sense of God's presence by continually conversing with him.

BROTHER LAWRENCE

COUNTRYMAN'S GOD

Who reaps the grain and plows the sod
Must feel a kinship with his God:

For there's so much on earth to see
That marks the hand of Deity.

When blossom springs from tiny shoot:
When orchard yields its luscious fruit:

When sap is running from great trees—
On all occasions such as these

The man who breathes fresh country air
Must know full well that God is there.

ROGER WINSHIP STUART

PRAYER AND WORK

Prayer is not a substitute for work; it is a desperate effort to work further and to be efficient beyond the range of one's powers. It is not the lazy who are most inclined to prayer; those pray most who care most, and who, having worked hard, find it intolerable to be defeated.

GEORGE SANTAYANA

FIELD OF LABOR

Go and toil in my vineyard,
Do not fear to do or dare;
If you want a field of labor,
You can find it anywhere.

From L'ENVOI

When Earth's last picture is painted, and the
    tubes are twisted and dried,
When the oldest colors have faded, and the
    youngest critic has died,
We shall rest, and, faith, we shall need it—lie
    down for an aeon or two,
Till the Master of All Good Workmen shall
    put us to work anew.

                    RUDYARD KIPLING

Nothing is really work unless you would rather
be doing something else.

                    JAMES M. BARRIE

MY TASK

To love some one more dearly ev'ry day,
To help a wandering child to find his way,
To ponder o'er a noble thought, and pray,
    And smile when evening falls.
      This is my task.

To follow truth as blind men long for light,
To do my best from dawn of day till night,
To keep my heart fit for His holy sight,
    And answer when He calls.
      This is my task.

                    MAUDE LOUISE RAY

HUMBLE TASKS

I long to accomplish a great and noble task, but
it is my chief duty to accomplish humble tasks
as though they were great and noble. The world
is moved along, not only by the mighty shoves
of its heroes, but also by the aggregate of the
tiny pushes of each honest worker.

                    HELEN KELLER

YOUR BEST FOOT FORWARD

Which sounds longer to you, 569,400 hours or
65 years? They are exactly the same in length
of time. The average man spends his first
eighteen years—157,000 hours—getting an education. That leaves him 412,000 hours from
age 18 to 65. Eight hours of every day are spent
in sleeping; eight hours in eating and recreation. So there is left eight hours to work in
each day. One third of 412,000 hours is 134,-
000 hours—the number of hours a man has in
which to work between the age of 18 and 65.
Expressed in hours it doesn't seem a very long
time, does it? Now I am not recommending
that you tick off the hours that you worked,
134,000, 133,999, 133,998, etc., but I do
suggest that whatever you do, you do it with all
that you have in you. If you are sleeping, sleep
well. If you are playing, play well. If you are
working, give the best that is in you, remembering that in the last analysis the real satisfactions in life come not from money and
things, but from the realization of a job well
done. Therein lies the difference between the
journeyman worker and a real craftsman.

                    H. W. PRENTIS, JR.

THE SISTERS

The waves forever move;
The hills forever rest:
Yet each the heavens approve,
And Love alike hath blessed
A Martha's household care,
A Mary's cloistered prayer.

                    JOHN BANISTER TABB

Don't worry and fret, faint-hearted,
    The chances have just begun,
For the best jobs haven't been started,
    The best work hasn't been done.

                    BERTON BRALEY

ACKNOWLEDGMENTS

Acknowledgment is made to the following for permission to reprint materials as indicated:

AMERICAN BAPTIST BOARD OF EDUCATION AND PUBLICATION for "The Meaning of Prayer" by Frances McKinnon Morton in *The Secret Place*.

AMERICAN BOOK COMPANY for extracts from *Living Issues in Philosophy* by Harold H. Titus, 4th ed., 1964.

APPLETON-CENTURY-CROFTS for extract from *Stepping Westward* by Laura B. Richards.

ASSOCIATION PRESS for extract from *Religious Living* by Georgia Harkness; extract from *Young People's Prayers* by Percy Roy Hayward; extract from *The Christian Character* by Stephen C. Neill; extract from *The Christian's God* by Stephen C. Neill; extracts by Edward S. Ames, Frederic S. Goodrich, Burris A. Jenkins, and Henry van Dyke from *Treasury of the Christian Faith*, ed. by Stanley I. Stuber.

THE BODLEY HEAD, LTD., AND HOLLIS & CARTER, LTD., for extract from *Seeds of Contemplation* by Thomas Merton.

JONATHAN CAPE, LTD., for extract from *All I Could Never Be* by Beverley Nichols.

CHRISTY & MOORE, LTD., for extract from "The Gate of the Year" by M. Louise Haskins.

COMET PRESS BOOKS for extracts by Allen A. Stockdale.

CURTIS BROWN, LTD., for extracts from *The Art of Living* by André Maurois.

J. M. DENT & SONS, LTD., AND E. P. DUTTON & COMPANY, INC., for extracts from *The Temple* by W. E. Orchard.

DOUBLEDAY & COMPANY, INC., for extracts from *The Open Door* and *The Story of My Life* by Helen Keller.

WM. B. EERDMANS PUBLISHING COMPANY for extract from *Aspects of Christian Social Ethics* by Carl F. H. Henry.

GUIDEPOSTS for "Aspiration" by Pamela Vaull Starr.

HARCOURT, BRACE & WORLD, INC., for extract from *Modern Man in Search of a Soul* by C. G. Jung.

HARPER & ROW, PUBLISHERS, for extract from *Not Minds Alone* by Kenneth Irving Brown; extracts from *Finding God in a New World* by William Adams Brown; extracts from *Man, the Unknown* by Alexis Carrell; extract from *Except the Lord* by Joyce Cary; "So Long as There Are Homes" and "Wait" from *Light of the Years* by Grace Noll Crowell; "The Day" from *Songs for Courage* by Grace Noll Crowell; "The Common Tasks" and "To One in Sorrow" from *Songs of Hope* by Grace Noll Crowell; extract from *Doctor Schweitzer of Lambaréné* by Norman Cousins; extracts from *Making Religion Real* by Nels F. S. Ferré; extract from *The Life of Mahatma Gandhi* by Louis Fischer; extract from *The Transformation of the Scientific World View* by Karl Heim, reprinted by Harper & Row, Publishers, and Student Christian Movement Press, Ltd.; extract from *Religious Perplexities* by L. P. Jacks; extract from *Profiles in Cour-*

age by John F. Kennedy; extract from *Strength to Love* by Martin Luther King, Jr.; extract from *Love and Marriage* by F. Alexander Magoun; "A Creed," "Earth Is Enough," "Outwitted," "A Prayer," "Revelation," and "Your Tears" from *Poems of Edwin Markham*, ed. by Charles L. Wallis, reprinted by permission of Harper & Row, Publishers, and Virgil Markham; "God Is There" by Madeleine Aaron, "Proof" by Ethel Romig Fuller, "Prayer" by Robert Freeman, and "Two Prayers" by Andrew Gillies from *Masterpieces of Religious Verse*, ed. by James Dalton Morrison; extract from *The Great Realities* by Samuel H. Miller; "How—When—Where," "A New Earth," "The Secret Place," "The Ways," and "Your Place" from *Selected Poems of John Oxenham*, ed. by Charles L. Wallis; extract from *A Guidebook to the Bible* by Alice Parmelee; "A Song of Service" by Marguerite Few and "Lord, Let Me Give and Sing and Sow" by Prudence Tasker Olsen from *Poems for Daily Needs*, ed. by Thomas Curtis Clark; extract from *This I Remember* by Eleanor Roosevelt; extract from *The Best of Dick Sheppard*; extract from *The Life of Faith* by Joseph R. Sizoo; extract from *On Active Service in Peace and War* by Henry L. Stimson; extract from *The Best of G. A. Studdert-Kennedy*; extract from *Our Common Loyalty* by Philemon F. Sturges; extracts from *The Common Ventures of Life* by Elton Trueblood; extract from *The Life We Prize* by Elton Trueblood; extract from *The Predicament of Modern Man* by Elton Trueblood; extract from *Ethics*, rev. ed., by Radoslav A. Tsanoff; extract from *Power to Manage Yourself* by Harold B. Walker; extract from *The Web and the Rock* by Thomas Wolfe; extracts from Henry Hodgkin and Wendell Willkie, "Childhood" by John Erskine, "Father, We Thank Thee" by Grenville Kleiser, and "The Teacher's Prayer" by Norman E. Richardson from *Worship Resources for the Christian Year*, ed. by Charles L. Wallis.

HARPER'S BAZAAR for extract by W. H. Auden.

HOLT, RINEHART AND WINSTON, INC., for extract from *The Indiscreet Years* by Larry Barretto; extract from *How to Be Happy Though Human* by W. Béran Wolfe.

HOUGHTON MIFFLIN COMPANY for extract from *What Men Live By* by Richard C. Cabot; extract from *My Antonia* by Willa Cather; extracts from *Doctor Hudson's Secret Journal* and *Green Light* by Lloyd C. Douglas; extract from *The Family* by Meyer Francis Nimkoff.

HYMN SOCIETY OF AMERICA for "When Life's Day Closes" by Thomas Tiplady.

JEWISH LABOR COMMITTEE for "What Is Brotherhood" by Peter E. Terzick.

LITTLE, BROWN AND COMPANY for extract from *Adventures in*

Two Worlds by A. J. Cronin; extract from *Time and Time Again* by James Hilton, published by Atlantic-Little, Brown and Company.

MACALESTER PARK PUBLISHING COMPANY for "Imperishables" from *Brothers All and Other Poems* by Charles Russell Wakely.

HAROLD MATSON COMPANY, INC., for extracts from *Answer Without Ceasing* and *Our Miss Boo* by Margaret Lee Runbeck.

DAVID MCKAY COMPANY, INC., for extract from *Human Destiny* by Lecomte du Noüy.

OPEN CHURCH FOUNDATION for "Slow Me Down, Lord" by Orin L. Crain.

OPTIMIST INTERNATIONAL for "The Optimist Creed."

PHILOSOPHICAL LIBRARY for extract from *Hasidism* by Martin Buber; extracts from *The World as I See It* by Albert Einstein.

RAND MCNALLY & COMPANY for "Gethsemane," "God, what a world," "The Goal," extract from "Our Lives," "Windows of the Soul," and "The Winds of Fate" by Ella Wheeler Wilcox.

FLEMING H. REVELL COMPANY for extract from *The Lord's Prayer* by Charles L. Allen; extract by Ralph A. Herring in *The Pulpit in the South*, ed. by Frank S. Mead.

REVIEW AND HERALD PUBLISHING ASSOCIATION for extract from *I Love Books* by John Snider.

THE RYERSON PRESS for extract from "Keep Thou Thy Dreams" in *Ballad of the Quest* by Virna Sheard.

SATURDAY REVIEW for extract by Mortimer J. Adler.

CHARLES SCRIBNER'S SONS for extract from *Joy in Believing*, ed. by Walter Russell Bowie; extract from *Human Nature in the Bible* by William Lyon Phelps; extract from *The Irony of American History* by Reinhold Niebuhr; "O World" from *Poems* by George Santayana; extract from *The Realm of the Spirit* by George Santayana.

THE SOCIETY OF AUTHORS for "Loveliest of Trees" by A. E. Housman; extracts from the writings of George Bernard Shaw.

THESE TIMES for extracts from L. Nelson Bell and E. Margaret Clarkson; "Life's Finest Gifts" and "A Salute to a Scoutmaster"; "The Measure of Love" by Taylor G. Bunch and "The Rose" by Patience Strong."

THE UPPER ROOM for extract from J. J. Rives.

A. P. WATT & SON for extract from "L'Envoi" by Rudyard Kipling, reprinted by permission of Mrs. George Bambridge, Doubleday & Company, Inc., The Macmillan Company of Canada, Ltd., Methuen & Company, Ltd., and A. P. Watt & Son.

Acknowledgment is made to the following for permission to reprint the materials indicated:

L. Gray Burdin for extract from Dale Carnegie; W. W. Coblentz for "The Housewife" by Catherine Cate Coblentz; Milton S. Harrison for "Awareness" by Miriam Teichner; Mrs. Edward P. Hutton for extract

from Edward P. Hutton; estate of Harry Kemp for "God the Architect"; Donald Craig Kerr for extract from *Design for Christian Living* by Hugh Thompson Kerr; Edward D. Landels for extract from "At Eighty-Three" in *Things New and Old* by Thomas Durley Landels; Jean MacArthur for "A Father's Prayer" by Douglas MacArthur; Louise Lindsey Merrick for "The Man Christ" by Therese Lindsey; Charlotte Baker Montgomery for "Courage" and "Let Me Grow Lovely" by Karle Wilson Baker; Ella H. Myer for "Kinship," "Thank God That I Can Trust," and "Windows" by Angela Morgan; LeRoy Alexander Percy for "Overtones" by William Alexander Percy; Daniel Rhoads for extract from H. W. Prentis, Jr.; Ora Searle for "Silence" by Charles Hanson Towne; Mrs. Jacob Zeitlin for extract from *Shaping Men and Women* by Stuart Pratt Sherman.

Acknowledgment is made to the following persons for permissions to reprint material from their writings:

Charles Angoff for "Home"; Charles F. Banning; Bruce Barton; Gail Brook Burket for "Prayer"; Anne Campbell for "The Choir Boy" and extract from "To My Child"; James Conant; Deane Edwards; K. Morgan Edwards; Dwight D. Eisenhower; Charles Burge Emerson; M. P. Ferguson; Harry Emerson Fosdick; Raymond B. Fosdick; Louis Ginsberg for "Love That is Hoarded"; John Heuss; William Ernest Hocking; J. Edgar Hoover; Frances Parkinson Keyes; Robert G. Lee; Elinor Lennen for "In the Beginning"; Phillips H. Lord; R. M. MacIver; Nenien C. McPherson, Jr.; Belle Chapman Morrill for "My Galilees"; Lewis Mumford; Ida Norton Munson for "Only the Human Heart"; Lawrence E. Nelson for "Beauty on Parade"; Reinhold Niebuhr; Angelo Patri; Daniel A. Poling; Nathan M. Pusey; Archibald Rutledge; Paul Scherer; Ralph W. Seager for "The Extravagance of God" and "Christian Courtesy" from *Beyond the Green Gate*; Fulton J. Sheen; Harold Shrylock; Joseph R. Sizoo; Ralph W. Sockman; Amos Alonzo Stagg; Adlai Stevenson; Roger Winship Stuart for "Countryman's God"; Gilbert Thomas for "The Unseen Bridge"; Harry S. Truman; Agnes Sligh Turnbull for extract from *Leaves of a Diary*; Jean Starr Untermeyer for "The Passionate Sword" from *Love and Need*; Harold B. Walker; Esther Baldwin York; Lin Yutang for extracts from *My Country and My People* and *On the Wisdom of America*.

INDEX OF PROSE AUTHORS

POETRY INDEX

This index includes first lines, titles, and poets.

INDEX OF TOPICS